Birgit Glorius, Josefina Domínguez-Mujica (eds.)
European Mobility in Times of Crisis

Culture and Social Practice

BIRGIT GLORIUS, JOSEFINA DOMÍNGUEZ-MUJICA (EDS.)

European Mobility in Times of Crisis
The New Context of European South-North Migration

[transcript]

This publication received financial support
by the German Academic Exchange Service (DAAD).

Bibliographic information published by the Deutsche Nationalbibliothek
The Deutsche Nationalbibliothek lists this publication in the Deutsche Nationalbibliografie; detailed bibliographic data are available in the Internet at http://dnb.d-nb.de

© 2017 transcript Verlag, Bielefeld

All rights reserved. No part of this book may be reprinted or reproduced or utilized in any form or by any electronic, mechanical, or other means, now known or hereafter invented, including photocopying and recording, or in any information storage or retrieval system, without permission in writing from the publisher.

Cover layout: Kordula Röckenhaus, Bielefeld
Printed in Germany
Print-ISBN 978-3-8376-3478-5
PDF-ISBN 978-3-8394-3478-9

Contents

1. Introduction
   Birgit Glorius, Josefina Domínguez-Mujica | 7

PART I: THE ECONOMIC AND FINANCIAL CRISIS AND ITS EFFECTS ON MOBILITY PROCESSES IN EUROPE

2. The economic crisis and the Southern European migration model
   Josefina Domínguez-Mujica, Tanausú Pérez García | 17

3. Young Italians on the move
   Armando Montanari, Barbara Staniscia | 49

4. Crisis and the resurgence of emigration from Greece: trends, representations, and the multiplicity of migrant trajectories
   Manolis Pratsinakis, Panos Hatziprokopiou, Dimitris Grammatikas and Lois Labrianidis | 75

PART II: STRUCTURE AND AGENCY IN EUROPEAN CRISIS MIGRATION

5. Study German to shape your future? – Motives for foreign language acquisition among Spaniards
   Birgit Glorius | 105

6. The changing migration projects of Spaniards in the UK. The case of Brighton
   Pablo Pumares | 133

7. A psychological perspective on adjustment of recent immigrants from Southern Europe in Germany. The correlation of adjustment with return intentions and personality predispositions for successfull adjustment
   Maria Wassermann | 161

8. **The role of intermediaries in Spanish emigration: past and present**
Dirk Godenau | 191

9. **Recruiting from Spain – a qualitative insight into Spanish-German labor migration projects**
Phillip Meinardus | 215

PART III: PERCEPTIONS AND DISCOURSES

10. **The recent international emigration of young Spaniards. The emigrants' narrative versus the official and media perception**
Ramón Díaz-Hernández, Juan M. Parreño-Castellano | 245

11. **The new emigration issue in the public and political debate in Spain. Official discourses and new forms of mobilization**
Ana López-Sala | 267

List of figures | 287

List of tables | 291

List of contributors | 293

1. Introduction[1]

BIRGIT GLORIUS AND JOSEFINA DOMÍNGUEZ-MUJICA

Since the onset of the economic and financial crisis, European internal migration changed significantly. While South European countries since the oil crisis of 1973 were rather immigration than emigration countries and their populations said to be reluctant towards migration, migration numbers increased considerably since 2008. Especially young and well educated migrants are leaving their home countries, nurturing the fear of brain drain back home.

The youth mobility topic is positioned – among other – in the context of a discussion on Europe needing a strong young generation. It is known that the profile of this young generation varies within Europe and that the socio-demographic characteristics of youth are inextricably linked to the differentiated demographic and migratory transition of the different countries. After the economic and financial crisis since 2008 and ongoing, we can distinguish a new stage in the model of Southern European migration. Despite the difficulties inherent to the availability of the statistical information on emigration, the databases allow us to get some evidences on the geographical mobility from Mediterranean countries, especially of the skilled young adults. This phenomenon has attracted the attention of scholars both in countries of origin and destination of emigrants and has been interpreted as a new juncture in the migratory transition of Southern Europe.

---

1   Most of the chapters collected in this anthology have been presented and discussed during an international conference at TU Chemnitz. This event – as well as the book publication – was made possible with the help of financial funding from the German Academic Exchange Service. The project: "Migration and Crisis. The example of Spain" was funded within the funding scheme "Academic Dialogue Southern Europe/Hochschuldialog Südeuropa" by the German Academic Exchange Service (DAAD).

Beyond the formulation of this model, the mobility choice of these young adults has been seen in the high unemployment rate and in the lack of career opportunities and transparency on the home labor market. Furthermore, it is unknown if the processes of demographic and social transformation as well as the increasing internationalization of society may serve as framing elements which are fuelling migration decisions. So far it is unidentified if the migratory movements in the context of the economic crisis will be of temporary nature or if they will lead to long-term absence and if these flows will endure as times go by. Therefore it is necessary to develop comparative studies in homeland and host land, with quantitative and qualitative analyses, that allow us for reading these processes concerning their durability, contextuality and their consequences for economy, politics and society. To know the new migratory linkages aroused from them and to improve their management can indeed contribute to a better integration of the European Union.

This publication aims to deepen our expertise by presenting a collection of most recent empirical research results on migration from Mediterranean Europe to Northern and Western European countries, notably to Germany, The Netherlands and the UK.[2] The authors of this joint volume use statistical data such as Eurostat or Census data and explore empirical studies on the topic; but they also present fresh results from a large number of quantitative surveys and qualitative interviews as well as media analyses. Based on a variety of scientific disciplines such as anthropology, human geography, psychology and sociology, the authors examine migration processes and practices, the management of migratory moves by institutional frameworks as well as public discourses about the 'crisis migration'. Specifically, the papers focus on the following topics:

- Processes: description of recent South-North migrations from a sociodemographic or regionalized perspective; characterization of migrants concerning age, gender, ethnicity and legal status; selectivity of migration, especially regional selectivity (e.g., effects of centre-periphery-relations, reasons for regional preference for specific destinations);
- Practices and strategies: examination of the motives, decision-making processes and migration strategies of migrants, in particular concerning the con-

---

[2] The editors would like to thank all contributors for their intensive work, the German Academic Exchange Service for its funding, the TU Chemnitz for hosting the conference and our student assistant Lisa Eichhorst for her thorough support during the editorial and layout process.

nectivity of career development and family formation; long-term mobility strategies and the decisive criteria for a specific target country;
- Institutional framing of migration processes: political and regulatory schemes; activities of public and private employment agencies, chambers, language schools, companies and other actors; and
- Perceptions and discourses: awareness and public opinions of the recent South-North migration processes from the perspective of politics and society in origin and destination countries; reflection on migration processes from the perspective of migrants; media discourses on migration in the context of crisis and demographic change.

The first part of this publication delivers a description of recent South-North migrations from a socio-demographic and regionalized perspective. It presents a characterization of migrants concerning age, gender, ethnicity and legal status and gives insight into the selectivity of recent migration, especially concerning regional selectivity. Opening the volume, Josefina Domínguez-Mujica and Tanausú Pérez García give an overview on the recent demographic and migration history of Southern Europe, aiming to highlight the most important features linking the profiles of those countries and differentiating them from Eastern, Western and Northern Europe. Based on 2011 Census data on unemployment, tertiary education and expatriation, the chapter aims to depict the relations between socio-demographic and migration characteristics of the young Portuguese, Spaniards, Italians and Greeks as opposed to those from Western and Northern Europe. This analysis displays socio-demographic features that may explain the importance of the recent emigration of young adults and, especially, of those with tertiary education from Southern to Western and Northern Europe, as well as to other destinations worldwide.

In chapter three, Armando Montanari and Barbara Staniscia give insight into recent mobility features of young Italians as a consequence of global economic crisis and its effects on the Italian economy and labor market. In their chapter, they elaborate on migration motives and mobility processes of young Italians and give an overview on socio-demographic characteristics of migrants or potential migrants, based on statistics and scientific reports on the phenomenon. They elaborate on Italian policy responses to what is called the 'fuga' – flight – in Italy and discuss the success of those measures to promote return migration from the migrants' perspectives. As a result, Montanari and Staniscia stress the role of psychological and cultural motivations, which are, often, the invisible factors affecting the decision to move, but which can hardly be measured through statistics.

Manolis Pratsinakis, Panos Hatziprokopiou, Dimitris Grammatikas and Lois Labrianidis draw our attention to Greece, the country which has been hit hardest by the crisis, recession and austerity measures. The chapter gives insight into the emigration trends and key features of 'crisis migrants' and how migration is reflected by the public discourse in Greek media. It then zooms into the case of recent Greek migrants to the Netherlands, providing a typology of different mobility trajectories and migration experiences. Thus, the authors intend to deconstruct a number of conventional assumptions, notably by situating the recent Greek emigration in a historical continuum with several structural preconditions predating the crisis. They furthermore discuss the qualitative dimension of mobility shifts and critically reflect on idealistic perceptions of life and work 'in Europe' often depicted in Greek media, and thus bring to the fore the ambivalence of mobility decisions and the multiplicity of individual pathways.

The second part of this volume examines the role of framing structures as well as on the actors' practices in the context of crisis migration. It analyses the migration motives and decision-making processes and gives insight into the migration strategies of migrants and individual consequences of migration. Furthermore it discusses the role of institutional support networks and specific polities in shaping the migration process.

The chapter of Birgit Glorius addresses the question of typical educational or sociodemographic features and other necessary prerequisites for the development and implementation of migration plans. She specifically focuses on the role of language proficiency and explores data from an online survey on mobility intentions and socio-demographic characteristics of Spaniards studying German in language schools such as the Goethe Institute. The results give insight into the variety of motives for language acquisition as well as on the connectivity of language proficiency, transnational social capital and mobility experiences with migration plans. On the basis of the survey data, Birgit Glorius shows different stages of migration preparation and explores the connection of spatial perceptions and mobility experiences, thus giving hints towards the question how large the share of individuals is, who actually put their migration intentions into practice.

Pablo Pumares then zooms into the lived realities of Spanish migrants, reporting on a qualitative study among Spanish migrants in the Brighton and Hove area (Sussex, UK). Using results from qualitative interviews, he explores profiles, experiences and future perspectives of young Spaniards who moved to the UK in the context of the financial and economic crisis. His study reveals the uncertainty of migrants regarding the duration of their stay in the UK, being torn between the desire to build up social and cultural capital and establish a career abroad, and feelings of homesickness and return intentions. Their narrations reveal their deep attachment to Spain and thus a high level of dissatisfaction with the political and economic realities back home. With his results, Pablo Pumares adds to the research literature on post-industrial liquid migration, a concept that so far mostly was applied for the example of migrations from Central and Eastern Europe.

The chapter by Maria Wassermann also explores integration experiences and return intentions, using quantitative survey data on the example of South European migrants in Germany. Framing her research with psychological considerations, she not only explores the effects of immigrant adjustment, but also personality predispositions like cultural empathy, flexibility, social initiative, emotional stability and open-mindedness for the development of return intentions. Furthermore, she gives insight into important differences of Spanish, Italian and Greek migrants in her study, indicating that Italian participants are most representative of a new generation of immigrants that make use of a transnational space of living, whereas Greek participants are most representative of traditional, economically driven migration.

In the next chapter, Dirk Godenau focuses on the role of private and public intermediation in Spanish labor migration to Germany. Taking on a historical perspective, he compares the structure of intermediaries during the period of *Gastarbeiter* migration in the 1960s and the recent institutionalization of migration. He shows the major changes of structure and agency of a *migration industry* under the conditions of free movement, where intermediation along the migration process concentrates on the labor market and settlement, with the latter including housing, education (e.g., language), and other social services (e.g., health). He shows the development and interlinkages of public and private services and the impact of migrant self-selection and self-organization on the structuration of the migration process. With his research, Dirk Godenau gives first hints towards the functioning of publicly funded recruitment initiatives, which are explored more deeply in the following chapter by Phillip Meinardus.

Based on a case study among German recruitment agencies, employers and migrants, Phillip Meinardus gives deeper insight into the decisive procedures for a successful recruitment of employees from abroad, as well as on the implementation of these procedures. He stresses the changes towards recruitment of qualified staff (in contrast to former *Gastarbeiter* migration) and details the steps of the recruitment and intermediation process of Spanish employees and trainees, exploring the perspectives of recruiters, employers, and migrants. Reflecting the results of his interviews, he points to the significance of soft factors for a successful acclimatization and integration and discusses the role of regional differences of a 'welcoming culture' in this respect.

The third part of this book focuses on the development of media discourses and on the connectivity of public representation and political discourses on crisis migration and the development of social movements, notably for the Spanish case. It highlights the development of stereotypical imaginations of Germany and Spain within the media and discusses how those stereotypes influence migrants' decision making processes. Furthermore, it shows how strongly reflections on migration are interwoven with general discussions on necessary reforms within the state administration and how emigrants are able to actively influence public opinion in their home country, thus fueling reform processes from below.

The chapter of Ramón Díaz-Hernández and Juan Parreño-Castellano explores the emotional constitution of Spanish youth and their family concerning emigration experiences, which appear as a mixture of disappointment, indignation and a sense of failure, mingled with the hope of a better life abroad. They contrast this picture with the public perception of crisis migration, based on the image projected by the government and the mass media, which is ranging between outright denial of the phenomenon to incomprehension, criticism and even irony. For their paper, Ramón Díaz-Hernández and Juan Parreño-Castellano use survey data of young emigrants as well as media analysis of a large range of printed and social media.

The final chapter by Ana López-Sala addresses current reconfigurations of Spanish society and political life brought about by the economic crisis. Taking the example of the social movement *Maroon Wave*, she explores the development of a new kind of external citizenry that is highly critical of the current government. Ana López-Sala depicts the *Maroon Wave* as part of a reaction to the inaction and indifference of the Spanish government to the plight of economic exiles, but also as an aspect of the general detachment from and lack of trust in Spanish institutions and traditional political parties observed in many sectors of Spanish society. However, contrary to other countries discussed in this volume, the disappointment and distrust of many migrants has not increased their feeling of detachment from Spanish society, but rather had the opposite effect: it has activated a desire to influence the political and social dynamics in the society of origin, with the objective of bringing about structural changes that will allow them to return.

These approaches to new processes of European mobility open innovative perspectives for researchers interested in the complex interplay between economy, society and politics within the European Union. Free movement is not only a fundamental principle of the European single market, but also a fundamental right of European citizens entitling them to move freely across borders and reside anywhere in the EU. Hence, the chapters compiled in this book open further research perspectives on the evolution of patterns and networks of intra-EU mobility and the scale and impact of this mobility on the social and economic systems of the sending and receiving countries. Finally, whether and how perceptions and attitudes towards migration are related to support for the welfare state can be extended in further investigations.

Chemnitz and Las Palmas, November 2016
Birgit Glorius & Josefina Domínguez-Mujica

Part I: The economic and financial crisis and its effects on mobility processes in Europe

2. The economic crisis and the Southern European migration model

JOSEFINA DOMÍNGUEZ-MUJICA AND TANAUSÚ PÉREZ GARCÍA

ABSTRACT

Many scholars from social sciences have considered Southern Europe, referring to Portugal, Spain, Italy and Greece, an area of common features with regard to political integration into the European Union, development of the welfare state and demographic and migration evolution, among other issues. The aim of this chapter is to draw attention to the recent demographic and migration history of Southern Europe, in order to offer an interpretation of the processes that have taken place since the turn of the century, differentiating the stage of economic growth (2001-2007) and the economic and financial crisis that followed (2008-2014). To this end population balance, natural change, fertility indicators, demographic structure, emigration and immigration data are analyzed, trying to highlight the most important features linking the profiles of those countries and setting them apart from Eastern, Western and Northern Europe, exemplified in the cases of France and Germany and the United Kingdom and Sweden, respectively.

The chapter aims to depict the relations between socio-demographic and migration characteristics of the young Portuguese, Spaniards, Italians and Greeks as opposed to those from Western and Northern Europe, offering a cluster analysis of the 2011 Census data on unemployment, tertiary education and expatriation. This analysis displays socio-demographic features that may explain the importance of the recent emigration of young adults and, especially, of those with tertiary education from Southern to Western and Northern Europe, as well as to other labor destinations in the world.

Keywords: Demographic profile, Economic crisis, Migration linkages, Skilled migration, Southern Europe

INTRODUCTION AND CONCEPTUAL FRAMEWORK OF THE RESEARCH

As stated by Baumeister and Sala (2015: 21), "Southern Europe is not a particularly prominent paradigm in academic discourse [...] however it represents an influential analytical category within social sciences". From this perspective many scholars have used the concept of a Southern European model, exploring the ways in which this region has been categorized in different areas such as historical and comparative political economy (Rhodes 2015). The study developed in this chapter mainly focuses on the demographic and migration trends of this geographical space in the early fifteen years of the 21st century, following the path of a differentiated evolution in the context of Europe that can be identified in the expressions "second demographic transition" as coined by Van de Kaa (1987, 1999, 2001, 2002) and "Southern Europe model of migration", used by King (2000, 2015), King/DeBono (2013) and King et al. (2014).

The major framing elements of this demographic and migration evolution analyzed are linked to economic and socio-cultural factors underlying two different stages in the period under examination, one of expansion (2001-2007) and the following of crisis (2008-2014). The evidences of the second phase distance Southern Europe from other countries with which it was converging during the expansion stage – Northern and Western Europe –, reinforcing the persistence of a differentiated course of demographic and migration history.

AN OVERVIEW ON THE DEMOGRAPHIC AND MIGRATION TRANSITION IN EUROPE

From a demographic point of view, Europe can be divided into three broad areas since the 1980s. On the one hand, Northern, Western and Southern Europe continued their victory over disease and death, however in Eastern Europe, the evolution of mortality followed an opposite way, with a clear relapse in the second epidemiological transition at the end of the 20th century. On the other hand, with respect to the fertility rates, the high fertility and demographic growth rates displayed by the Southern countries until the 1980s inverted, and these countries showed the lowest fertility rates in the last thirty years and, consequently, a greater aging pace, while in the Northern and Western European states fertility rates are higher and demographic aging has slightly slowed down. Thus, from the point of view of demographic evolution and population structures, it is possible to talk of a Mediterranean model to characterize a group of countries with demographically stagnant and aged populations, generally in the midst of a 'second demographic transition' or a 'second demographic revolution' (Van de Kaa 1987; King 2000; Cavounidis 2002; Reques 2002; Ribas-Mateos 2004; Arango et al. 2009; Sobotka 2009; King/DeBono 2013).

Regarding international migrations, three distinctive sub-groups of EU states can be identified. With respect to Eastern Europe, with the exception of the former Yugoslavia, external emigration only took place in the post-socialist period. After the fall of the totalitarian regimes, this geographical area became an important source of migration, and this trend increased with the enlargement of the European Union – a trend that reinforces the predominance of emigration over immigration. A second group of countries, those of Northern and Western Europe, despite some junctures with some ups and downs, have maintained their attraction for immigrants. Finally, Italy, Spain, Portugal and Greece that until 1973 were countries of emigration because 'political and economic hardship and lack of opportunities acted as motivating factors compelling people to search for prospects in more advanced European economies or across the Atlantic' (Fonseca/McGarrigle 2014: 51). After the oil crisis, they underwent a migration transition, becoming states of both emigration and immigration (Domínguez-Mujica/Guerra-Talavera 2009) and increasing their appeal as receiving countries in the post-Cold War period.

Now the question is what has happened during the economic and financial crisis (2008-2014)? Does it have altered or re-altered the migration trends in Europe? In the South, the inflows of foreign workers have declined; return migration to sending regions and re-emigration to other countries have increased; and the emigration of Portuguese, Greek, Spanish and Italian nationals has grown noticeably. We witness in words of King (2015: 157) "the Return to the Center-Periphery Dynamic".

The demographic and migration indicators corresponding to the years of the crisis allow us to update the peculiarities of this Southern model, and to better define the region's demographic evolution as well as these countries' migration profile. To this end, the chapter will compare different indicators of the mentioned countries in Southern Europe with those of two in Northern Europe (Sweden and United Kingdom) and two in Western Europe (Germany and France).[1]

Population change and its drivers

The relationship between demographics and economics has been a 'leitmotiv' in the social sciences already during the last two centuries, and until today, knowledge how periods of economic growth and decline interact with demographic changes continues to be a key element in social research. The long-term population processes, with their changes and cycles, are crucial factors interacting with the socio-economic history. This leads us to study and interpret demographic and migration indicators of the Southern countries as a differentiated model in the European evolution, persisting through the first fifteen years of the 21st century.

When comparing demographic trends in the countries analyzed during both the period of economic growth (2001-2007) and the recession that followed (2008-2014), we can see that all of them except Germany[2] experienced a positive growth during the first stage. Specifically, from January 1, 2001 to January 1, 2008, population growth added 12.8 per cent to the total population in Spain (more than five million people); between three per cent and five per cent to the total population in France, United Kingdom and Sweden (more than three million people, more than two and a half million people and more than 300,000 people, respectively); and between two and three per cent in Italy, Portugal and Greece (more than one and a half million people in Italy, 222,565 in Portugal, and 224,948 in Greece). Germany was the only country with a slightly negative total growth (-0.05 per cent), the equivalent to a loss of 42,000 inhabitants.

During the period of recession (from January 1, 2008 to December 31, 2014), the same trends persisted in France, Sweden, the United Kingdom and Germany, in other words, demographic growth rates were positive in the first three countries and negative in the last, although the situation changed in 2015 given the

---

1 We have used the terms employed by the United Nations Statistics Division, which includes both Sweden and the United Kingdom in Northern Europe; France and Germany are included in Western Europe and Portugal, Spain, Italy and Greece in Southern Europe.
2 In an international comparison, Germany stands out as the country with a history of more than 40 years of negative natural population growth (Weber 2015), despite the positive economic evolution. However, it is beyond the scopes of this chapter to investigate the reasons for this exceptional process.

large-scale arrival of refugees. The growth rates reached 6.1 per cent in Sweden and 5.2 per cent in the United Kingdom, whereas in the case of Western Europe, France cut down its growth rate to 3.7 per cent and Germany's negative growth became even stronger (-1.3 per cent).

As to the Southern countries, Greece and Portugal reversed their growth patterns, displaying a population decline of -2.2 per cent and -1.7 per cent respectively, whereas both Spain and Italy continued to show positive growth rates. However, in the first case they fell down to a mere 1.7 per cent whilst Italy was the only Southern country to display an increase in its pace of growth during the crisis (3.6 per cent) (tables 2.1, 2.2, 2.3).

Table 2.1: Population change in the countries analyzed during the stages of economic expansion and recession

Countries	Total Change (2001-2007)	Total Change (2008-2014)
Greece	2.08	-2.25
Spain	12.83	1.69
Italy	2.97	3.65
Portugal	2.15	-1.69
Sweden	3.38	6.15
United Kingdom	4.36	5.19
Germany (including former GDR)	-0.05	-1.27
France	4.97	3.66

Source: Eurostat

Table 2.2: Population change in 2001-2007 and its demographic drivers

Demographic drivers	Selected countries
Population growth due to:	
Mostly natural change	France
Mostly net migration	Greece, Spain, Portugal, Sweden, United Kingdom
Only net migration	Italy
Population decline due to:	
Only natural change	Germany

Source: Eurostat

Table 2.3: Population change in 2008-2014 and its demographic drivers

Demographic drivers	Selected countries
Population growth due to:	
Mostly natural change	Spain, United Kingdom*, France
Mostly net migration	Sweden, United Kingdom*
Only net migration	Italy
Population decline due to:	
Only natural change	Germany
Mostly net migration	Greece, Portugal

*The values are identical

Source: Eurostat

Natural change, demographic aging and population structures

With regard to the natural change, during the stage of economic expansion, with the exception of Germany, all countries displayed a positive balance, with France and the United Kingdom showing the highest rates of natural growth, about 4.0 per cent and 3.5 per cent, respectively (figure 2.1).

Figure 2.1: Crude rate of natural population change

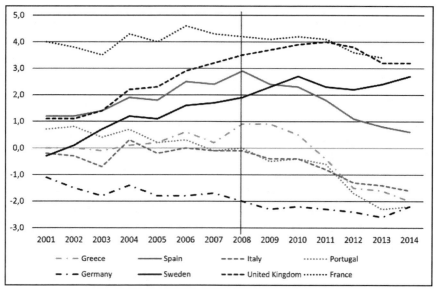

Source: Eurostat

This trend remained during the period of recession in Northern and Western Europe, with positive rates, at exception of Germany, in line with their higher crude birth rates (average rates of 12.4 per 1,000 in Sweden, United Kingdom and France). Nonetheless, the natural growth rates in the South experienced a marked drop, coming close to -2.0 per cent in 2014, with the exception of Spain that maintained a positive balance until first half of 2015 (average crude birth rates of 9.4 per 1,000 in Southern countries).

This recent evolution is only a further stage in the general reduction in birth rates that has been taking place in Southern Europe since the 1970s and 80s, which was temporarily halted by these countries' attractiveness for immigrants during the first few years of the 21st century, up until 2008. This pattern came about because these countries had been countries of extremes as far as demographic modernization was concerned. The sharp drop in the general death and child death rates, the resulting longer longevity at all ages and the steep decline in fertility rates have favored the intensity of the demographic transition.

Population aging is a long-term trend which began several decades ago in Europe. "This aging is visible in the development of the age structure of the population and is reflected in an increasing share of older persons coupled with a declining share of working-age persons in the total population" (Eurostat 2015:

1). However, this aging process has not taken place uniformly throughout Europe. As far as Northern and Western Europe are concerned, with the exception of Germany mentioned above, the recovery in fertility and birth rates have given rise to populations that are aged but stationary, whose pyramids display children, young people and adults cohorts of similar dimensions, there being no great differences between them as we go from the period of economic growth to the recession that followed it. If at all, there is a slight increase of the older population (figure 2.2).

In the case of the Southern European countries analyzed, the reduction in birth rates, the emigration of former immigrants and the impact of emigration on young nationals have given rise to increasingly onion-shaped population pyramids with remarkable shares of adults between the ages of 35 and 45 in 2014 (figure 2.3). Thus, if we add the current emigration trends to the reduction in birth rates, in a period of 20 to 25 years the ageing process will be extreme and an important proportion of the population will reach the age of retirement.

Figure 2.2: Age Pyramids of selected countries of Northern and Western Europe

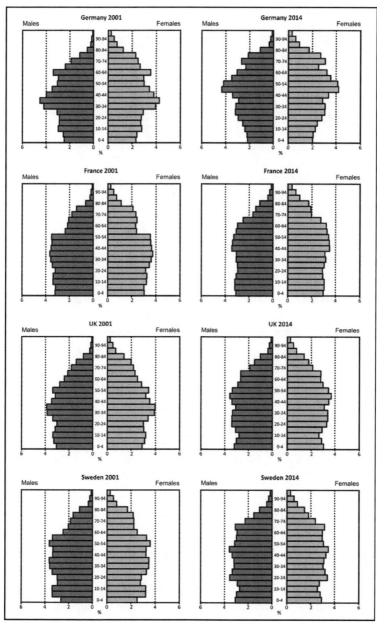

Source: Eurostat

Figure 2.3: Age Pyramids of selected countries of Southern Europe

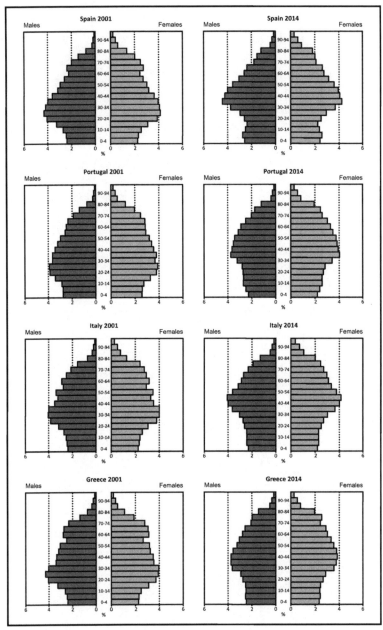

Source: Eurostat

The migratory patterns in the selected countries

In the model of the two successive demographic transitions proposed by Lesthaeghe and Van de Kaa (Van de Kaa 1999), the second demographic transition could "be compared to a cyclone irresistibly sweeping south from Scandinavia and gradually engulfing the South of Europe [...]" (Van de Kaa 2001: 3487) but the empirical evidence shows that at any given point in time each country or region has its own demographic heritage and cultural endowment (Van de Kaa 2002). And this is what has happened with the role of migration in the second demographic transition.

According to Van de Kaa, the assumptions underlying the second part of the demographic model are that the industrialized countries began to attract immigrants after three decades of fertility decline and, consequently, immigration became even more of a determinant of population growth when, from the early 1990s onward, the number of applicants for political asylum rose considerably and irregular migration gained importance (2002). In addition, the enlargement of the European Union in May 2004 involving eight Central and Eastern European countries, along with Malta and Cyprus, and the accession of Bulgaria and Romania in January 2007, triggered important flows of migrants from Eastern to Western and Northern Europe and became a crucial factor in the population growth of these last countries, despite the transitional measures adopted to delay the free access of these nationals to the labor markets in some of them. This cyclone also reached the Southern Europe countries, as shown by the fact that between 2001 and 2008 all of them displayed a positive net migration rate (table 2.4).

During the years of recession, as we have already indicated, immigration rates have not fallen in the countries of Northern and Western Europe – in fact, in some cases there is even an increase. However, in Southern European countries, which had followed the same pattern up until 2007-2008, undergoing their own migration transition, the trend changes. With exception of Italy, which continues to play the role of gateway to Europe for immigrants from Eastern Europe (Ukraine, Moldavia, Albania), Western Asia (Syria) and Africa (Libya), the other Southern countries examined (Portugal, Spain and Greece) closed the gap between emigration and immigration in 2008 and 2009 and, from 2010 on,[3] they returned to the net emigration that had characterized them in the past.

---

3   The so-called 2015 "refugees crisis" has been excluded in this analysis.

Table 2.4: Net migration rate of the countries of Southern Europe (2001-2008)

Countries	Net migration rate %
Greece	1.96
Spain	10.80
Italy	3.06
Portugal	1.83

Source: Eurostat

Figures 2.4 and 2.5, based on emigration and immigration data (base 100 in 2009), reveal the diverging migration trends of Northern and Western European countries during the recession years, on the one hand, and of Southern European countries on the other.

Figure 2.4: Net migration rate (base 100) of countries of Northern and Western Europe (2010-2013)

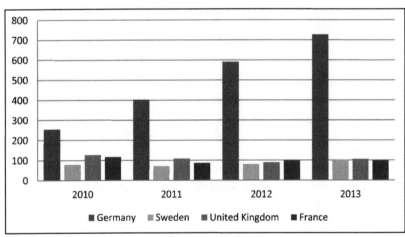

Source: Eurostat

Figure 2.5: Net migration rate (base 100) of the countries of Southern Europe (2010-2013)

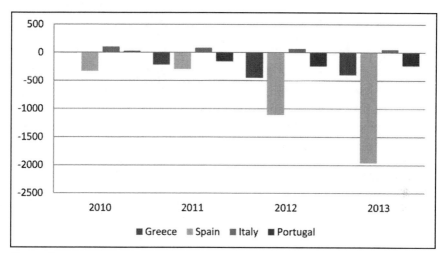

Source: Eurostat

THE PROFILE OF SOUTHERN EUROPEAN YOUNG ADULTS DURING THE CRISIS (2008-2015)

As indicated above, the Southern European model is characterized by a group of countries demographically stagnant as a consequence of decreasing fertility rates, a phenomenon that has had immediate effects on family structure and indirect effects on the meanings and values that society bestows on childhood, youth, adulthood and old age, in other words, on the social construction of the different age groups. Concerning this last circumstance, Southern Europe's socio-demographic model is characterized by a lengthening of young people's residential, work and family dependency, because families invest their economic resources and focus their expectations on their descendants' upward social mobility, "in a context characterized by weak family policies that force them to be responsible for the well-being of their members" (Ribas-Mateos 2004: 1053). Nevertheless, despite their best efforts, the families' emotional and financial investment in the well-being of descendants has failed in this new scenario (Domínguez-Mujica et al. 2016) and young people have been severely hit by the economic recession, especially since 2011, as a consequence of high youth unemployment (Díaz-Hernández et al. 2015).

Development of the crisis and effects on European youth

Between 2008 and 2009 Southern European countries entered into a process of recession that was triggered by the collapse of Lehman Brothers Holdings Inc. Economic activity stabilized in 2010, but the purported green shoots that announced an economic recovery in Mediterranean countries proved ephemeral. In April 2010, the Greek government requested a 'bailout loan' and became the first country in the Eurozone to receive a program of international financial assistance (110 billion€).

At the same time, there were growing doubts in the European Commission as to the sustainability of public debt in other countries with particularly large budget deficits. In the same year 2011, the Spanish government's commitment to budgetary cuts and tax rises – in exchange for European financial support (via the ECB) – contributed to the precipitation of the second recession of the Spanish economy. In Portugal's case, after having repeatedly denied the need for a bailout, on April 7, the government resorted to the European Financial Stability Facility and to the International Monetary Fund (financial assistance worth 78 billion€). Finally, the Italian economy, which did not require financial assistance, underwent a severe contraction as from the last quarter of this year and showed negative rates in 2012.

One of the most important consequences of this economic stance has been the sharp increase of youth unemployment. According to ILO figures (2015), between 2000 and 2014, youth unemployment rates rose by 11.7 percentage points in Spain (53.2 per cent rate of youth unemployment), 12 percentage points in Portugal (34.8 per cent rate of youth unemployment), 14.8 percentage points in Italy (42.7 per cent rate of youth unemployment) and 19.4 percentage points in Greece (52.4 per cent rate of youth unemployment).

This situation also fosters a new attitude among young people, who have now come to regard mobility and new experiences more positively, notably as a sign of a more cosmopolitan identity. To a certain extent, this explains the fact that the willingness to migrate at a time of crisis has been higher among those with top-class degrees and postgraduate qualifications (Parreño-Castellano et al. 2016). In most European nations, "a higher education level among young people leads to a decline in youth unemployment rates, but in Spain, Greece, Italy and Portugal the exact opposite occurs" (Hernández Peinado/Montero González 2013: 677). In addition, there is a collective feeling of deep frustration among young adults regarding the conditions in their home country (Bygnes 2015; Triandafyllidou/Gropas 2014). This includes the feeling of being rejected by political leaders and institutions, and the practice of recommendations or family contacts as opposed to merit (King et al. 2014).

Some evidence from 2011 censuses

Aiming to find statistical evidence for diverging patterns between Southern European and Northern and Western European countries, we have elaborated a comparative analysis of data gathered in the 2011 censuses by means of the new Eurostat tool known as Census Hub. This analysis displays some socio-demographic features that may explain the importance of the recent emigration of young adults between the ages of 20 and 39, notably of those with tertiary education. This should be particularly revealing, given the fact that the Census was conducted in the year of the second great economic recession, the effects of which are still felt at present, and which coincided with the sovereign debt crisis in these countries.

As a statistical procedure we used cluster analysis. The first step was the selection of indicators after an exploratory analysis based on the following criteria: young adults; tertiary education; unemployment; emigration.[4] The second step was a principal components factor analysis based on the existence of statistically significant correlations between selected variables, measured for the Northern, Western and Southern countries. To do this, a correlation matrix was prepared using the KMO (Kaiser-Meyer-Olkin's) measure of sampling adequacy and

---

[4] The indicators used are the following: unemployment rate (>15 years); unemployment rate (20-39 years); rate of population with tertiary education (>20 years); rate of population with tertiary education (20-39 years); rate of active population with tertiary education (total population); rate of active population with tertiary education (20-39 years) with respect to active population (20-39 years); rate of unemployed population with tertiary education (total population); rate of unemployed population with tertiary education rate (total population) with respect to the active population with tertiary education (total population); rate of unemployed population with tertiary education (20-39 years) with respect to the unemployed population (20-39 years); rate of unemployed population with tertiary education (20-39 years) with respect to the active population with tertiary education (20-39 years); rate of active expatriates with tertiary education (total population) with respect to the active expatriates (total population). The only exceptions are The Netherlands and Austria. The first because their census data do not provide information with regard to the population working abroad and the second because its rate of population with tertiary education is much lower than those of any other country considered in this study.

Bartlett's test of Sphericity. These checks show the following results: the determinant of the correlation matrix was 4.227E-012; KMO was 0.587 and Bartlett's test of Sphericity 0.000. The total variance demonstrates that two components explain 84.36 per cent of the total. The representation of the component plot in rotated space is depicted in figure 2.6, where two different factors can be identified. The variables related to tertiary education coalesce around this first axis (F1) and those related to activity, employment and emigration coalesce around the second axis (F2).

A cluster and a dendrogram were elaborated with the values of these components, using Ward's linkage method (rescaled distance cluster combine) (figure 2.7).

Figure 2.6: Component Plot in Rotated Space of the countries in Northern, Western and Southern Europe

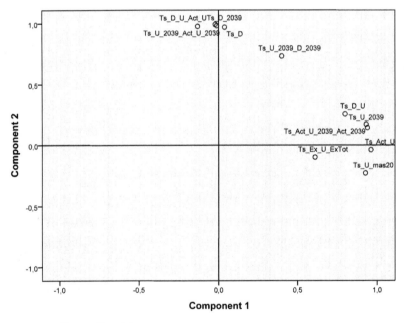

Source: Eurostat

Figure 2.7: Dendrogram resulting from Cluster Analysis

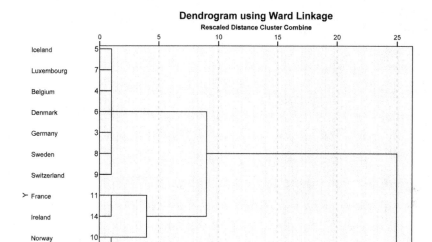

Source: Eurostat

The result of the Cluster Dispersion identifies four distinct conglomerates, with a higher proximity between the conglomerate one and two (Northern and Western Europe) and with a higher proximity between conglomerates three (Italy and Portugal) and four (Spain and Greece), but with a pronounced distance between the first group (conglomerates one and two) and the second group (conglomerates three and four) (figure 2.8). Thus, the results demonstrate that the employment and educational trends of young people from Southern Europe are similar within this geographical area, differing clearly from the profile of those in Northern and Western Europe and contributing to perpetuate emigration processes from the South.

Figure 2.8: Conglomerates resulting from Cluster Analysis

Country	FAC1	FAC2	C
Switzerland	0,29	-0,51	
Sweden	0,09	-0,74	
Denmark	-0,11	-0,58	
Belgium	-0,23	-0,54	C1
Luxembourg	-0,23	-0,38	
Iceland	-0,23	-0,45	
Germany	-0,33	-0,89	
UK	1,35	-0,31	
Norway	1,09	-1,20	C2
Ireland	1,08	0,72	
France	0,73	0,13	
Portugal	-1,76	0,26	C3
Italy	-2,22	0,31	
Spain	0,86	2,56	C4
Greece	-0,40	1,63	

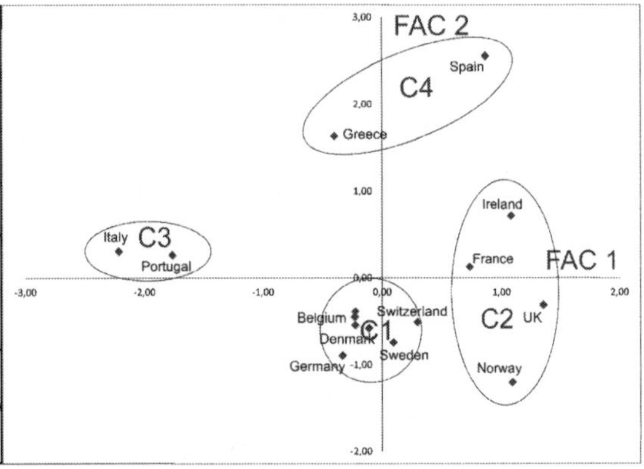

Source: Eurostat

MIGRATION LINKAGES BETWEEN SOUTHERN COUNTRIES AND NORTHERN/WESTERN COUNTRIES

In the 1960s and early 1970s, before the oil crisis, central and Northern European countries were an important destination for emigration flows from Southern Europe. During the late 1970s, and throughout the 1980s and 1990s, this historical trend lost importance while there was an increase in the flow of returnees, and at the same time Southern Europe itself became more attractive for immigrants, as the fact that these countries started to enact their laws on foreign nationals at this time reveals: Portugal in 1981 (Law 37/1981), Spain in 1985 (Organic Law 7/1985), Italy in 1986 (Law 943/1986) and Greece in 1991 (Law 1975/1991) (Silveira 2011).

Unlike what had been happening in the traditional receiving countries, many of the immigrants arriving in Southern Europe did so with no residence or working permits, drawn by the informal economy (Reyneri, 2001; Solé et al. 2001; Reyneri et al. 2006; Arango/Baldwin-Edwards 2014). The sending regions where these emigrants came from were Northern Africa, Morocco in particular; former Eastern Bloc countries, after the fall of the Berlin Wall (Romania, Albania, etc.) (Baldwin-Edwards 2007); some Asian countries, such as Pakistan and Bangladesh; other African countries, like Senegal and Nigeria; and in the case of Spain and Portugal, their former colonies.

The crisis, as has been noted, has altered some of these migration patterns: immigration has dropped, the flow of returnees has increased and at the same time the number of young people emigrating abroad has risen. Hence, the countries of Northern and Western Europe have become again an important destination for Southern European emigrants. The data gathered by Statistics Sweden (SCB), the United Kingdom's Office for National Statistics (ONS) and Germany's *Statistisches Bundesamt* (StBA), based on surveys and administrative records, reveal that up until 2008 the annual growth rate in the number of residents born in Greece, Italy, Portugal and Spain had been barely positive or negative. But between 2009 and 2014, the rise in the number of residents of Southern European origin was significant (table 2.5).

Table 2.5: Annual growth rates in the number of residents born in Greece, Italy, Portugal and Spain (2004-2008 and 2009-2014)

	Sweden		United Kingdom		Germany		France	
	2004-2008*	2009-2014	2004-2008*	2009-2014	2004-2008*	2009-2014	2004-2008*	2009-2014**
Greece	0.58	7.06	-6.62	15.86	-2.28	4.54		
Italy	2.45	6.60	-1.34	7.27	-1.14	2.76		-1.50
Portugal	2.17	4.04	5.97	8.86	-0.49	3.89		0.62
Spain	2.89	9.04	8.82	17.78	-0.63	10.30		-0.73

* Information on the years prior to 2004 is scarce or non-existent.
** We have not taken into account information gathered by France's Institut National de la Statistique et des Études Économiques (INSEE), because it only provides data for the period 2009-2012 and none on Greek nationals desegregated from other immigrants.

Sources: SCB, ONS, StBA and INSEE

Among these residents, there is a number of young people that have emigrated to other European countries, taking advantage of the EU legal framework that allows for the free movement of persons within the Union (Schengen Treaty); to other destinations with job opportunities for skilled immigrants: USA, Canada, China, United Arab Emirates, etc.; to countries in the midst of an expansive economic cycle, such as Chile, Peru, Brazil – up until 2013 –, etc.; or to countries with close post-colonial ties (Angola and Mozambique, in the case of the Portuguese, and Latin American countries, in the case of Spanish emigrants), which the crisis has strengthened (Avila-Tàpies/Domínguez-Mujica 2015).

The geographical profile of this new diaspora is described in table 2.6, although these figures correspond to registered emigrants and, consequently, their number is likely to be much higher. Emigrants born in Spain migrated first of all to Ecuador[5] (12.5 per cent of the 72,449 emigrants in 2013), United Kingdom (10.2 per cent), France (9.9 per cent), Germany (8.8 per cent), USA (7.2 per cent) and Switzerland (4.6 per cent), according to the micro-data files of Residential Variation Statistics of the National Statistics Institute of Spain (INE).

When this table is compared to that of the Spanish-born population residing abroad by January 1, 2013 (figure 2.9), several similarities can be observed. For example, France, the country with the largest number of Spanish residents (118,072) has also attracted an important flow of recent migrants, as is the case of Germany (54,358), the fourth country in terms of Spanish residents and fourth destination of recent emigrants.

Figure 2.9: Spaniards residing abroad (people born in Spain) in 2013

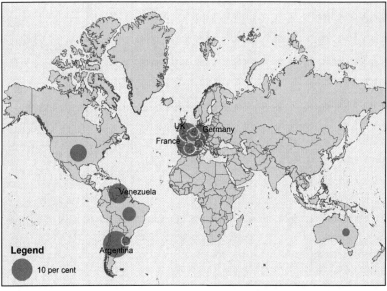

Source: Residential Variation Statistics of the National Statistics Institute (INE), Spain

---

5 Their ages indicate that they are mostly children (born in Spain) accompanying their parents (born in Ecuador), former immigrants returning to their country of origin.

The situation is similar in the UK (45,098), Switzerland (44,289) and the USA (42,938), which, having already had an important number of Spanish-born residents, have attracted a substantial number of emigrants during the crisis. On the other hand, Argentina, which is host to the second largest community of Spanish residents (92,453) or Venezuela (55,850), in third place, have attracted a much smaller group of emigrants over the last few years, which indicates that some of the emigration flows of the past have not been revitalized recently. Likewise, in the case of countries with important flows, such as Ecuador or Morocco, where the communities of resident Spaniards are relatively small (6,634 and 3,005, respectively) the figures reflect the return of Ecuadorians and Moroccans who, having arrived in Spain during the period of economic growth, have now migrated back to their homeland together with the children they have had while in Spain.

As far as Portugal is concerned, even though emigration had been constant since World War II, the flows had decreased towards the middle of the first decade of the 21st century, but during the crisis, particularly between 2010 and 2013, the number of emigrating Portuguese nationals grew by over 50 per cent, stabilizing at around 110,000 persons per year between 2013 and 2014 (Observatório da Emigração 2015). Their main destination was the UK, according to the Observatório (30,121 in 2013), followed by Switzerland with 20,039, France with 18,000 (2012) and Germany with 10,121 (2013). Spain, with 5,923 emigrants, was followed by Luxembourg (4,590), Angola (4,351), Belgium (4,227), Mozambique (3,759), Brazil (2,913) and the Netherlands (2,079). Other destinations did not exceed a thousand emigrants in the year of reference.

A comparative analysis between these flows and the Portuguese-born population residing abroad reveals some similarities and differences (table 2.6 and figure 2.10).

Table 2.6: Outflows from Italy, Spain, Portugal and Greece in 2013

Destination country	More than 1% of total emigrants of the reporting countries			
	From Italy*	From Spain**	From Portugal++	From Greece+
Austria	1.69			
Belgium	2.96	3.30	3.82	
Spain	4.82		4.80	
France	9.72	9.90	16.29	

Ireland	1.18			
Italy		1.30		
Luxembourg			4.15	
The Netherlands	1.53	1.50	1.88	
Andorra		1.20		
United Kingdom	15.79	10.20	27.26	
Germany	13.94	8.80	9.16	
Switzerland	12.03	4.60	18.13	
Angola			3.94	
Morocco		1.10		
Mozambique			3.40	
Canada	1.32			
United States of America	5.87	7.20		
Dominican Republic		1.10		No data
Argentina	2.12	3.30		
Bolivia		1.30		
Brazil	4.14	2.10	2.64	
Colombia		4.00		
Chile		2.40		
Ecuador		12.50		
Peru		2.00		
Uruguay		1.00		
Venezuela		4.20		
China	1.20	1.10		
United Arab Emirates				
Australia	1.90			
Other countries	19.79	15.86	4.53	
TOTAL OUTFLOWS	82,095	72,449	110,511	117,094

*Italian citizenship ** Born in Spain ++ Born in Portugal +Greek citizenship

Sources: Istituto Nazionale di Statistica (Italy); Instituto Nacional de Estadística (Spain), Observatório da Emigraçao (Portugal) and Hellenic Statistical Authority (Greece)

Figure 2.10: Portuguese residing abroad (people born in Portugal) in 2013

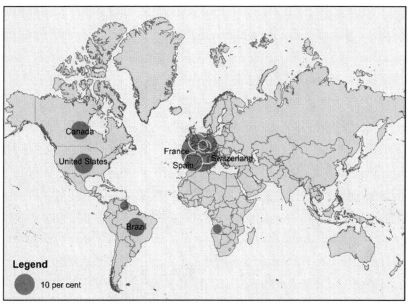

Source: Observatório da Emigraçao (OEm), Portugal

France, which continues to be the country with the largest community of Portuguese nationals residing abroad (592,281 in 2013), was not the main destination of Portuguese migrants during the crisis, but the third, with 16.3 per cent of the total flow of emigrants. The UK, on the other hand, has been the main destination for Portuguese migrants over the last few years – over one in every four Portuguese emigrants settled in the UK in 2013 (27.3 per cent), even though it is the eighth country in terms of the number of Portuguese nationals residing abroad (107,000 in 2013). Despite these slight differences, a comparison with past flows indicates that the recent destinations of Portuguese emigration flows abroad do not differ much. Eleven countries have been the destination of over one per cent of residents, and in nine of them there are important communities of Portuguese residents. The exceptions are The Netherlands and Mozambique, both of which have attracted recent inflows of migrants even though their resident Portuguese communities are rather small compared to other destinations. Conversely, Canada and the USA, despite their large Portuguese expatriate communities, have attracted a small number of immigrants in 2013, 629 and 918 respectively.

Since the Italian Istituto Nazionale di Statistica (ISTAT) only offers information on Italian emigration flows but not information on Italians residing abroad (stock), we have made use of those data on flows in 2013 and of the information provided by the Fondazione Migrantes on Italian nationals who reside abroad (figure 2.11).

Figure 2.11: Italians residing abroad (people with Italian citizenship) in 2013

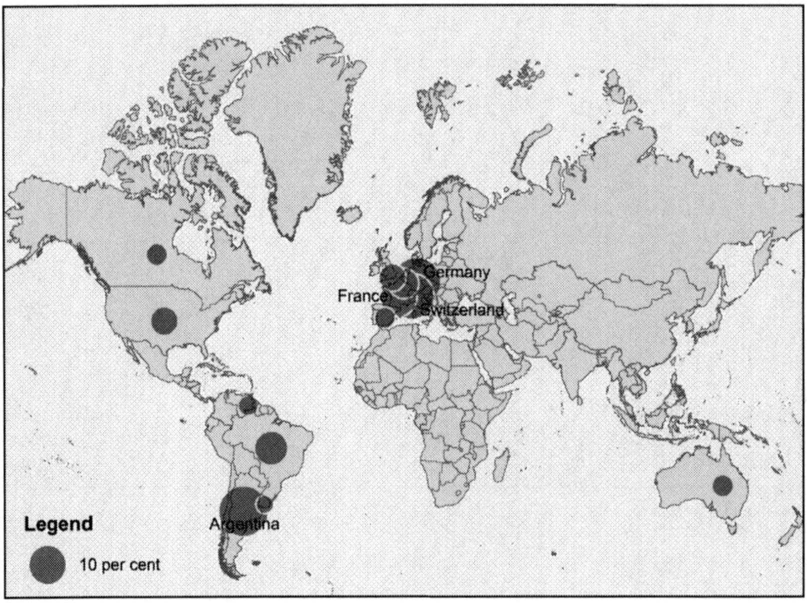

Source: Fondazione Migrantes. Italy

Table 2.6 shows that the five most important destinations for Italian migrants abroad have been the United Kingdom (12,962), Germany (11,441), Switzerland (9,872), France (7,976) and the USA (4,822). Among them, both Germany and Switzerland have large communities of residing Italian nationals.

The emergence of the UK as a recent destination is not in line with the size of the Italian expatriate community, the reverse of what has happened in Argentina, where recent flows are of little significance, despite the high numbers of Italian or Italo-Argentinian residents. Finally, Austria, Ireland and The Netherlands, with no Italian expatriate colonies, have become recent destinations for Italian migrants, unlike Uruguay and Venezuela, which have traditionally had relatively important numbers of Italian residents.

In the case of Greece, as indicated by Cavounidis (2013: 72), "the sharp increase in unemployment in the labor market since the last trimester of 2008 together with the worsening of terms of employment have caused many Greeks to seek employment abroad, especially younger population groups that have been characterized by particularly high unemployment levels". Ifanti et al. (2014), who have examined the specific case of 'physicians' brain drain' in recent years, agree. But, unfortunately, the Hellenic Statistical Authority only publishes data on the total of outflows (117,094 in 2013) because no official data on immigration or emigration have been available since the Greek statistical authority stopped collecting migration data in 1977 (Cavounidis 2015). Nevertheless, according to the IOM office in Athens, the main countries attracting the attention of prospective Greek migrants in 2012 were Germany, Australia and the United States, as well as some countries of the Middle East. Finally, according to the website EURES, the highest contribution to this outflow was of those with higher education and under 35 years of age (Cavounidis 2013).

In total, 117,094 Greeks, 110,511 Portuguese, 82,095 Italians and 72,449 Spaniards emigrated abroad in 2013. The intensity of emigration with respect to the total population has been highest in Portugal, with an emigration rate of 1.15 per cent, followed by Greece (1.07 per cent), Spain (0.18 per cent) and Italy (0.13 per cent).[6] Nevertheless, there are notable coincidences among the main countries of emigration.

During the economic and financial crisis, for Italians and Portuguese the key destination has been the United Kingdom; for Spaniards as well, with the exception of Ecuador for the reasons mentioned above. France is the third destination for Portuguese and Spaniards and the fourth for Italians. Germany, the first destination for Greeks, according to IOM, is the second for Italians, the fourth for Portuguese and Spaniards. Switzerland occupies the second position for Portuguese, the third for Italians and the sixth for Spaniards. Finally, the United States of America is the third for Greeks, the fifth for Italians and Spaniards and, in the case of Portuguese, it is only the twelfth. Other common and important destinations are Belgium, The Netherlands and Brazil. In any case, the greater attraction of countries like Germany, the United Kingdom or France is the result of their larger populations and, thus, larger job markets, along with the fact of their membership to the European Union area of free movement of persons.

In conclusion, the United Kingdom, France, Germany and Switzerland, and to a lesser extent the United States of America, are the most attractive countries for the recent emigrants from Southern Europe. There is, however, a certain degree of dispersion of destinations, particularly so in the cases of Italy (19.8 per cent migrate to countries where inflows are unsubstantial) and Spain (15.9 per cent), and to a lesser extent in the case of Portugal (4.5 per cent), which confirms

---

6   The emigration rates have been calculated using the data available in Eurostat on the reporting population (birth or citizenship, depending on the information of flows) of these different countries (the average of population on January, 1 2013 and 2014).

one of the most outstanding characteristics of migration flows in the context of globalization, the fact that any country can become a potential destination for migrants and, especially, for those highly skilled young adults with no job expectations in their countries of birth.

FINAL REMARKS

The definition of a population model requires a long-term analytical approach. Regarding evolution patterns in Europe since World War II, some authors have established three main models corresponding to Eastern European countries on the one hand, Northern and Western Europe on the other, and a third model for Southern Europe. Placing the focus on the two latter groups of countries underlines some distinct differences between them, both from the point of view of demographic transition (natural change) and migration transition.

Focusing in demographic evolution of Southern Europe, since the 1980s and 1990s of the twentieth century, these countries contracted their fertility and birth rates to such a degree that the aging process sped up. This evolution intermingles with social factors related to a model of protector families where the household efforts are invested in the social upbringing of increasingly slimmer cohorts. But, in a context of lack of labor expectations, the external emigration becomes an important option for these young people.

Regarding the migration evolution, at the turn of the century, Southern European countries had undergone a change in their traditional negative net migration rates, but the economic and financial crisis that broke out in 2008 – and deepened in 2011 – hit them hard, and gave rise to new migration outflows.

It is difficult to establish whether this recent process has added a new component to their population evolution, or whether it suggests that the period during which Southern European countries attracted an inflow of immigrants was short-lived, and thus have returned to their age-long tradition of emigration. In other words, whether emigration is a structural factor, and consequently the years during which immigrants settled in Southern Europe were merely a transient circumstance. Anyway, the population factors triggering the emigration processes are very different since the majority of them came from a population surplus, as a consequence of the high fertility rates in the past, regardless of the economic difficulties and lack of expectations of people from rural areas or urban workers scarcely qualified. Conversely, at present, the emigration processes affect young people best formed and skilled and cohorts increasingly smaller, contributing to the shortage of generational replacement.

At the same time, there is no doubt that the demographic features of Northern and Western European countries attract immigrants given their aged population structure and relative scarcity of young people. This 'demographic vacuum' in these migration-receiving countries and the unmet demand of labor take place at the same time as two diverging economic evolutions during the second part of the economic crisis – growth in Northern and Western Europe and a recession in Southern Europe. As a result, the combination of growing labor demand with shrinking labor supply in the destination countries (pull factors) interacts with the surplus supply of young highly skilled workers in the origin countries (push factor) and plays a determining role in the migration patterns analyzed.

An in-depth analysis of recent outflows and of the profile of emigrants might shed some light on the study of the current migration patterns in Southern Europe, because as has been mentioned, Southern Europe's socio-demographic model is characterized by a lengthening of young people's home, work and family dependency, but high unemployment during the crisis has contributed to a new attitude among them, who have reacted with a greater inclination to emigrating abroad than in previous stages. To this we should add a collective feeling of deep frustration with conditions in the home country and the rejection felt by these young adults towards political leaders and institutions. In words of King (2015: 158) "the recent increase in highly qualified emigrants from Southern Europe is not just a result of the 2008 financial crisis, but reflects a much deeper structural crisis in graduate unemployment".

Consequently, the 2011 Census data reveal a longer path in some demographic and migration processes drawing a common profile of youth in Southern Europe and set it apart from that of Northern and Western European countries. Furthermore, the geographical linkages between Southern Europe, on the one hand, and Northern and Western Europe, on the other, demonstrate the persistence of former migration trends and the similarities in the choice of destination, common to young generations from the different Southern countries. The attraction of the labor markets of the United Kingdom, France, Germany and Switzerland and, to a lesser degree, Belgium, The Netherlands, Luxembourg, Sweden, Norway, Austria, etc. contributes to reinforcing internal migration circuits within the EU member states and Norway and Switzerland. Finally, beyond Europe, the United States of America, Canada and some countries from Latin America, Asia, Oceania and Africa, with emerging economies or post-colonial relations constitute second-tier destinations for the newly skilled younger generation of Southern Europeans.

REFERENCES

Arango, Joaquín/Bonifazi, Claudia/Finotelli, Corrado/Peixoto, Joao/Sabino, Catarina/Strozza, Salvatore/Triandafyllidou, Anna (2009): "The making of an immigration model: inflows, impacts and policies in Southern Europe." In: IDEA Working Paper 9, August 31, 2016 (https://www.researchgate.net/profile/Claudia_Finotelli/publication/265142874_The_making_of_an_immigration_model_inflows_impacts_and_policies_in_Southern_Europe/links/54f984ef0cf28d6deca4ceb9.pdf).

Arango, Joaquín/Baldwin-Edwards, Martin (eds.) (2014): Immigrants and the informal economy in Southern Europe, London: Routledge.

Avila-Tàpies, Rosalia/Domínguez-Mujica, Josefina (2015): "Postcolonial migrations and diasporic linkages between Latin America and Japan and Spain." In: Asian and Pacific Migration Journal 24/4, pp. 487-511.

Baldwin-Edwards, Martin (2007): "La migración en la región del Mediterráneo." In: Vanguardia. Dossier, 22, pp. 18-26.

Baumeister, Martin/Sala, Roberto (eds.) (2015): Southern Europe? Italy, Spain, Portugal, and Greece from the 1950s until the present day, Frankfurt: Campus Verlag.

Bygnes, Sussane (2015): "Are They Leaving Because of the Crisis? The Sociological Significance of Anomie as a Motivation for Migration." Sociology, Doi 0038038515589300.

Cavounidis, Jennifer (2015): The Changing face of Emigration. Harnessing the potential of the New Greek Diaspora, Washington: Migration Policy Institute, August 31, 2016 (http://www.migrationpolicy.org/research/changing-face-emigration-harnessing-potential-new-greek-diaspora).

Cavounidis, Jennifer (2013): "Migration and the Economic and Social Landscape of Greece." In: South-Eastern Journal of Economics 1, pp.59-78.

Cavounidis, Jennifer (2002): "Migration in Southern Europe and the Case of Greece." In: International Migration 40/1, pp. 45-70.

Díaz-Hernández, Ramón/Domínguez-Mujica, Josefina/Parreño-Castellano, Juan (2015): "Una aproximación a la emigración española durante la crisis económica: herramientas de estudio." In: Ar@cne. Revista electrónica de recursos en Internet sobre Geografía y Ciencias Sociales 198, pp. 1-26, December 10, 2015 (http://www.ub.edu/geocrit/aracne/aracne-198.pdf).

Domínguez-Mujica, Josefina/Díaz-Hernández, Ramón/Parreño-Castellano, Juan (2016): "Migrating Abroad to Get Ahead: The Emigration of Young Spanish Adults During the Financial Crisis (2008-2013)." In: Josefina Domínguez-

Mujica (ed.), Global Change and Human Mobility, Singapore: Springer, pp. 203-224.

Domínguez-Mujica, Josefina/Guerra Talavera, Raquel (2009): "The new demographic and social challenges in Spain: the aging process and the immigration." In: Geographical Review of Japan Series B 81/1, pp. 4-15, December 10, 2015 (https://www.jstage.jst.go.jp/article/geogrevjapanb/81/1/81_1_4/_article).

Eurostat (2015): Population and Housing Census. Database. 2011 Census Hub. December 10, 2015 (https://ec.europa.eu/CensusHub2/query.do?step=select HyperCube&qhc=false).

Eurostat (2015): DATABASE, December 10, 2015 (http://ec.europa.eu/eurostat/data/database).

Eurostat (2015): Eurostat Statistics Explained. Population structure and ageing, December 10, 2015 (http://ec.europa.eu/eurostat/statistics-explained/index.php/Population_structure_and_ageing).

Fondazione Migrantes (2015): Rapporto Italiani nel Mondo 2013, Dati statistici, December 10, 2015 (http://www.chiesacattolica.it/pls/cci_new_v3/V3_S2EW_CONSULTAZIONE.mostra_pagina?id_pagina=49458&rifi=guest&rifp=guest).

Fonseca, Maria Lucinda/McGarrigle, Jennifer (2014): "Immigration and Policy: New Challenges after the Economic Crisis in Portugal." In: Impacts of the Recent Economic Crisis (2008-2009) on International Migration, Mexico City: Universidad Nacional Autónoma de México, pp. 51-75.

Hellenic Statistical Authority (2015): Migration Flows 2014, December 10, 2015 (http://www.statistics.gr/en/statistics/-/publication/SPO15/-).

Hernández Peinado, Manuel/Montero González, Bárbara (2013): "Un enfoque regional de la relación de los jóvenes con el Mercado de Trabajo." In: José Antonio Camacho Ballesta/Yolanda Jiménez Olivencia (eds.), Desarrollo Regional Sostenible en tiempos de crisis, Granada: Universidad de Granada, pp. 671-690.

Ifanti, Amalia/Argyriou, Andreas/Kalofonou, Foteini/Kalofonos, Haralabos (2014): "Physicians' brain drain in Greece: A perspective on the reasons why and how to address it." In: Health Policy 117/2, pp. 210-215.

ILO-OIT (2015): Tendencias mundiales del empleo juvenil 2015. Promover la inversión en empleos decentes para los jóvenes, December 10, 2015 (http://www.ilo.org/wcmsp5/groups/public/---dgreports/---dcomm/documents/publication/wcms_412025.pdf).

Institut National de la Statistique et des Études Économiques (2015): Population. Étrangers – Immigrés, December 10, 2015 (http://www.insee.fr/fr/themes/theme.asp?theme=2&sous_theme=5&type=3&nivgeo=0&produit=OK).

Istat (2014): "Migrazioni Internazionali e Interne della Popolazione Residente.", Istat Statistiche Report, December 10, 2015 (http://www.istat.it/it/files/2014/12/Migrazioni-internazionali-e-interne-Anno-2013.pdf?title=Migrazioni+della+popolazione+residente++-+09%2Fdic%2F2014+-+Testo+integrale.pdf).

King, Russell (2000): "Southern Europe in the changing global map of migration." In: Russell King/Gabriella Lazaridis/Charalambos Tsardanidis (eds.), Eldorado or Fortress? Migration in Southern Europe, London: Macmillan, pp. 1-26.

King, Russell (2015): "Migration and Southern Europe. A Center-Periphery Dynamic?" In: Martin Baumeister/Roberto Sala (eds.), Southern Europe? Italy, Spain, Portugal, and Greece from the 1950s until the present day. Frankfurt: Campus Verlag, pp. 139-169.

King, Russell/DeBono, Daniela (2013): "Irregular migration and the 'Southern European model' of migration." In: Journal of Mediterranean Studies 22/1, pp. 1-31.

King, Russell/Lulle, Aija/Conti, Francesca/Mueller, Dorothea/Scotto, Giuseppe (2014): "The Lure of London: A Comparative Study of Recent Graduate Migration from Germany, Italy and Latvia." In: Working Paper, 75, University of Sussex., December 12, 2015 (https://www.sussex.ac.uk/webteam/gateway/file.php?name=mwp75.pdf&site=252).

Observatório da Emigração (2015): Relatório Estatístico 2015. Migração total e indicadores de enquadramento, December 10, 2015 (http://observatorioemigracao.pt/np4/home).

Office for National Statistics (2015): Population Database, December 10, 2015 (http://www.ons.gov.uk/ons/taxonomy/index.html?nscl=Population#tab-data-tables).

Parreño-Castellano, Juan/Domínguez-Mujica, Josefina/Díaz-Hernández, Ramón (2016): "Migrations and mobility abroad of Spaniards at a time of crisis. The state of the question." In: Rosa Cañada Torrecillas (ed.), Aportación Española al 33rd International Geographical Congress, Madrid: AGE, pp. 176-187.

Reques Velasco, Pedro (2002): El nuevo orden demográfico, Madrid: BBVA.

Reyneri, Emilio (2001): "Migrants' involvement in irregular employment in the Mediterranean countries of the European Union." In: International Migration Papers (IMP), Geneve: ILO, p 66.

Reyneri, Emilio (2006): "De la economía sumergida a la devaluación profesional: Nivel educativo e inserción en el mercado de trabajo de los inmigrantes en Italia (From Underground Economy to Occupational Downgrading: Education Levels and the Labour Market Insertion of Immigrants in Italy)." In: Reis, 116/6, pp. 213-237.

Rhodes, Martin (2015): "Southern Europe in Social Sciences. 'A Southern European Model'?" In: Martin Baumeister/Roberto Sala (eds.), Southern Europe? Italy, Spain, Portugal, and Greece from the 1950s until the present day, Frankfurt: Campus Verlag, pp. 51-76.

Ribas-Mateos, Natalia (2004): "How can we understand immigration in Southern Europe?" In: Journal of Ethnic and Migration Studies 30/6, pp.1045-1063.

Silveira Gorski, Héctor C. (2011): "Análisis de los datos de las personas extranjeras detenidas, internadas y expulsadas en España, Grecia, Italia y Portugal. In: Revista Crítica Penal y Poder 1, pp. 117-140.

Sobotka, Tomáš (2009): "Migration continent Europe." In: Vienna Yearbook of Population Research (Data & Trends), Vienna: Vienna Institute of Demography, pp. 217-233.

Solé, Carlota/Alarcón, Amado/Gubert, Florence/Parella, Sonia/Ribas, Natalia (2001): "El impacto de la inmigración en los países del sur de Europa. El caso de Grecia, Italia y Portugal." In: Carlota Solé (ed.), El impacto de la inmigración en la economía y en la sociedad receptora, Barcelona: Anthropos, pp. 249-277.

Statistika Centralbyran Statistics Sweden (2015): Befolkning, December 10, 2015 (http://www.statistikdatabasen.scb.se/pxweb/sv/ssd/?rxid=fc360676-fabd-4727-9596-692adddb11c1).

Statistisches Bundesamt (2015): Bevölkerungsstände, December 10, 2015 (https://www.destatis.de/EN/FactsFigures/SocietyState/Population/Population.html).

Triandafyllidou, Anna/Gropas, Ruby (2014): "'Voting With Their Feet': Highly Skilled Emigrants from Southern Europe." In: American Behavioral Scientist 58/12, pp. 1614-1633.

Van de Kaa, Dirk J. (1987): "Europe's second demographic transition." In: Population bulletin 42, pp. 1-59.

Van de Kaa, Dirk J. (1999): "Europe and its population: the long view." In: European Populations, Rotterdam: Springer Netherlands, pp. 1-49.

Van de Kaa, Dirk J. (2001): "Demographic Transition, Second." In: International Encyclopedia of the Social & Behavioral Sciences, Amsterdam: Elsevier, Vol. 5, pp. 3486-3488.

Van de Kaa, Dirk J. (2002). "The idea of a second demographic transition in industrialized countries." In: Paper presented at the Sixth Welfare Policy Seminar of the National Institute of Population and Social Security, August 31, 2016 (http://websv.ipss.go.jp/webj-ad/WebJournal.files/population/2003_4/Kaa.pdf).

Weber, Hannes (2015): "Could Immigration Prevent Population Decline? The Demographic Prospects of Germany Revisited." In: Comparative Population Studies 40/2, pp. 165-189. Doi: 10.12765/CPoS-2015-05en, August 31, 2016 (http://www.comparativepopulationstudies.de/index.php/CPoS/article/viewFile/136/201)

3. Young Italians on the move

ARMANDO MONTANARI AND BARBARA STANISCIA

ABSTRACT

Since the beginning of the global economic crisis, 2007-2008, Italy has become increasingly unattractive as a country. The general economic situation and the employment situation in particular are negative, and Italians' perception of their own country even more so. One response from young Italians is what has been called the *fuga* – flight. The number of young Italians moving abroad has been increasing steadily since 2008 and almost half of students say they would be willing to move abroad when they finish their education. The essay responds to the main questions posed by the problem: (i) the characteristics of the young people who have moved abroad or who intend to do so; (ii) the main reasons behind the decision to move abroad; (iii) the destinations most attractive to young Italians; and (iv) the (un)successfulness of the policies that Italy is putting in place to promote return migration. The essay bases its considerations on the statistics and the many scientific reports on this phenomenon. We shall not, however, underestimate the psychological and cultural motivations which certainly play a role but which can hardly be measured through statistics. Psychological and cultural motivations are, often, the *invisible* factors affecting the decision to move.

Keywords: Economic crisis, Italian society, Mobility of young Italians, Return mobility policies

INTRODUCTION

The crisis that began in 2007-2008 has been the most significant one for Italy since World War II. It was caused by: (i) economic phenomena: the international economic and financial situation; (ii) structural phenomena: the negative trend in productivity and, consequently, in international competitiveness; decreased average company size; international specialization; insufficient investment in R&D; and (iii) institutional phenomena: inefficient market regulation; poor management of public services; lack of infrastructure resources and human capital (Svimez 2015).

Since the beginning of the global economic crisis, which began with the 2007-2008 financial crisis, Italy has become increasingly unattractive as a country. The general economic situation and the employment situation in particular are negative, and Italians' perception of their own country even more so. Mistrust and pessimism are the dominant sentiments; anger and resignation together seem to have a stranglehold on the future. One response from young Italians is what has been called the *fuga* – flight. The number of young Italians moving abroad has been increasing steadily since 2008 (Istat 2014b) and almost half of (adult) students say they would be willing to move abroad when they finish their education (Rosina 2013). Young people in the other southern European countries (Portugal, Spain, Greece) have had a similar reaction to the crisis, as demonstrated by, among others, King et al. (2014) and Domínguez-Mujica and Pérez-García in this volume (Domínguez-Mujica/Pérez-García 2017). In Italy, however, it is a reaction not only to the economic crisis but also to a structural one that has struck the country independently of the recent economic problems. The economic crisis revived the periphery-core flows from Southern Europe (but also from the East) seen in the first decades of the postwar period.

Despite all this, Italy is still the fourth most important economy in the European Union (CountryWatch 2015) and, since the second half of 2014, the first signs of recovery, albeit slowly, have been seen, and have been confirmed by 2015 performance (Istat 2015a; Svimez 2015). For 2016, the European Commission estimates a slight increase in GDP (+1.4 per cent) and employment (+1.1 per cent) compared to 2015. This growth should be reinforced in 2017, for which GDP and employment growth are estimated at +1.3 per cent and +1 per cent, respectively, over the previous year (European Commission 2016).

In this chapter we will attempt to propose an analysis of the real situation in the country, to present the conditions in which Italian young people are living, the significance of their international mobility – and the main reasons for it –, and the policies that Italy is putting in place to promote return migration.

Our main research question is: how important, in absolute and relative terms, international youth movements are? Should those movements be considered as permanent migration or temporary mobility? Which are the main causes of it? In which context do they take place? Which is the long term perspective? With those questions in mind, we will analyze the main characteristics of Italian economy and labor market, highlighting the North-South divide in terms of performance. We will present the Italian *sentiment* in the years of crisis, the attitudes of the young people, their relationship to their own future and expectations. Acknowledging that there is an increase in the youth migration-mobility, we will introduce in the discussion the policies that the Italian government is putting in place. We will use secondary data from official international and national statistics (Eurostat, Istat), targeted reports (Svimez), and sample surveys carried out by international and national institutions (Eurobarometer, Istituto Giuseppe Toniolo).

In the international literature the debate concerning youth mobility is rapidly increasing. A comprehensive review of the researches concerning youth mobility in the European Union is proposed by King et al. (2016) with a specific *focus* on three main typologies: (i) students' mobility, (ii) mobility of the high-skilled and of (iii) the low-skilled. There are two main interpretations of the mobility of the young persons, emerging from the literature: (i) mobility can be considered as a choice and a voluntary act: it is a way to gain new experiences, to explore the world, to acquire new skills and competences, to favour personal growth, to boost one's own career, and to improve one's own life (Altbach 1989; King/Ruiz-Gelices 2003; Ackers 2005a, 2005b; Williams/Baláž 2005, 2008; Findlay 2010; Findlay et al. 2012; Staniscia 2012; King/Raghuram 2013; Montanari/Staniscia 2014; Perkins/Neumayer 2014; Williams/Baláž 2014); (ii) mobility can be considered as a necessity and a forced act: it is a way to escape from difficult economic and social conditions, from unemployment, from difficulties in progressing in one's own career, and from problematic family life (Istat 2010, 2011, 2012a, 2012b; King/Conti 2013; Istat 2014a, 2014b; King et al. 2014; Istat 2015a, 2015b; Domínguez-Mujica/Pérez-García 2017). Information and data that we will present show the impossibility of assessing which of the two hypotheses is correct and that there is evidence that both of them concur in explaining the Italian flows.

In the international debate, attention is also posed on the spatial effects of youth mobility: which are the consequences for the regions of origin in the short and long term? Discourses on brain drain and the loss of human capital (Bhagwati/Hamada 1974; Findlay/Gould 1989; Salt 1992; Montanari 1993, 1995; Bhagwati/Hanson 2009; Boucher/Cerna 2014) with the consequence of

regional marginalization emerge (Jouen 2014). This is one of the risks envisaged by some researchers concerning the Italian Mezzogiorno (Southern Italy) (Svimez 2015). In this chapter we will try to introduce the problem of the North-South divide in Italy and the relationship between regional disequilibria and migration.

A COUNTRY IN CRISIS: ITALY FROM 2008 TO TODAY

A country losing wealth and jobs

The Italian crisis can be measured through a range of factors. The first of these is economic in nature and concerns the country's economic growth. In the 2008-2014 period, the Italian GDP showed a decrease in five years out of seven – with a minimum value of -5.5 per cent (in 2009) and a maximum value of 1.7 per cent (in 2010) (Istat 2015a) – and the per capita GDP decreased from 27,600€ in 2008 to 26,500€ in 2014 (Eurostat 2016a). In the Euro Area, 2009 and 2010 were also the years when the GDP's highest and lowest values for the period were recorded; these values were, however, higher than Italy's at -4.5 per cent and 2.1 per cent respectively (Eurostat 2016a); in the Euro Area the per capita GDP increased from 28,800€ in 2008 to 29,800€ in 2014 (Eurostat 2016a). In the 2008-2014 period, the real GDP increased by about 0.7 per cent in the European Union and fell by 0.9 per cent in the Euro Area and by 9 per cent in Italy (Svimez 2015). Average GDP performance in Italy, therefore, was lower than in the Euro Area and in the European Union over the 2008-2014 period.

The second economic factor that draws attention to the criticality of Italy's situation is the vitality of its businesses and its real estate market. As of December 31, 2008, there were 5,316,104 enterprises actively operating in Italy; this number had dropped to 5,144,383 as of December 31, 2015 (Demografia Imprese 2016). Since the beginning of the crisis the total number of active businesses in Italy decreased by 3.2 per cent. The change in number of active enterprises[1] has been negative every year (varying between -0.7 and -1.5) since 2008. Between April 2009 and December 2015, 2,580,490 businesses were created and 2,592,276 closed (Demografia Imprese 2016). From 2008 to 2014 the number of residential real estate transactions in Italy decreased by 39 per cent overall; in the

---

1   This index measures the difference between the number of businesses that were started and those that were closed over a given period.

capitals of provinces this effect was less marked but still negative, decreasing by 27 per cent (AgenziaEntrate 2016).

The third critical factor – economic in nature but with significant social consequences – involves the labor market. During the 2008-2014 period the number of employed persons in Italy decreased by 3.5 per cent, the unemployment rate rose from 6.7 per cent to 12.7 per cent and the unemployment rate for people aged 15 to 39 years rose from 9.8 per cent to 19.9 per cent. During this same period the number of employed persons in the EU-15 decreased by 1.5 per cent, the unemployment rate rose from 7.2 per cent to 10.5 per cent and the unemployment rate for people aged 15 to 39 years rose from 9.1 per cent to 13.9 per cent (Eurostat 2016b). The decrease in employment in Italy was especially significant for Italian citizens (-6.6 per cent) and only partially compensated for by the increase in employment for foreigners (+35.7 per cent) (Svimez 2015). In 2014 the employment rate in the EU-28 was 64.9 per cent and had increased over the previous year, though it remained lower than in 2008 (65.7 per cent). Italy also showed substantial improvement from 2013 to 2014 but still less than the EU-28 average: the employment rate in Italy, in 2014, was 55.7 per cent, nearly three percent lower than in 2008 (Istat 2015a).

The average performance of Italy's labor market was lower than the average in EU countries over the 2008-2015 period. Nevertheless, in the past year, there have been signs of recovery and employment is growing again in certain sectors (including agriculture, hotels and catering, education, health, services for families), for certain age groups (people aged over 50 years) and for some contract types (fixed term and part time).

A country divided in half and out of faith

The economic and employment crisis that Italy is experiencing – and slowly recovering from – looks much more serious in the South: from 2007 to 2014 GDP in Southern Italy fell by 13 per cent, while in the Centre and North, the drop was 7.4 per cent (Svimez 2015). The GDP per capita in 2014 in the South stood at 16,975€, while in the Central/North zones it was 31,586€, with a differential which fell during the 2001-2009 period but is now on the rise again. Both domestic and foreign demand (consumption and exports) decreased, as did investment, especially the public one.

During the 2008-2014 period, household consumption fell 13.2 per cent and in the South there were no signs of recovery in 2014 (Svimez 2015). The data on food consumption are especially negative: -15.3 per cent over the 2008-2014 period. Gross fixed capital formation during the 2008-2014 period fell by 38.1 per cent in the South of Italy but by 27.1 per cent in the Centre-North; the decline was especially significant in the industrial sector at -59.3 per cent (Svimez 2015). In the 2008-2014 period, employment in the South decreased by 9 per cent; in the same period, it fell by 1.4 per cent in the rest of the country (Svimez 2015). Employment in the South in 2014 was the lowest recorded since 1977 (Svimez 2015).

The forecasts for 2016 are for recovery, albeit very slight: GDP in the South (+0.7 per cent), consumption (+0.8 per cent), gross fixed capital formation (+0.5 per cent), employment (+0.6 per cent) (Svimez 2015). These cautiously positive predictions, if fulfilled, would nonetheless not reduce the significant gap in growth and development between the Centre-North and the South of Italy.

Italians' confidence in the future of their country is low: in 2014, 37 per cent of Italians thought that the economic situation would get worse over the next twelve months and 36 per cent thought that it would not improve; 43 per cent thought that the employment situation would get worse over the next twelve months and 32 per cent thought that it would not improve; 60 per cent of Italians thought that the country's most serious problem was unemployment; 58 per cent of Italians thought that the situation in their country was going in the wrong direction (European Commission 2014b).

Mistrust also affects the value system; in 2013, 58 per cent of Italians thought that corruption was widespread and 74 per cent believed that the problem had become more severe in the former three years (EC 2013); nevertheless, 90 per cent of respondents stated that they had never witnessed or been involved in instances of corruption.

Overall, Italians' dissatisfaction with their lives is increasing. From 2009 to 2014, the Social Climate Index[2] for Italy dropped from -1.9 to -3 (European Commission 2014a). This negative perception is also to be found, though less markedly, in other countries in Southern and Eastern Europe (Spain and Portugal have better indices, though still negative). The index for Italy is particularly negative – and worsening since 2009 – for satisfaction with the employment situation (-6.7 in 2014), the economic situation (-6 in 2014), the cost of living (-4.8 in 2014) and the efficiency of public administration (-4.8 in 2014) (European Commission2014a).

---

2 An index on a scale from -10 to +10 which considers EU citizens' perception of their own conditions, the general situation of their country and social protection and inclusion in their country.

YOUNG ITALIANS

Defining today's young Italians is not a simple task. Rosina (2013) describes adulthood as an age characterized by concrete steps – leaving school, entering the world of work, going to live on one's own, starting a family – and points out that these steps are no longer necessarily sequential in contemporary Italian society, nor does everyone go through them at the same age. Scabini and Marta (2013: 24) describe youth as a transitional and uncertain age, where "meaningful self-realization" triumphs over commitment, where multiple options are explored, where choices are always reversible. In the context of the analysis of the mobility of young Italians – the context of the economic crisis – this paper has selected a broad interpretation of the concept of youth, placing it between 15 and 39 years, thus including parts of adolescence and adulthood in an *extended youth*. Youth is, in fact, defined by the local, social and cultural context in which one lives, and the Italian economic crisis has created individuals who are, in a sense, *forced to stay young*, with uncertainty and reversibility imposed on their choices.

In 2015 there were 17,094,688 residents of Italy between 15 and 39 years of age (Istat 2016b). 16.76 per cent were between 15 and 19 years old and 18.03 per cent between 20 and 24 years; young people between 25 and 29 years accounted for 19.2 per cent; those from 30 to 34 accounted for 21.13 per cent and 24.88 per cent of young people were aged between 35 and 39 years. But what are these young people like? And what particular characteristics define them?

We will begin with their home environment, the family. Young Italians have a very strong and positive bond with their families; they feel protected and reassured by them and it is from them that they acquire the confidence to achieve their own autonomy, to cultivate their talents and to believe and hope for the future (Rosina/Sironi 2013; Scabini/Marta 2013). They see their family as a *haven more than a prison*, a safe place where they can always be welcomed. Young Italians are delaying ever longer the moment when they will move out, establish an independent life and start a new family unit. This can be attributed to two equally important factors, one cultural and the other economic. We will look at these in detail.

Italy is a Mediterranean country where the model for familial relations is based more on the principle of solidarity than on individual independence and autonomy (Dalla Zuanna/Micheli 2004). Such *strong* bonds do not push young people to leave home but rather make it socially acceptable to stay, even for an extended period. These bonds also make it possible to return home even after having left, should one's life plans fail (e.g., failure in university studies, failure of a marriage).

As we have seen, Italy is a country facing an economic and employment crisis. This makes independence very difficult for young people and induces a delay in the plan to begin an autonomous life, even for those who have a job, as it is often not a permanent job and one that doesn't pay well. Young people's employment problems translate into reduced autonomy: 89 per cent of young people between 18 and 24 years old manage to get by only with economic help from their families, as do 43 per cent of those between 25 and 34 years and 28 per cent of those between 35 and 40 years old (Coldiretti-SWG 2013). In addition, 89 per cent of young people between 18 and 24 live with their parents; this percentage drops to 48 per cent for young people aged between 25 and 34 years, and 26 per cent for those between 35 and 40 years (Coldiretti-SWG 2013). The notion of youth in Italy has become very broad, indeed. In Italy, especially in the South, the family compensates for the lack of subsidies and adequate public services.

Young Italians are studying less and less; the number of students enrolled in Italian universities in relation to population has been in decline in recent years, especially with respect to students from poorer families, particularly in the South, and in the fields of the social sciences and humanities (Viesti 2016). This is true both in absolute and relative sense, taking into account the demographic trends bringing to a reduction of the youth component in the Italian population. Along with the economic crisis that has struck families, we are seeing a crisis of confidence in the system and in the ability of a university degree to ensure the future graduate a job and an income that would justify the family's investment.

A survey conducted in 2011 on young Italians who graduated in 2007 shows that those who stayed in Italy after graduating are less satisfied with their job than those who reside abroad, especially as regards compensation and opportunities for advancement. Only 13.9 per cent of young people interviewed said they were very satisfied with their wages and only 18.1 per cent described themselves as very satisfied with their careers (Istat 2012a). Young Italians also consider themselves overqualified for the duties they perform: only 25.2 per cent said they were very satisfied with their use of the knowledge they acquired at university (Istat 2012a).

In 2014 the employment rate for young people aged 15 to 34 years was 55.1 per cent in the EU-28 while in Italy it was 39.1 per cent. The employment gap is even wider for university graduates: 56.7 per cent in Italy and 77.8 per cent in the EU-28 (Istat 2015a). In the 2008-2014 period, employment among young people from 15 to 34 years in Italy decreased by 27.7 per cent; the decrease was particularly significant in the South: -31.9 per cent (Svimez 2015). As employment has decreased, an increase has been seen in job instability and uncertainty, with 'non-standard' work arrangements on the rise (Svimez 2015). The difficult employment situation affects not only undereducated young people but also those with secondary school diplomas or university degrees. In the 2008-2014 period, employment among young people from 20 to 34 years with a secondary school diploma fell by 22.1 per cent and among young university graduates by 17.6 per cent. The decrease was larger in the Centre-North for the secondary school graduates but more significant in the South for university graduates (Svimez 2015). In 2014 the employment rate for secondary school graduates aged 20 to 34 was 46.5 per cent in the Centre-North and 24.7 per cent in the South; for university graduates the figures were, respectively, 64.7 per cent and 31.9 per cent (Svimez 2015). A comparison with the rest of Europe makes the situation even clearer. In 2014, three years after graduation from secondary school or university, 76 per cent of EU-28 young people were employed; in Italy only 45 per cent (Svimez 2015).

Continuing to make comparisons with Europe, we can note that, in 2014, 42.1 per cent of Europeans (EU-28) between 15 and 34 years were employed, but only 34.1 per cent in Italy. The Italian figure is heavily influenced by the situation in the South, where only 23.9 per cent of young people between 15 and 34 were employed. The figure that perhaps best represents the imbalance in the economy, employment and confidence in the South is the NEET (Not in Education, Employment, or Training) rate: 38.7 per cent in 2014, higher than in Greece (29.5 per cent) and Spain (22.4 per cent), to name two other Mediterranean European Countries. That rate has increased in Italy by 25.4 per cent since the beginning of the economic crisis (Svimez 2015).

The youth unemployment rate (young people between 15 and 24 years), in December 2015, was 19.7 per cent in the EU-28 and 22.0 per cent in the Euro Area. In Italy, the youth unemployment rate (young people between 15 and 24 years) in December 2015 was 37.9 per cent (Eurostat 2016c), a figure which, although very high, showed significant improvement compared to 2014, when it was 43 per cent (56 per cent in the South and 35 per cent in the Centre-North) (Svimez 2015).

Young Italians are, for the most part, "moderately pessimistic" but with a "desire not to give up" Rosina (2013: 18) which induces them not to despair in the future. They have great self-confidence and a desire to get involved and show their worth, but are at high risk for de-motivation when their expectations are continually frustrated (Rosina 2014). Those who are very pessimistic are, however, increasing in number (Triani 2014).These young people do not believe in the political structures and traditional institutions, especially those with which they have no direct contact. However, they believe in the value of the European Union, perhaps because they are hoping for a means of salvation (for) or escape (from) Italy; they are very much at odds with the previous generations, who they feel are partially responsible for their current predicament; they believe in the value of schooling; they are more conscious of religion and spirituality than the young people of the past; they are digital natives and they use the internet naturally but are aware of its potential "traps"; they hope for change in Italian society but they are convinced that this change cannot come from the internet and grassroots movements (Rosina 2013).

YOUNG ITALIANS ON THE MOVE

EU policies to promote mobility of young people within the EU

EU policies are – clearly and openly – aimed at promoting movement of young people within the EU, for both study and work purposes. The existence of a European Higher Education Area – which came out of the Bologna Process – and of an EU research and scientific area (Ackers 2005a; Ackers 2005b), of the ERASMUS and SOCRATES programs promote the mobility of both university students and scientists.

One of the key actions of the Lisbon Strategy is "the removal of obstacles to physical, labour and academic mobility" (Commission of the European Communities 2005). This is an ambitious aim, strongly linked to the need of solving regional/national labor market imbalances. The European Community has the scope to create a pan-European labor market where occupational and geographic mobility is facilitated. A specific effort is put in integrating the youth component in this open market, through policies directed to human capital, education, vocational training. Since the Lisbon Strategy, then, the mobility policies for youth are, in the vision of the European Commission, strictly linked to (and as a way to solve) European labor market dynamics. This orientation is confirmed by the Europe 2020 Strategy where the flagship initiative "Youth on the Move" (European Commission 2010a) is recalled "to enhance the performance of education systems and to facilitate the entry of young people to the labour market" (European Commission 2010b). The Commission highlights once again the link between youth mobility for education and training, reduction of unemployment and promotion of entrepreneurship. The year before, 2009, a Green Paper on "Promoting the learning mobility of young people" (Commission of the European Communities 2009) has been issued in which the mobility aimed at acquiring new skills and competences has been recognized as one of the main ways, especially for young persons, to improve their *employability* and their *personal development* (Commission of the European Communities 2009). The learning mobility is also recognized as a pre-phase for a future job-mobility, recommended in a period of economic crisis. The European Commission supported the idea of youth mobility as a tool to improve skills, acquire competences, improve employability, with initiatives complementary to "Youth on the Move", like "Agenda for New Skills and Jobs" (European Commission 2010c) and "Your first EURES job". The first one considers the need to remove regulatory and non-regulatory obstacles to transnational mobility as a way to promote employment; the second one created in several European Countries, offices to favor the matching of demand and supply in a European labor market.

All the above mentioned recommendations, initiatives and strategies have focused their attention on the European young citizen considered in his/her individuality. They have not paid attention to the regions and territories those persons belong to. This is in line with the spirit and aim of the Lisbon Strategy that prioritized the axis of Single Market over the Cohesion Policy. The Cohesion Policy, launched in 1988, had the aim of integrating the existing European funds for territorial development (European Agricultural Guarantee Fund-EAGGF, European Regional Development Fund-EDRF, European Social Fund-ESF) in order to reduce European inequalities (Jouen 2014). The Cohesion Policy was intended to be a way to promote growth in less favored regions and for disadvantaged communities in marginal areas. The Cohesion Policy was based on the strong assumption of Tommaso Padoa-Schioppa of very low geographical mobility of Europeans (Jouen 2014). It was promoted by Jacques Delors during his Presidency of the European Commission as a form of solidarity among Member States and as the second tier together with the European Single Market.

The factors that motivate young people to move and the characteristics of those who do so

The motivations that drive young people to mobility are numerous and diverse. They include both personal and collective considerations and are determined by specific local, historical, social and economic conditions.

One reason young people move abroad is to improve their education by enrolling in a course of study internationally (Altbach 1989; King/Ruiz-Gelices 2003; Findlay 2010; Findlay et al. 2012; Staniscia 2012; King/Raghuram 2013; Montanari/Staniscia 2014; Perkins/Neumayer 2014). An experience abroad offers new and exciting experiences on a personal level, for increasing one's human capital, skills and competences, including language skills, and tacit knowledge (Williams/Baláž 2005, 2008) and to improve future employability.

International mobility characterizes academia and researchers (Altbach 1989; Mahroum 2000; Ackers 2005a, 2005b) and highly skilled workers, with the local risk of brain drain and the individual risk of brain waste (Bhagwati/Hamada1974; Findlay/Gould 1989; Salt 1992; Montanari 1993, 1995; Bhagwati/Hanson 2009; Boucher/Cerna 2014). In a period of crisis like this one, even low-skilled young people have greater motivation to move, driven by push and pull factors: high unemployment in their native region and better wages at their destination.

Monetary factors are not the only ones that push young people to migrate. Young people with career aspirations are more geared towards moving internationally while those with strong roots in their own communities and stronger family ties are less so. Personal inclination toward risk-taking and the ability to handle unfamiliar situations in new contexts are two factors that strongly influence the decision to move (Williams/Baláž 2014). According to a panel of experts from nine countries (Latvia, Sweden, Ireland, the United Kingdom, Germany, Slovakia, Romania, Spain, Italy) who took part in a research project on the mobility of young Europeans (YMOBILITY)[3], the main factors that influence the mobility of young people – aside from reasons related to economics (wage differentials and career opportunities), employment (moving to more efficient labor markets) and personal development (to improve one's educational capital and knowledge) – include individual and relational factors, such as having networks of friends and family that live abroad, having had previous experience abroad and having a high tolerance for risk.

What motivations drive young Italians to move abroad? King and Conti (2013) divide motivations of young Italian graduates who moved to London into three categories: (i) economic situation and career prospects, (ii) possibility of self-development and (iii) criticism for the cultural and ethical values of Italian society. They find this mobility to be closely related to the freedom of movement within the EU territory, the short distance and the availability of low-cost flights. King and Conti (2013) and King et al. (2014) place great emphasis on the criticisms that young Italian graduates who moved to London express for their own country. They criticize its lack of organization and its enormous administrative problems. They criticize the widespread habit of finding jobs through personal networks and not through formal channels; they criticize the lack of recognition

---

3   www.ymobility.eu.

for merit. They complain about the existence of powerful groups that control the country and of a gerontocracy that blocks young people of merit from career opportunities. They believe that Italy does not invest in the future and therefore does not invest in the younger generations.

The objective challenge of measuring the phenomenon

Quantifying the mobility of Italian young people is not an easy task because of the variety of available, not necessarily coordinated, sources of statistics. The difficulty is also due to the fact that young Italians who move within the EU territory do not necessarily document their movements officially. The challenge is so great that the President of Italy's National Statistical Office Istat was driven to write "La misura degli italiani residenti all'estero: un problema di non facile soluzione" (*Measuring Italians residing abroad: a problem not easy to be solved*) (Istat 2012a: 5).

A primary and important source of statistics for Italy is Istat's data on changes of residence from the municipal population registries. The changes recorded show names entered in or cancelled from the register for moves from one municipality in Italy to another, and from an Italian municipality to one in another country. This source includes data starting from 1955, dealing only with residents in Italy –whether Italian citizens or foreigners– and measures the flows of residents, both entering and leaving. These data, however, give an imprecise picture of the situation because many Italian citizens (and foreigners) move abroad without cancelling their names from the population registers, especially if they consider the move not to be a permanent one, even if it is long-term.

Other sources include: the archive of the Consular Registries (Ministry of Foreign Affairs and International Cooperation); the central archive of the Registry of Italians Resident Abroad – AIRE, since 1990 (Ministry of the Interior); for the years 2003 and 2011, the Survey of Italians abroad (Ministry of Foreign Affairs and International Cooperation and Istat). These data provide a count of Italians resident abroad. These sources carry out administrative –not statistical– functions and therefore do not satisfy the requirements of comprehensiveness, quality and completeness of the information (Istat 2012a). Furthermore, they only count Italians who are abroad longer than twelve months, because registration is not obligatory for shorter stays. Even then, many Italians who are legally required to register do not actually do so. Data on return migrants are provided by the Census of Population and Housing taken every ten years (the most recent available is for 2011).

The size of the phenomenon

On January 1, 2012, the estimated Italian population resident abroad was 3,916,023 and had increased by 1.1 per cent in just less than nine years (compared with residents abroad on March 21, 2003); 57.4 per cent of Italians resident abroad reside in a European country; the most significant concentrations are, in descending order, in Germany, Switzerland, France, Belgium and the United Kingdom; 37.3 per cent reside in America; the most significant concentrations are, in descending order, in Argentina, Brazil, the United States and Canada (Istat 2012a) (table 3.1).

In the 2008-2014 period, 407,114 Italians moved abroad and 208,277 returned from abroad; net migration of Italian citizens to foreign countries from 2008 to 2014 was therefore negative -98,837 individuals. The number of persons moving abroad is steadily increasing (increased by 125 per cent over the 2008-2014 period), while the number of returnees oscillates but shows a negative trend (Istat 2016a).

The significance of these figures can be seen when they are compared with those for the previous period (2001-2007): 284,576 Italians moved abroad and 330,392 returned. The balance, therefore, was positive: 45,816 persons (Istat 2010).

These figures are even more significant – in percentages – in an analysis of the data for young Italians (aged 18 to 39 years), of whom 208,818 moved abroad during the 2008-2014 period and 72,904 returned, for a negative migration balance totaling 135,914. The number of young people (from 18 to 39 years) moving abroad is steadily increasing (increased by 115 per cent over the period), while the number of returnees oscillates but shows a negative trend (Istat 2016a). In general, the preferred destinations, in Europe, are Germany, the United Kingdom, Switzerland and France and, outside Europe, the United States and Brazil (Istat 2012b, 2014a, 2014b, 2015b).

Table 3.1: Some relevant figures concerning youth migration in Italy

Time Span	Mobility Features	Numbers/Shares
2012	Italian citizens resident abroad	3,916,023
	In Europe	57.4%
	In America	37.3%
2001-2007	Italian citizens who moved abroad	284,576
	Italian citizens who returned from abroad	330,392
2008-2014	Italian citizens who moved abroad,	407,114
	of which young Italians (18-39 years old)	208,818
	Italian citizens who returned from abroad,	208,277
	of which young Italians (18-39 years old)	72,904

Source: Istat 2010; Istat 2012a; Istat 2016a

During the 2008-2011 period, the percentage of Italians over the age of 25 years with a university degree who moved abroad was always greater than the percentage of those who returned. The situation stabilized in the 2012-2013 period, when the percentage of graduates who moved abroad was almost equal to that of returning graduates. The trend showed some change in 2014, when the percentage of university graduates returning from abroad was 34.7 per cent of the total and that of graduates moving abroad was 30 per cent of the total. It will be necessary to wait for 2015 data to see if 2014 marked a turnaround or simply an exception (Istat 2012b, 2014a, 2014b, 2015b). The favorite destination for university graduates is London (Istat, 2012b, 2014a, 2014b, 2015b) for the quality and style of life as well as the employment and career opportunities it offers.

Of those who graduated in 2007 and were living abroad in 2011, the largest group had degrees in the humanities (25.1 per cent of the sample), while it was in the sciences that the highest percentage of graduates moving abroad was recorded (3.7 per cent of the total). More males than females made the move, respectively 2.6 per cent and 1.8 per cent of those who left university in 2007. Graduates from the northern regions of Italy were particularly likely to move abroad; 63.6 per cent of respondents stated that the opportunity to find a more specialized job than in Italy was very important in the decision to move abroad and 60.7 per cent say that the prospect of better pay was very important. This is also confirmed by their wages: in Italy the average salary declared by the respondents was 1,402€ per month, while abroad it was 1,891€ per month; 39.4 per cent of the graduates have intellectual, scientific or highly specialized professions and 38.7 per cent have technical professions. They come from a favorable family background in cultural and economic terms; more than half (52.2 per cent) of university graduates living abroad have a father in an intellectual, scientific, highly specialized or technical job; nearly half (44.7 per cent) have at least one parent with a university degree.

Between December 2009 and February 2010, a sample survey[4] was conducted of 18,568 people, mostly young people, who earned a PhD in Italy between 2004 and 2006. The survey showed that 6.4 per cent of respondents lived abroad (Istat 2011). The main destination countries are France, the United States and the United Kingdom. The origins of the respondents were, in descending order, Northern Italy (8.4 per cent of doctoral students who have moved abroad lived in the North before starting university), the Centre (6.5 per cent of doctoral students who have moved abroad lived in the Centre before starting university) and the South (4.4 per cent of doctoral students who have moved abroad lived in a region in Southern Italy before starting university). Males (7.6 per cent) showed greater inclination to move abroad than females do (5.1 per cent). Those with PhDs in the physical sciences were also more likely to go (22.7 per cent were abroad). Factors that influenced the decision were: (i) the education level of the parents, (ii) the age at which the doctorate was completed, (iii) having spent time abroad during the PhD program, (iv) international experiences after completing the PhD, (v) the intention to work in the research sector and (vi) the difficulty of finding a position in Italy corresponding with the advanced degree acquired (Istat 2011).

ITALIAN POLICIES THAT ENCOURAGE OUTBOUND OR RETURN MOBILITY OF YOUNG ITALIANS

When the crisis began, the Italian government was already working to reverse the brain drain, which was already well under way (Avveduto/Brandi 2004; Becker et al. 2004; Morano-Foadi 2006). In 2008 the government issued Decree Law 185/2008, subsequently converted into Law 2/2009. This legislation provided tax incentives for researchers and university instructors returning from abroad. Its purpose was to encourage a return of talent back to Italy, but its suc-

---

4 The survey is conducted every three years, by the Italian National Institute of Statistics in the general framework of the surveys carried out for analyzing the transition from education to work. It is implemented through a CATI (Computer Assisted Telephone Interviewing) technique. It concerns all the persons who have got a PhD in the given period. The valid answers obtained were 70% of the total. An estimation procedure was, then, implemented in order to cover the missing data.

cess was limited because the tax incentives did not come with a tenured position (Boeri 2014).

At the end of the 2010, that is, at the height of the economic crisis, Law 238/2010, also known as *Legge Controesodo* (counter-exodus law) was enacted to promote development through human, cultural and professional experience accrued by EU citizens under 40 years old, who had resided in Italy continuously for at least 24 months, and who had studied or worked abroad and then decided to return to Italy. This law reduced the income tax base by 80 per cent for women and 70 per cent for men. The tax benefits were applied from January 28, 2011 until the end of fiscal year 2013. It was subsequently extended to the end of 2015.

The process to enact the law was a circuitous one. After it was approved, it was only in June 2011 that the decrees to implement it were issued, and another year would pass before the Italian Tax Agency (Agenzia delle Entrate) issued the circular to implement it. On May 4, 2012, the Tax Agency then drew a distinction between those abroad for work and those abroad for education. The former would need to have a university degree and have resided outside Italy for at least 24 months while continuously employed, self-employed or working as entrepreneurs. The latter were required to have been resident in Italy for at least 24 months, to have been resident abroad for at least two years, and to have obtained a university or post-graduate degree abroad. The numerous doubts about the Law's interpretation were hardly an encouragement to anyone who might have wanted to take advantage of its benefits. According to the Tax Agency, 3,838 Italians decided to use the benefits provided by the *Legge Controesodo* and return in 2011. The majority (93 per cent) were employed while only 7 per cent had self-employment or business income. Although in previous years most of the young people leaving had been men, women made up the majority of those who used the Law 238/2010 (60 per cent). In 2012, 2,087 people took advantage of that law, about half as many as the year before. Women accounted for most of that decrease, while the percentage of professionals and entrepreneurs rose to 14.3 per cent. This increase is explained by the worsening of the economic crisis and by the Law's increased visibility during 2012. The Tax Agency has not released figures for the subsequent years but some observers have estimated that between 2011 and 2015 about 10,000 Italians used the *Legge Controesodo*.

Assolombarda, the Industrial Association of Lombardy, presented (November 25,2013) the platform "Fonderia dei Talenti" (Talent Foundry) to facilitate the discovery of young talents who had moved abroad and to help them connect with Italian industry. On the basis of this initiative, a series of public and private agencies sponsored a series of annual conferences: *Mee Talentsche* was first held in Milan (2012) and then regularly in the following years in Naples (2013), Perugia (2014) and Milan (2015).

From the beginning, the Law's application gave rise to extensive discussion, and in particular was given coverage by the economic newspaper Il Sole 24 Ore. The newspaper interviewed several young Italians living abroad who could have used Law 238/2010 to return to Italy. Francesco – a 30-year-old radiologist who works in France – said he would be willing to pay higher taxes but would want better working conditions in Italy. He referred specifically to the style of the organizations. "In Italy you need recommendations, but in France, if they see a young person who shows interest, they ask him to stay." Francesco was offered a good career opportunity and an attractive salary and decided to remain in France (Il Sole 24 Ore, May 4, 2012). Alex – a 33-year-old engineer who lives in the USA, where he was hired as a permanent employee with a salary about six times higher than what he could earn in Italy – says: "Tax breaks to come back to Italy? They are not enough to convince me to come back, because in my country I wouldn't find a job."(Il Sole 24 Ore, May 5, 2012) Federico – a 37-year-old software developer in the USA – wonders: "Come back for tax incentives? The problem in Italy is the bureaucracy." (Il Sole 24 Ore, May 5, 2012) Andrea is a 30-year-old entrepreneur in Brussels; he believes that: "It isn't about the taxes; I'd happily pay them in my country, if conditions were different." (Il Sole 24 Ore, June 29, 2012) ISTAT, however, in 2015 declared that the change in returns recorded in 2014 could be partly attributed to the effectiveness of the *Legge ControEsodo* (ISTAT 2015b).

The law was then extended through 2017 by Law 192/2014. This was later cancelled with the introduction of Law 147/2015, "Provisions bearing measures for business growth and internationalization." Article 16 of this Law defines a new "special regime for repatriated workers". Three important changes were introduced: (i) the tax bonus was reduced to 30 per cent regardless of gender; (ii) the tax bonus was granted to all Italians living abroad regardless of age; and (iii) the period of residence abroad was extended to five years with a commitment to stay in Italy for at least two years. The new rules created great alarm among those who had benefited from the previous Law 238/2010 and who had made the decision to return on the basis of a financial plan that partially relied on reduced taxes. Aside from the recent controversy over the unexpected change in the legislation, other factors contributed to the initiative's limited success in encouraging return migration. The Italian economy is dominated by small and medium-sized enterprises which, in many cases, fail to use a systematic approach and to make contact with highly-skilled workers who reside abroad but who might be prepared to return to Italy if an opportunity presented itself. Lanvin and Evans

(2016) consider Italy uncompetitive in terms of ability to attract talents, ranking it twenty-sixth in Europe and forty-first in the world. This leaves Italy in a situation of reduced international mobility, with limited inbound and outbound flows. This hinders the country's ability to promote its strengths. Among the many variables taken into consideration, Italy ranks particularly low in its institutional environment, seen as unfavorable to businesses, and in the rigidity of its labor market. Italy is positioned better in mid-level skills (labor and vocational skills – eighteenth place) but lower in high-level skills (tertiary educated workforce – sixty-sixth place).

Conclusions

The statistical data relating to the mobility of young people are certainly numerous and have allowed us to irrefutably demonstrate a series of objective consequences of the economic crisis that has affected Italy in recent years. We have noted, however, that the phenomenon can be only partially explained using the official statistical data. In fact, flows of young people remain largely invisible in official statistics precisely because the movements are constantly changing, but also because the very concept of freedom of movement within the European Union has been embraced with great enthusiasm especially by young people. Collections of official statistics are prepared according to long-established national and international parameters and are not equipped to adapt to rapidly occurring phenomena the causes of which cannot always be identified and measured.

Public opinion and the media also rely on sometimes obsolete methods to assess the situation. For example, the term 'mobility' can be misinterpreted and is easily confused with the concept of 'flight'. In the EU of the future, young people should move freely from one city or country to another according to their life goals. Mobility involves periods of both outbound and return flows, periods of production and of recognition, and periods of consumption, for example for education or tourism. The term 'flight', however, has a negative meaning, one of absolute rejection. It can be used for political purposes, to indicate disaffection and therefore opposition to a government or to an administration. Even scholars play a role in these unrealistic lines of thinking. Rather than verifying whether a *flight* of young people is actually taking place, they set to work studying the motivations behind it, thus substantiating the theory of its existence.

According to Eurostat data, the expatriates of all ages who left Italy during the years of the crisis are about half as many as those who left other major European countries such as Germany, France and the UK. A 'flight' would have affected all the demographic components. Italians, and therefore young Italians, do not actually move to other countries in an indistinctive way, but they choose specific locations. In the UK, for instance, they are concentrated in London. Some predict that in 2016 the Italian population in London will become the largest of any city outside Italy. Italians who move to London are of all ages; there is no specific prevalence of young people[5]. No one would express surprise if there were a significant migratory flow in the USA from one State to New York. The situation in the USA cannot certainly be compared with that of the EU, but perhaps in this case going abroad has been the result of an attitude rather than of a political process. This is confirmed by the fact that Italian emigration, even during the crisis, was limited to EU countries.

Cultural and psychological elements are a significant component of the decisions that affect human mobility at a time when the culture is in a somewhat *liquid* state. We can objectively refer to young Italians' lack of faith in their administration's ability to resolve the economic and social problems that the economic crisis posed for all of European society. This is demonstrated by the fact that Italians have less confidence in their own country than citizens of other Southern European countries, who are often living in worse social and economic conditions.

The structure of Italian society has always been founded on the family. In this period of crisis the family's role has become even more important. When seeking solidarity, young people remain with (or return to) their families. If they are looking for autonomy and individual independence they go abroad. Young people move to major cities like London to put themselves to the test and to prove their worth away from the flaws of Italian society, which is still very conservative and reluctant to recognize the merits and qualities of its citizens.

Social networks play an important role in this process. The uninterrupted communication we now experience has shown that it is possible to go abroad, that life may be difficult, but that success is also a possibility. Social networks help to solve the practical problems of a new life abroad, but also help in finding a position. Furthermore, they ensure continuous contact with home, which, all in

---

5 Following the results of the referendum held in June 2016, Great Britain has decided to leave the EU. Young Italians living in the UK have immediately reacted to this. Their immediate concern is the uncertainty about the way the new situation will be managed and its outcomes, more than the risks associated with the decision to leave the EU. According to some empirical evidences, several young Italians residing in the UK and working with a regular contract are already looking for a solution to return to Italy; several others are starting the procedures to acquire British citizenship.

all, is very close and can be cheaply and easily reached through the new transportation modes.

Acknowledgments

The research leading to these results received funding from the Horizon2020 YMOBILITY project (Youth Mobility: Maximizing Opportunities for Individuals, Labour Markets and Regions in Europe), grant agreement no 649491. Project website: www.ymobility.eu.

REFERENCES

Ackers, Louise (2005a): "Moving people and knowledge: scientific mobility in the European Union." In: International Migration 43, pp. 99-131.

Ackers, Louise (2005b): "Promoting scientific mobility and balanced growth in the European Research Area." In: Innovation: The European Journal of Social Science Research 18/3, pp. 301-317.

Agenzia delle Entrate (2016): "Osservatorio del mercato immobiliare. Banche dati." February 8, 2016 (http://www.agenziaentrate.gov.it/wps/content/Nsilib /Nsi/Documentazione/omi/Banche+dati/Volumi+di+compravendita/ Compravendite+immobili+residenziali/).

Altbach, Philip G. (1989): "The new internationalism: foreign students and scholars." In: Studies in Higher Education 14/2, pp. 125-136.

Associazione per lo sviluppo dell' industria nel Mezzogiorno (Svimez) (2015): Rapporto Svimez 2015 sull'economia del Mezzogiorno, Bologna: il Mulino.

Avveduto, Sveva/Brandi, Maria Carolina (2004): "Le migrazioni qualificate in Italia." In: StudiEmigrazione 41/156, pp. 797-830.

Becker, Sascha O./Ichino, Andrea/Peri, Giovanni (2004): "How large is the 'brain drain' from Italy?" In: Giornale degli Economisti e Annali di Economia 63/1, pp. 1-32.

Bhagwati, Jagdish N./Hamada, Koichi (1974): "The brain drain, international integration of markets for professionals and unemployment." In: Journal of Development Economics 1, pp. 19-42.

Bhagwati, Jagdish N./Hanson, Gordon (2009): Skilled immigration today: Prospects, problems, and policies, Oxford: Oxford University Press.

Boeri, Tito (2014): "In Italia tanto brain drain e poco brain gain." In: Confindustria (ed.), People first. Il capitale sociale e umano: la forza del Paese, Rome: S.I.P.I. Editore, pp. 137-151.

Boucher, Anna/Cerna, Lucie (2014): "Current policy trends in skilled immigration." In: International Migration 52/3, pp. 21-25.
Coldiretti-SWG (2013): "I giovani e la crisi." December 7, 2015 (http://www.coldiretti.it/).
Commission of the European Communities (2005): Common Actions for Growth and Employment: The Community Lisbon Programme. COM (2005) 330 final, pp. 1-10.
Commission of the European Communities (2009): Green Paper. Promoting the Learning Mobility of Young People. COM (2009) 329 final, pp. 1-22.
CountryWatch (2015): Italy Country Review 2015, Houston, Texas: CountryWatch.
Dalla Zuanna, Gianpiero/Micheli, Giuseppe A. (2004): Strong family and low fertility: A paradox?, Dordrecht: Kluwer Academic Press.
DemografiaImprese (2016): "Demografia Imprese Open Data Explorer." February 8, 2016 (http://www.mc.camcom.it/uploaded/Allegati/Promozione/Charts/Open-Data-Imprese-Attive.htm).
Domínguez-Mujica, Josefina/Pérez-García, Tanausú (2017): "The economic crisis and the Southern European migration model. A comparative analysis." In: Birgit Glorius/Josefina Domínguez-Mujica (eds.), European Mobility in Times of Crisis. The new context of European South-North Migration, Bielefeld: Transcript-Verlag.
European Commission (2010a): Youth on the Move. An Initiative to Unleash the Potential of Young People to Achieve Smart, Sustainable and Inclusive Growth in the European Union. COM (2010) 477 final, pp. 1-26.
European Commission (2010b): Europe 2020. A strategy for smart, sustainable and inclusive growth. COM (2010) 2020, pp. 1-37.
European Commission (2010c): An Agenda for New Skills and Jobs. A European Contribution Towards Full Employment. COM (2010) 682 final, pp. 1-22.
European Commission (2012): Towards a job-rich recovery. COM (2012) 173 final, p. 1-27.
European Commission (2013): Special Eurobarometer 397. Corruption. January 7, 2016 (http://ec.europa.eu/public_opinion).
European Commission (2014a): Special Eurobarometer 418. Social climate. January 7, 2016 (http://ec.europa.eu/public_opinion).
European Commission (2014b): Special Eurobarometer 415. Europeans in 2014. January 7, 2016 (http://ec.europa.eu/public_opinion).
European Commission (2016): European economic forecast. Winter 2016. Institutional Paper 20. February 22, 2016 (http://ec.europa.eu/economy_finance/publications/eeip/ip020_en.htm).

Eurostat (2016a): National accounts. January 11, 2016 (http://ec.europa.eu/euro statEurostat/web/national-accounts/data).
Eurostat (2016b): Labour market. January 11, 2016 (http://ec.europa.eu/eurostat/ data).
Eurostat (2016c): Unemployment statistics. February 12, 2016 (http://ec.europa. eu/eurostat/statisticsexplained/index.php/Unemployment_statistics).
Findlay, Allan M. (2010): "An assessment of supply and demand-side theorizations of international student mobility." In: International Migration 49/2, pp. 162-190.
Findlay, Allan M./Gould, William T.S. (1989): "Skilled international migration: A research agenda." In: Area 21/1, pp. 3-11.
Findlay, Allan M./King, Russell/Smith, Fiona M./Geddes, Alistair/Skeldon, Ronald (2012): "'World class?' An investigation of globalisation, difference and international student mobility." In: Transactions of the Institute of British Geographers 37/1, pp. 118-131.
Istituto Nazionale di Statistica (Istat) (2010): Movimento migratorio della popolazione residente, Rome: ISTAT.
Istituto Nazionale di Statistica (Istat) (2011): Indagine 2009 sull'inserimento professionale dei dottori di ricerca. Mobilità interna e verso l'estero dei dottori di ricerca, Rome: ISTAT.
Istituto Nazionale di Statistica (Istat) (2012a): Indagine conoscitiva sulle politiche relative ai cittadini italiani residenti all'estero. Audizione del Presidente dell'Istituto Nazionale di Statistica Enrico Giovannini al Senato della Repubblica, Rome: ISTAT.
Istituto Nazionale di Statistica (Istat) (2012b): Migrazioni internazionali e interne della popolazione residente. Anno 2011, Rome: ISTAT.
Istituto Nazionale di Statistica (Istat) (2014a): Migrazioni internazionali e interne della popolazione residente. Anno 2012, Rome: ISTAT.
Istituto Nazionale di Statistica (Istat) (2014b): Migrazioni internazionali e interne della popolazione residente. Anno 2013, Rome: ISTAT.
Istituto Nazionale di Statistica (Istat) (2015a): Rapporto Annuale 2015. La situazione del Paese, Rome: ISTAT.
Istituto Nazionale di Statistica (Istat) (2015b): Migrazioni internazionali e interne della popolazione residente. Anno 2014, Rome: ISTAT.
Istituto Nazionale di Statistica (Istat) (2016a): Data on in-flows and out-flows of Italian citizens. January 10, 2016 (http://dati.istat.it/#).
Istituto Nazionale di Statistica (Istat) (2016b): Popolazione residente al 1 gennaio 2015 per età, sesso e stato civile. February 12, 2016 (http://demo.istat .it/pop2015/index.html).

Jouen, Marjorie (2014): The single market and cohesion policy dyad: battered by the crisis and globalisation (Notre Europe, Policy Paper 108), Paris: Notre Europe, pp. 1-18.

King, Russell/Ruiz-Gelices, Enric (2003): "International student migration and the European 'Year Abroad': effects on European identity and subsequent migration behavior." In: International Journal of Population Geography 9/3, pp. 229-252.

King, Russell/Conti, Francesca (2013): Bridging the divide: the gap between the study of internal and international migration, with an Italian example (Willy Brandt Series of Working Papers in International Migration and Ethnic Relations, 1), Malmö: Malmö University, pp. 1-56.

King, Russell/Raghuram, Parvati (2013): "International student migration: Mapping the field and new research agendas." In: Population, Space and Place 19/2, pp. 127-137.

King, Russell/Lulle, Aija/Conti, Francesca/Mueller, Dorothea/Scotto, Giuseppe (2014): The lure of London: a comparative study of recent graduate migration from Germany, Italy and Latvia (Working paper 75, University of Sussex-Sussex Centre for Migration Research), Brighton: University of Sussex, pp. 1-39.

King, Russell/Lulle, Aija/Morosanu, Laura/Williams, Allan M. (2016): International youth mobility and life transitions in Europe: questions, definitions, typologies and theoretical approaches (Working Paper 86, University of Sussex-Sussex Centre for Migration Research), Brighton: University of Sussex, pp. 1-61.

Lavin, Bruno/Evans, Paul (eds.) (2016): The Global Talent Competitiveness Index, Talent attraction and international mobility, 2015-16, Fontainebleau: INSEAD.

Mahroum, Sami (2000): "Scientists and global spaces." In: Technology in Society 22, pp. 513-523.

Montanari, Armando (1993): "Italian skilled and graduate emigration." In: Susan Biggin/Vladimir Kouzminov (eds.), Proceedings of the international seminar on "brain drain" issues in Europe, Venice: UNESCO Regional Office for Science and Technology for Europe, pp. 286-294.

Montanari, Armando (1995): "Skilled migration from Italy." In: Studi Emigrazione 32/117, pp. 42-53.

Montanari, Armando/Staniscia, Barbara (2014): "International tertiary students: Is Rome an attractive destination?" In: Eurolimes 17, pp. 169-183.

Morano-Foadi, Sonia (2006): "Key issues and courses of the Italian brain drain." In: European Journal of Social Research 19/2, pp. 209-223.

Perkins, Richard/Neumayer, Eric (2014): "Geographies of educational mobilities: exploring the uneven flows of international students." In: The Geographical Journal 180/3, pp. 246-259.
Rosina, Alessandro (2013): "Introduzione." In: Istituto Giuseppe Toniolo (ed.), La condizione giovanile in Italia. Rapporto Giovani 2013,Bologna: il Mulino, pp. 7-20.
Rosina, Alessandro (2014): "Introduzione." In: Istituto Giuseppe Toniolo (ed.), La condizione giovanile in Italia. Rapporto Giovani 2014, Bologna: il Mulino, pp. 7-22.
Rosina, Alessandro/Sironi, Emiliano (2013): "Diventare adulti in tempo di crisi." In: Istituto Giuseppe Toniolo (ed.). La condizione giovanile in Italia. Rapporto Giovani 2013, Bologna: il Mulino, pp. 75-95.
Salt, John (1992): "Migration processes among the highly skilled in Europe." In: International Migration Review 26/2, pp. 484-505.
Scabini, Eugenia/Marta, Elena (2013): "Giovani in famiglia: risorsa o rifugio?" In: Istituto Giuseppe Toniolo (ed.), La condizione giovanile in Italia. Rapporto Giovani 2013, Bologna: il Mulino, pp. 23-48.
Staniscia, Barbara (2012): "Mobility of students and attractiveness of universities. The case of Sapienza University of Rome." In: International Review of Sociology, DOI:10.1080/03906701.2012.696967.
Triani, Pierpaolo (2014): "In che cosa credere? A chi dare fiducia?" In: Istituto Giuseppe Toniolo (ed.), La condizione giovanile in Italia. Rapporto Giovani 2014, Bologna: il Mulino, pp. 99-121.
Viesti, Gianfranco (ed.) (2016): Università in declino. Un'indagine sugli atenei da Nord a Sud, Rome: Donzelli Editore.
Williams, Allan M./Baláž, Vladimir (2005): "What Human Capital, Which Migrants? Returned Skilled Migration to Slovakia from the UK." In: International Migration Review 39, pp. 439-468.
Williams, Allan M./Baláž, Vladimir (2008): International migration and knowledge, London: Routledge.
Williams, Allan M./Baláž, Vladimir (2014): "Mobility, risk tolerance and competence to manage risks." In: Journal of Risk Research, 17/8, pp.1061-1088.

4. Crisis and the resurgence of emigration from Greece: trends, representations, and the multiplicity of migrant trajectories[1]

MANOLIS PRATSINAKIS, PANOS HATZIPROKOPIOU, DIMITRIS GRAMMATIKAS AND LOIS LABRIANIDIS

ABSTRACT

In the context and conjuncture of the crisis affecting the Eurozone as whole, yet shaking mostly its 'weakest links', rising unemployment and steep decreases in salaries and welfare allowances are cited as push factors contributing to what is seen as the emergence of a new emigration wave from Southern Europe. This is especially true for Greece, the country which has been hit hardest by the crisis, recession and austerity, and their social and political consequences. In Greece, there is extended media coverage of this new emigration, which is presented as an one-way option for certain population segments, notably the young and the highly skilled, and hence a drain of the most dynamic part of the country's labor force. Despite this media attention, however, little is known about the current intensification of emigration from Greece and its characteristics, as well as the experiences of the country's new 'crisis migrants'.

This paper aims to partly fill in this gap. It begins by sketching the broad picture and identifying key trends, before moving on to explore key issues in the emerging public discourse. It then zooms into the case of recent Greek migrants to the Netherlands, providing a typology of different mobility trajectories and

---

1   The chapter partly draws from research conducted by the first author for the EUMIGRE project, funded by the EU's Horizon 2020 research and innovation programme under the Marie Skłodowska-Curie grant agreement No 658694.

migration experiences. Through this, we intend to deconstruct a number of conventional assumptions. Firstly, by situating new Greek emigration in a historical continuum, whereby its structural preconditions predated the crisis. Secondly, by identifying the qualitative dimensions of rupture through which the intra-EU mobility from Greece has undergone a shift from a career choice to one largely motivated by necessity. Finally, by highlighting those aspects that problematize idealistic perceptions of life and work 'in Europe' often depicted in Greek media, we bring to the fore the ambivalence of mobility decisions and the multiplicity of individual pathways.

Keywords: Crisis, Emigration, Greece, Intra-EU mobility, Migrant trajectories

INTRODUCTION

In post-war decades Greece emerged as an emigration country and a net exporter of labor (Fakiolas/King 1996: 172-4). By the mid-1970s, net migration rates had turned positive primarily due to the return of former Greek emigrants, especially from European destinations such as (West) Germany. It is around the same period when recruitment of foreign labor was first registered; from the 1980s Greece also begun to attract (limited numbers of) refugees and international students, and, by the early 1990s, the country became a de facto destination for international migrants. This turnaround coincided with similar pathways of other southern European countries (King 2000). Since then, immigration has become a crucial factor of societal change, largely monopolising public debates and academic research.

In the meanwhile, emigration had in fact never ceased as such, but remained insignificant as compared to the inflows. A renewed public discussion has recently appeared, in which rising unemployment and cuts in salaries and allowances, in the context of debt crisis, recession, austerity and their socio-political consequences, are cited as push factors contributing to the emergence of a new emigration wave. At an early phase, this discussion has largely been shaped by a study of Greek professionals leaving in search of better career opportunities abroad – a trend which has always been in place, but became more prominent since the 1990s and intensified with the crisis (Labrianidis 2011; 2014). Out-migration receives increasing media attention, and is presented as a one-way option for the young and the highly skilled, and hence a drain of the most dynamic part of the country's labor force.

Despite growing media coverage, however, still little is known about the current intensification of emigration and its qualitative dimensions. Moreover, increasingly politicised media discourses tend to overlook certain issues while others remain silenced. Not only the pre-existing structural conditions tend to be forgotten, but also the diversification of emigration flows is often ignored. A major shift that is underway concerns the transition from emigration as a career choice to a pathway imposed by need. As such, it may affect primarily the young and highly skilled, but spans to include other population segments: migrants, minorities, people of older age and lower educational attainments. As ever, 'objective' structural factors ('the crisis', etc.) are refined into a multiplicity of subjective motivations, trajectories and experiences in destination places. Depending on conditions there and prospects at home, as well as on the individuals' or households' circumstances and plans, mobility pathways can be temporary or ambivalent.

Aiming to partly fill in such gaps and to account for neglected aspects, this chapter focuses on the resurgence of Greek emigration at times of crisis by combining two different angles: the view from the sending country, and that at the destination. It is divided in two broad sections, each drawing on a variety of sources. In the first section, we overview the evidence deriving from official statistics and academic studies on the topic in order to sketch the broad picture of (what we know about) current emigration trends. We then explore media debates so as to highlight key points in the emerging public discourse, based on a review of 60 original newspaper items published between 2010 and 2015. In the second section, we zoom into one of the emerging destinations, the Netherlands. Building on qualitative research conducted in the context of two research projects and on survey material deriving from engagement with a Greek community organization,[2] we provide a typology of Greek 'crisis' migration to this country. The

---

2 Most of the qualitative data presented in the second section were collected as part of Pratsinakis' aforementioned EUMIGRE project. The chapter also builds on additional material from the recently completed project "Outward Migration from Greece during the Crisis" (2015-2016), funded by the National Bank of Greece through the London School of Economics' Hellenic Observatory (Research Tender 3-NBG3-2014; cp. Labrianidis/Pratsinakis 2016). The Netherlands survey was conducted during 2013-14 by Grammatikas through his involvement in the Greek community organization "Neoafihthendes", providing information and support to newcomers in The Hague, Rotterdam and Amsterdam, in which Pratsinakis also volunteered. The first section draws on collective work and on Hatziprokopiou's review of media articles.

chapter closes with a concluding section, in which we revisit key findings and summarise our arguments.

THE RESURGENCE OF EMIGRATION FROM GREECE

Even if the establishment of the right to free movement, employment and settlement across the European Union for Greek citizens in the 1980s allowed for unrestricted mobility, this never took the form of mass outflows. Until recently, Greeks were notably registered among the least mobile Europeans. A 2005 Eurobarometer survey unveiled that Greeks (second after the Cypriots) were the least favourable towards long distance mobility (European Commission 2006). Another Eurobarometer, conducted in 2009, showed that only eight per cent of Greeks envisaged working abroad (the lowest after Italians), while the share of those who would consider working in some other country in case of unemployment was well below the EU average (European Commission 2010). This was soon due to change in the shadow of the crisis.

In this section we overview existing evidence on new emigration and explore aspects of the emerging media discourse. The former relies on relevant academic studies and official data, evincing key figures and trends. The latter draws from a collection of nearly 100 newspaper (online and print) articles directly or indirectly accounting for the issue of outmigration from Greece, published between 2010 and 2015. These were identified during two main rounds of systematic Internet searches: one out of five during December 2013-January 2014, and most of the remainder during December 2015-January 2016. Of these, we have selected 60 original items, which we reviewed with the aim to explore media discourses on new emigration from Greece.[3]

Emigration trends

Albeit limited, emigration in the recent past was more frequent among specific groups: emigrants of the post-war waves and their offspring moving between Greece and European destinations (Fakiolas/King 1996: 175), Muslims from the minority of Thrace spending spells of employment in Germany or Turkey

---

3 We searched on Google, rather than excavating into specific media; and – for the analysis hereby presented – we have limited ourselves to national and general news media, rather than local or specialized ones, and tried to maintain some balance between original articles and news duplicated in several media.

(Pratsinakis 2002: 69ff.), as well as increased number of students abroad (Karamessini 2010: 260). Above all, there has been a continuous outflow of professionals that started becoming prominent in the 1990s, increasingly to Europe (Labrianidis 2011). Yet, highly skilled migration was largely a matter of choice for the middle and upper social classes; most emigrants left the country for reasons beyond employment as such, subjectively justifying their choice as an "escape" from a parochial Greek society, and as a desire to explore the world and live as cosmopolitans (Labrianidis 2011: 196f).

Labrianidis' (2011) pioneering study, based on an online survey conducted in 2009-10 that generated a sample of 1821 individuals and plenty of qualitative information, revealed the reality of "brain drain" as a trend predating the crisis, attributed not to the "over-education" of the young (against conventional earlier assumptions), but rather to structural malfunctions of the Greek productive model of the past decades, partly a (domestic) reason for the crisis. Accordingly, the inability of the labor market to absorb graduates has been primarily due to the private sector's failure to invest in high added-value products and services and expand knowledge-intensive sectors requiring highly skilled personnel (Labrianidis 2011; 2014). The crisis seems to intensify such trends, as job opportunities shrink and public sector employment is not a possibility anymore as a result of restrictions in new recruitments (ibid.; Pelliccia 2013; Triandafyllidou/Gropas 2014).

Yet the crisis undermines the employment prospects not only for graduates, but for the entire workforce. To give just an obvious example: the annual average unemployment rate in 2015 was nearly 25 per cent, almost double that of 2010 and more than triple than in 2008 (figure 4.1); in the last quarter of 2015, nearly half of young people aged 20-24 were unemployed, and over 37 per cent of those 25-29 years old. In a context of GDP contraction of more than one quarter between 2008-2014, the same period has also seen steep decreases in earnings and welfare provisions and allowances. The combined effects of recession, extreme austerity, and a generalised mistrust towards institutions and disillusionment from the political system have changed drastically mobility intentions. Despite the previously recorded scepticism, many were forced by the circumstances to change their views on mobility in a very short time span.

Figure 4.1: Migration Flows (2008-2014)

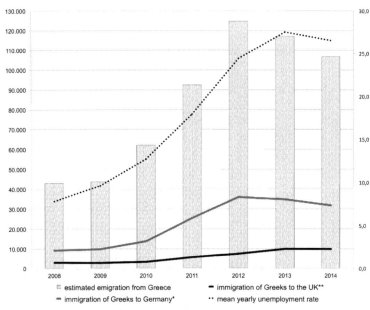

Source: Hellenic Statistical Authority, Genesis, DWP

Even if actual emigration is not systematically recorded as such, official data evince that there are already many who have taken that step. Figure 4.1 illustrates estimated numbers of emigrants, released annually by the Greek Statistical Authority since 2008. Accordingly, over half a million people left Greece in the period 2010-2014: emigration rates surged after 2009, peaked in 2012 and since then appear to decline, yet the numbers leaving annually now well exceed 100,000. Unpacking the composition of the outflows and the emigrants' destinations, however, is a complex matter in many respects.

First and foremost, significant shares of those leaving are foreign nationals.[4] Albanians, for example, who constitute the majority of Greece's immigrants and

---

4   When we first drafted this chapter and at least until April 2016, the Hellenic Statistical Authority's emigration estimations were also available on the Eurostat database for the years 2008-2013 (Population and social conditions: Emigration by sex, age group and citizenship, http://appsso.eurostat.ec.europa.eu/nui/show.do?dataset=migr_emi1 ctz&lang=en), including breakdown by citizenship. Accordingly, during 2008-2010 over half of emigrants were foreign nationals, while during 2011-2013 Greek nation-

are severely affected by rising unemployment, may take advantage of proximity and (since 2011) visa-free travel in the EU to return, temporarily at least, perhaps before seeking work elsewhere while maintaining their residence in Greece (Gemi 2014: 3, 11-13). Similarly, ethnic Greek migrants from the former Soviet Union may also seek work abroad as they have been doing before the crisis (Pratsinakis 2013: 104), while an invisible segment of the outflow concerns former Greek emigrants and their children, who had in the meanwhile settled in Greece and now return anew to their old host countries (Cavounides 2014: 29). Pre-existing links, alongside "pull" factors in terms of job demand and remuneration in specific sectors explain the persistence of "traditional" post-war destinations, as suggested by recent studies: Australia (Tamis 2014), the USA (Mihopoulos 2014), Canada (Konstandinidis 2014), or Germany (Georgiou et al. 2013; Damanakis 2014). Nevertheless, the range of destinations is highly diverse, spanning from the Balkans, Eastern Europe, the Middle East, or East Asia (Triandafyllidou/Gropas 2014: 1624; Labrianidis/Pratsinakis 2016: 13-14). The majority, however, head to EU countries, with Germany and the UK attracting approximately half of the outflows (Labrianidis/Pratsinakis 2016; figure 4.1).[5]

A recent study by Labrianidis and Pratsinakis (2016) conducted a nationwide representative survey to 1,237 households in Greece, gathering information for 248 emigrants. About one third of them left Greece after 2010 while the rest had migrated in earlier decades, allowing for three interesting observations of changes over time. Firstly, the emigrants' average age grows by emigration decade: from 24.3 years in the 1990s to 28.3 years in the 2000s and 30.5 years among post-2010 emigrants, while eleven per cent of the latter took the decision to migrate in their fourties. Secondly, the largest part of post-2010 emigrants (approximately two thirds) comprises of people with university degrees, yet there is a considerable growth in the shares of postgraduate degree holders and graduates of medical and engineering schools, while significant proportions (approximately one third) have lower qualifications. In addition, there seems to be a relationship between the emigrants' educational background and their choice of destination: e.g., the UK seems to attract primarily those with higher education, while Germany and other former guest worker's destinations such as the Netherlands

---

als form more than 50% of those estimated to leave. At the time of revising the chapter (June 2016), this data was not any more available on the EUROSTAT database.

5   Official statistics illustrated on figure 4.1 show that, between 2010-2014, more than 141,000 Greek nationals have registered with a local authority in Germany (including e.g., students and dependent family members), while nearly 36,000 have received a National Insurance number in the UK (thus not including students or dependents).

attract also people with middle or low skills. Thirdly, we see increased representation of lower income groups, representing 28 per cent among post-2010 emigrants, which is almost the double in comparison to their share during the previous decade.

The crisis thus not only feeds the resurgence of Greek emigration in terms of volume, but also brings qualitative changes. A major transformation seems to be underway: migration is now more a matter of need rather than one of choice. Even though the motivations of "crisis" migrants are not limited to mere economic need but are rather framed in a wider context of lack of prospects in the country, as well as positive evaluations of life and work abroad, worsening conditions in the Greek labor market and concerns about employment and income are primary motives for many.

At the same time, Labrianidis and Pratsinakis (2016) underline the difficulties of adaptation in destination places. One out of five of their survey respondents were not able to find a job within the first six months; a similar proportion were working below their qualifications and six per cent were unemployed, while some 15 per cent had already returned back to Greece. Moreover, qualitative material from their study, in accordance to previous research (Georgiou et al. 2013; Damanakis 2014: 151-159; Triandafyllidou/Gropas 2014: 1626-1629), show that difficulties may be more widespread[6], with a considerable segment of the emigrants who have not secured employment before emigration, including people of high educational backgrounds, ending up in low-skilled jobs for significant periods before they manage to find jobs matching their qualifications. In addition, although unrecorded in official statistics, the question of return is a reality beyond vague hopes or even actual plans, sometimes linked to temporary migration projects or subsequent mobility steps and livelihoods between 'here' and 'there'.

Dimensions of an emerging media discourse

Having outlined the broad picture and major trends of emigration from Greece at times of crisis, we now move on to explore relevant media debates. Our review

---

6   These results should be treated with caution due to the methodology of Labrianidis' and Pratsinakis' (2016) survey, according to which it is primarily not the migrant her/himself providing the answer but another member of the household, most commonly the parent. We may well assume that the emigrant paints a more positive image of his/her situation to his/her parent, hence adaptation difficulties may actually be more common as the qualitative data show.

of news articles reveals an emerging public discourse on new Greek emigration, which appears to be highly selective, often emotional and largely politicised. We focused on content, examining key themes, points of emphasis and perspectives, which allow us to broadly sketch the development of Greek media debates. In out attempt to dig back in time, we have not come across any articles on out-migration before 2010, and observed an exponential growth of news coverage from just a few items in 2010 and 2011, to nine in 2012, eleven in 2013, twelve in 2014 and 23 in 2015. Most are mere news, reporting on latest statistics and figures, relevant studies and surveys, or personal stories; some combine facts and opinion, while about 16 per cent are commentaries. A general overview of the media reviewed and articles examined is given in table 4.1.

Labrianidis' (2011) study has largely set the tone, monopolising early reports in 2010-2011. Soon after the publication of his book, he introduced a public debate entitled "Should I stay or should I go in crisis-ridden Greece" on 6 June 2011 (organised by the international think tank "intelligence squared"), which attracted considerable media attention focusing descriptively on his main findings and arguments. Yet the deepening of the crisis, alongside escalating emigration trends, seem to have inspired a direct association between his study and the worsening conditions due to recession. Media reports on the book itself have been recurring over the years as a reference point often complemented by new evidence, yet misleadingly linking the findings to the crisis and ignoring that its empirical basis actually predated it. The titles of such reports are indicative: "139,000 scientists out of Greece" (Imerisia, June 24, 2011); "New emigration wave: the Greeks, the crisis, and the routes of flight" (Ethnos, January 28, 2012).

Table 4.1: Overview of media articles reviewed

Media type	
1. Online versions of print newspapers (national range, general interest) Kathimerini (9), To Vima (5), Ethnos (4), Avgi (2), Eleftherotypia (2), Real News (1)	23 (38.3%)
2. Online-only news media (general news) TVXS (6), news247 (4), huffingtonpost (4), iefimerida (3), greekreporter (2) Greece Tribune (1), protagon, i.gr (1), zougla.gr (1), newsit.gr (1), enikos (1), sky.gr (1)	26 (43.3%)
3. Online versions of special interest or local newspapers Lifo (2), Imerisia (2), Ardin (2), Macedonia (1), Popaganda (1), Parallaximag (1), 7imeres (1), personal newsblog (1)	11 (18.3%)
Year of publication	
2010	2 (3.3%)
2011	3 (5.0%)
2012	9 (15%)
2013	11 (18.3%)
2014	12 (20.0%)
2015	23 (38.3%)
Article type	
A. mere reportage	39 (65.0%)
B. reportage, combined with or based on testimonies	11 (18.3%)
C. opinion and analysis	10 (16.7%)

Source: Authors' own elaboration

A major theme has expectedly been that of rising unemployment affecting disproportionally the young; the periodic updating of relevant statistics was often covered with reference to emigration. Titles speak for themselves: "Unemployment banishes the young: almost half Greeks of productive age look for work abroad" (in.gr, December 19, 2012); "Greece drives her children away: youth unemployment at 58 per cent" (Macedonia, January 9, 2014). Even if the link between unemployment and emigration is not a direct one, the case is made by incorporating additional evidence deriving e.g., from opinion surveys on emigration intensions, or trends in job searches or CVs uploaded on the EURES or Europass job portals. Including questions about migration intentions has been a novelty in opinion polls administered e.g., by market research companies or employment agencies. Although these are often isolated questions and results do not necessarily correlate with other variables, they tend to be overemphasised in the media, underlining intentions as reality rather than as an indication of the general mood.

Emigration is thus primarily pictured as a brain drain, directed mostly to European destinations, although their diversity is not ignored: "Greeks leave abroad for work: big increases in the flow towards Britain, Germany, Norway and Belgium" (Tsakiri 2014); "Which countries are Greek scientists-migrants heading to: brain drain" (TVXS, October 19, 2015). However, specific countries and professions have attracted more publicity: about one out of four of the articles reviewed focus on Germany. Reporting on official Destatis statistics on recent immigration to the country, for instance, tend to emphasize information on Greeks: "Record-high migration of graduates towards Germany: new wave" (TVXS, January 18, 2014). Over ten percent of news items are about doctors, mostly heading to Germany: "A flow of Greek doctors, as Germans emigrate" (Kathimerini, December 12, 2013); "More than 7,000 Greek doctors have left abroad due to the crisis" (Lifo, December 21, 2015).

The focus on Germany is no incidental: not only this is a major destination of new emigrants, as it has been in post-war times, but it is also the country blamed for the harsh austerity imposed on Greece as a condition for its bailout. Conditions there are occasionally depicted as far from ideal, revealing cases of difficult adaptation or even exploitation in the labor market, often by the older generation of former guest workers or by recruitment agencies: "Greeks exploit Greeks in Germany" (Galanis 2012); "Shocking testimony of a Greek migrant in Germany" (Dimou 2013); "Neomigrants are victims of exploitation" (Fotiadi 2014); "Berlin's psychic clinics getting full of Greeks" (Ethnos, October 28, 2015).

Still, despite reporting on difficulties, mostly referring to the emigrants experiences in Germany, the overall tendency is to prettify conditions abroad, especially by highlighting successful individual cases of professionals 'who made it'. Media articles are increasingly informed by personal stories and migrants' own insights, which feed the news alongside official data and survey results. Sometimes these depict changes over time in individuals' migration trajectories, or provide information for prospective migrants in specific countries or sectors: "A young Greek doctor in Germany" (Lifo, July 15, 2013); "Looking for a job in

London" (protagon, July 27, 2014); "A Greek woman leaves abroad" (Stathopoulou 2015). In such accounts, the option of leaving Greece is presented as a unidirectional and irreversible path. It is only in 2015 that we first encounter articles on the issue of return, not simply reporting on emigrants' intentions, but also through direct accounts of people who have already taken this step: "I have come back to Greece, but what for?" (Martinou 2015); "Return in crisis-ridden Greece" (Papadopoulos 2015).

Emigration has thus reappeared as both a reality and a societal concern increasingly evident in media discourses, a side effect of the crisis, recession and austerity. Its scale and volume have become significant enough to inspire works of art and TV shows alike. We are aware of at least three relevant theatre plays: one performed in 2013 ("Telemachus, or should I stay or should I go", featuring amateur actors who have been migrants themselves), and two in 2015 ("I want a country...", "Kangaroo"). Moreover, the brain drain from the perspective of emigrants has been the subject of numerous TV shows, including a documentary entitled "The great escape" (focusing especially on ophthalmologists), screened on a national channel on August 6, 2015. Although media debates have to an extent been politicized since the early years, emigration is increasingly depicted as a political issue, depending on different standpoints in the media: the "migration of 200,000 young talented Greeks" is labeled a "crime" (Imerisia, January 19, 2015) and brain drain is pictured as a "slow-burning bomb" (Kambouris 2015). This politicization also relates to the rise of emigration in policy agendas. Government change since January 2015 signaled for the first time an interest in taking action, with the new Prime Minister announcing a "long-term plan so that the thousands of young researchers currently employed at universities and research centers abroad return to the country. This bleeding must stop as it negatively affects the growth prospects of the Greek econom".[7] As in other policy domains, this proved to be far from straightforward.

Concerns about the prospects of recovery of a country deprived of its young educated workforce seem to give shape to a hegemonic discourse in which emigration appears as loss, placing greater emphasis on its (negative) impact on the economy rather than on the lives of the migrants themselves. Highlighting successful cases may be read as attempt to boost the wounded national sentiment, forming hence the other pole in an ambivalent presentation of emigration, which

---

7   Prime minister's A. Tsipras speech, during the programmatic statements of the then newly-elected Government, January 08, 2015 (http://www.primeminister.gov.gr/english/2015/02/08/primeministers-a-tsipras-speech-during-the-programmatic-statements-of-the-government).

on the one hand laments the 'bleeding' of the nation, while, on the other, depicts it as an (easy) way out from a wrecked economy and a corrupt and inefficient state. The outflow of immigrants is only scarcely mentioned, and in the few cases it does (e.g., "Economic migrants fleeing Greece massively"; Tsiros 2014), it is described as an entirely separate trend, while the emigration of older people, the lesser educated, or minority groups is totally neglected. The diversity and complexity of outflows, their underlying structural roots, as well as the motivations, aspirations, trajectories and experiences of emigrants remain thus poorly understood. We next explore some of these, shifting our perspective towards an emerging European destination.

GREEK MIGRATION TO THE NETHERLANDS AT TIMES OF CRISIS

The sailors who found work in and around the Rotterdam harbor as peddlers and shipbrokers, and the entrepreneurs who started cigarette factories or fur businesses in the early 20th century were the forbearers of a more extensive Greek immigration to the Netherlands in postwar times (Lindo 2000: 126). In contrast to other nationalities, largely migrating in the framework of bilateral agreements, the majority of Greek 'guestworkers' arrived on their own initiative, or by way of informal recruitment channels, mostly via Belgium and (less frequently) Germany (Vermeulen et al. 1985). A bilateral agreement was eventually signed in 1966, just a year before an economic downturn in the Netherlands and the coup d'état in Greece, therefore it did not result in much recruitment (Lindo 2000: 128). In the following years, immigration subsided taking place mostly through family reunification. Free EU mobility for Greek citizens since the 1980s triggered modest flows, including students and people from the Muslim minority of Thrace, while a limited in scale emigration of professionals was underway already from the late 1990s. By the late 2000s, the Greek population in the Netherlands counted approximately 13,900 people, showing modest annual increases in the previous 15 years, to a large extent due to natural growth. Within five years since the outbreak of the crisis in Greece, the registered population surged by almost 40 per cent, reaching 19,217 people in 2014. Taking into account that several newcomers may not register, as indicated by our research, we may estimate that the increase was significantly higher, considerably diversifying the established Greek community in the country.

This section builds on qualitative material and survey data, in order to draw a comprehensive picture of new Greek migration to the Netherlands. The survey was conducted by Grammatikas as part of his involvement in the Greek community organization "Neoafihthendes" (meaning "newcomers" in Greek). More specifically, a set of exploratory key-informant interviews were initially conducted (Autumn 2013), which helped us understand the broad picture and organize the survey which was administered during December 2013-February 2014. This was posted online on various relevant Facebook groups and further disseminated via personal email lists and key figures of the community. It deliberately targeted Muslims from Thrace, as an example of the migration of minority groups (which should also include Albanians and 'Soviet' Greeks), of whose presence we were aware though they were not captured by the online survey. Their participation was achieved in a series of meetings, organized with the help of their associations, to provide information about life and work in the country. These gathered more than 120 people, 44 of whom filled in the questionnaire face-to-face, making up a share of about 28 per cent among 158 total respondents of the survey. Even though survey respondents were not selected via random sampling, which would be in any case impossible given the lack of a sampling frame, we actively tried to increase the diversity of the sample by recruiting respondents through a variety of diversified entry points to increase representativeness. Comparing our results with available official sources and through information we collected by systematically monitoring social media webpages set up by newcomers, we were able to assess that they are largely indicative of the trends within the new Greek emigrant population in the Netherlands, at least with the exception of minority Muslims from Greece who were purposively sampled.

The qualitative material was collected through participant observation in the Greek community house in Amsterdam, conducted by Pratsinakis as part of his ongoing Individual Fellowship Marie Curie project EUMIGRE, as well as through his engagement with the same community organization during November 2015-June 2016. We also use material from eigth in-depth interviews he conducted over this period in the context of the same project and three more interviews the same author had contributed to the project "Outward Migration from Greece during the Crisis" (Labrianidis/Pratsinakis 2016). On the basis of this diverse material, we identified different categories of recent migrants from Greece to the Netherlands in terms of their emigration patterns, the types of jobs they are doing, the degree to which those jobs match their qualifications, their experiences of settling in, and the ways they frame their experiences.

In agreement to the general trends earlier outlined, emigration to the Netherlands concerns primarily, but not exclusively, educated young adults. Sixty six per cent of survey respondents have tertiary education, while nearly half are between 20-30 years old, followed by more than one third in their thirties. Yet, emigration is materialized following different mobility strategies and settlement pathways. Several people, commonly with lower educational backgrounds, emigrate for short-term periods as target earners. They work seasonally in agriculture or horticulture aiming to contribute to the family income at home (as most minority Muslims do), in small contracting projects or Greek taverns, to respond to immediate financial need or support themselves in wait of a job opening in Greece. Some may also come for short periods, to inquire into employment possibilities and life conditions through a first-hand experience of everyday life in the Netherlands. Many more arrive with more permanent settlement intentions, often hosted by friends or relatives who are already settled, after having collected enough information about life in the country but without having found a job. Others apply for jobs from Greece, sometimes declaring the local address of friends or kin in wait to be called for an interview, and some do secure employment in the Netherlands before settling in the country. We next draw on a range of different individual cases, as a step towards a typology of new Greek migration to the Netherlands

Highly skilled migrants who have secured a job before arrival

Most of the emigrants who already have a job upon arrival do so in specific economic sectors for which there are gaps and/or increased demand. Such gaps do not necessarily concern chronic shortages and do change following labor market developments: for instance, a few years ago one could rather easily find employment as a dentist even without considerable working experience and without speaking Dutch, yet this is not possible anymore as the dentists' job market got saturated in the meantime. High-demand sectors include the nine so-called "topsectoren" prioritised by the Dutch State in its attempt to retain a leading position or boost its competitiveness in the international market.[8] In these, there is global recruitment of people with a background in technology, applied and life sciences for positions linked to innovation, or for dynamic start-ups, in the context of the so-called global competition for talent. A recent study (Ooijevaar et al. 2015) approximating the 'expat' population in the Netherlands counted 770

---

8   Those nine sectors are: Agro and Food, Chemistry, Creative Industries, Energy, High Tech Systems and materials, Life Sciences and Health, Logistics, Horticulture and Starting Materials, Water.

Greek-born employees matching this profile at the end of 2011;[9] despite its limitations, this gives an indication of their shares at about one tenth of Greeks in the country: at the end of 2011 the registered Greek population counted 15,052 people, of whom 7,483 were Greek-born and in working age. According to our survey, 23 per cent of respondents fit in this category, with 18 per cent working for multinational companies or international organizations. They are thus not a negligible segment of recent migrations.

For Greeks employed in such positions, emigration decisions are largely based on career opportunity considerations, and location/city options are weighted in terms of valued quality of life. They are also increasingly informed by perceptions about the lack of opportunities for career advancement, for those who did have employment in Greece, and by experiencing shrinking employment opportunities, for those who were unemployed. A rather separate category concerns professionals sent to the Netherlands by their international companies. Their emigration decisions are directly linked to the needs of their companies, which commonly provide them with substantial help with settling in, and are framed within a perspective attributing special value to international mobility for career advancement. Even if the mobility of this category of people is the least typical case of crisis-driven migration and actually predated the crisis, it is not always entirely unrelated as the case below suggests.

Tasos works for a big multinational company, and had just settled in Amsterdam when we spoke in January 2016. He told us that gradually it had become clear to him that sooner or later he would have to leave Greece if he was to keep (and advance) his position. It was the lack of alternative employment options in Greece that made international mobility appear as a necessity more than ever before, and led him eventually to take the decision to move. When he learned about an opening in Amsterdam he found it an attractive opportunity and, together with his wife, both in their early forties, they decided to emigrate. Tasos was concerned about how migration will affect his everyday life and worried of the impact it will have on his relationship. They had past experience of relocating in another city within Greece a few years ago, which did not work out positively especially as his wife was not able to find employment there. Despite his worries, however, he was excited about the experience of living abroad and was convinced that being eager to pursue career opportunities is what people should

---

9   The report counted foreign-born employees either working in hospitals and universities or receiving high salaries irrespectively of their sector of employment. The data exclude the self-employed, do not provide information on the year of arrival and are rather out-dated given the growth of Greek emigration since 2012.

be after today. In his view, there always is labor demand, somewhere; one should be simply ready to meet it by following developments and being where one is needed.

Migrants in search for employment

In this rather broad category, we encounter people whose decisions to emigrate are less shaped by career considerations but primarily by a strong urge to escape crisis-ridden Greece and are hence eager to hasten their emigration projects, including graduates whose skills are not in much demand or people seeking work in sectors where recruitment does not take place through online solicitations. Most migrants come to the Netherlands to enquire for work opportunities with a certain amount of money ranging from a minimum of 2,000 to a few thousand Euros. Many have difficulties in their way to find employment matching their qualifications, and may end up in low-skilled jobs for considerable periods of time even if they are highly educated. Language barriers may be one of the reasons why their labor market integration proves to be difficult in practice, irrespectively of their skills. Among our survey respondents, some 85 per cent considered that limited knowledge of Dutch poses significant hindrances in everyday life and employment opportunities and claimed to be willing to upgrade their language skills by undertaking language classes. Knowing people in the Netherlands was reported to be equally important.

Yannis left Greece in late 2013 quitting his IT job, as he was heavily disappointed with the situation in the country and felt insecure for the future, seeing "no potential for improvement in the years to come". He decided to move to Amsterdam where a good friend of his lived. It took him six months to find his first job and another six months to find one in his field, living in various temporary housing arrangements in the meantime. He told us he would not have made it without his savings, since for a long period his earnings were well below his costs. After a year in his new job Yannis got promoted and was offered a long term contract with a good salary. He then rented out an independent apartment in Leiden, where he was joined by his wife and newborn son. He currently sees no reason of returning, and he would rather avoid re-migrating, at least in the short term, exhibiting a much less mobility-oriented attitude than Tasos.

Kostas, a trained hematologist, chose to migrate to Amsterdam in 2012 because his aunt Rina runs a restaurant there. He was hosted at her place and worked in her restaurant until he earned enough money to rent his own flat. He then found a second job in a café nearby and a few months later he was offered an annual contract in a museum restaurant. In the meantime, he had been learning Dutch looking for jobs matching his credentials. A similar pathway was earlier followed by Rina's son-in-law Petros, an engineer. After 1.5 years working in several restaurants in Amsterdam, Petros found a well-paid job in his field. It was taking longer for Kostas to find such a job but he was not disappointed. Although he told us that things are considerably more difficult in the Netherlands presently than in 2009, when Petros arrived, Kostas was rather confident that sooner or later he would find a good job too. He was not considering going back, as saw no chances of finding any work in Greece. In a follow up conversation, he had indeed managed to find employment in a company in a field close to his profession. He was happy with this development even though he confessed he did not expect it would take him three years to meet this goal.

In many cases, people like Kostas prefer staying abroad over returning back even if they have to work in low skilled jobs for prolonged periods of time. In Greece similar jobs are paid much less and usually do not provide social security, while they are also associated with a low social status. They thus stay abroad aiming to upgrade their language skills and build social networks that will help them to eventually find better jobs. It is this promise for a brighter future that keeps them abroad, even though there are also those who may decide to return. According to official data (Ooijevaar 2015), approximately 20 per cent of the 2008-2010 arrivals left within a year. Even if a considerable part concerns students leaving the country after completing their degrees, we may well assume that other cases are also included: people who are disillusioned with their experience in the Netherlands or whose life circumstances have changed, and may thus return to Greece or even emigrate instead to other destinations in search for better employment opportunities or more attractive career prospects.

Students into migrants

Part of the 'newcomers' are former students at Dutch Universities who overstay after graduation. Some have come recently with that goal in mind, treating their studies as a first step to materialise their emigration; others were already students before 2010 and, although they were not originally planning to seek employment, as the crisis started deepening in Greece they were confronted with the dilemma 'to stay or return'. It should be generally noted that student migration from Greece to the Netherlands has been on the increase in recent years: students comprise about a quarter of annual arrivals, with more than 2,000 Greeks studying in the country at the moment.[10] Greeks are the 6th most populous nationality in Dutch Universities and the 3rd in postgraduate degree programmes, with approximately 75 per cent of Greek students enrolled for a Masters degree (Huberts 2015: 26). As observed by Labrianidis and Pratsinakis (2016), those who study social sciences and arts and humanities seem to experience more difficulties in finding a job matching their background as compared to those who have studied medicine, applied sciences or IT, which in some cases makes their mobility and settlement projects rather ambivalent.

For instance, Aliki came to Amsterdam for postgraduate studies in the Social Sciences in 2014 and decided to stay. In the meantime, she found work in a cafeteria to support her living. Due to her demanding work schedule eventually she could not keep pace with the requirements of her studies. She thus decided to temporarily freeze her studies in order to raise the funds to redo the program in the following year. Chrysa, on the other hand, came with her boyfriend to follow an MA program in Political Science, but after her studies she could not find employment matching her qualifications. Being unemployed for one year, she decided to work voluntarily in an organisation which eventually hired her after eight months.

Yet, for others, the transition from studies to work turns out way beyond their aspirations, leading them to reconsider their migration projects. One such case is Anna's, who had graduated from the same programme as Aliki and had also tried to stay in Amsterdam but did not manage to find any job meeting her expectations. She returned to Greece only to leave again within a few months, this time for Brussels. On the other hand, Achilleas, who studied Social Sciences in Amsterdam, decided to prolong his stay working in a big international hotel. After some time there, however, and having looked for job opportunities in his field, he felt that he had no chance in getting any job matching his qualifications, mainly due to insufficient language skills and lack of social networks. Fully absorbed by the work rhythms of his hotel job, he felt that he was losing contact with his field of study. Although he was paid a salary way above what he would be paid Greece, he decided not to renew his contract and looked instead for a job related to his studies back home, even a low paid one. In a follow up discussion, he had managed to find a job related to his field on a three-month renewable contract, and was preparing his trip.

---

10 Holland became an attractive destination for studies due to the good reputation of Dutch Universities, the large number of study programs in English and, increasingly, the relatively low tuition fees, especially after the rise of tuition in UK Universities.

Migrants in precarious and exploitative conditions

A recent report (Booi et al. 2014: 24) unveiled that 18 per cent of the Greeks in Amsterdam were found to live in the poverty line. This category includes those who are forced to live with limited resources during their first steps in the country, as earlier recorded, but also people who stagnate in conditions of precarious living. Moreover, some report exploitative working conditions and discrimination in the labor market, particularly those working in low-skilled manual jobs or in the hotel and catering sector (especially in Amsterdam). The examples here draw on a diverse range of cases facing precarious and/or exploitative conditions, temporarily or in the long run. They come from the experiences of people who migrated at a later stage in their life course, the lesser educated, or minority groups.

The former case includes couples or even single parents emigrating in their late forties or older, who seem to be driven by pressing financial need and/or concerns about their children's future. Some leave their children behind and support them by sending money back home; others relocate together with their children aiming to build a life in the Netherlands which they consider better for the future of their offspring. The choice of destination is often linked to relatives living in the country, though this is not always the case. For instance, Eleni arrived after selling off her property in Greece to buy a house in Heerlen, where she relocated together with her (adult) son and daughter. They are currently making a living on her Greek pension and by renting out one room of their apartment, while her son and daughter try to find their way in the Dutch labor market which was the goal of their relocation.

Secondly, discrimination in the labor market may affect emigrants irrespective of their qualifications and sectors of work, although it is reportedly much more common among those with lower education attainments. More than half of the survey respondents reported experiences of labor market discrimination and/or negative stereotyping. The latter was the case especially in the early years of the crisis, when Greeks in the Netherlands were stigmatized as lazy and corrupted, and were scapegoated "as if they were to be blamed for the European Crisis", in the words of a survey respondent. Other respondents referred to cases of more direct discrimination, such as receiving lower wages than their Dutch counterparts, or employers not recognizing their qualifications, etc.

Although broader stereotyping now seems to have lessened, some people we have talked to in Amsterdam also reported exploitation in their work. Yorgos, for example, who does not have university education, came to Amsterdam looking for work in 2012. He found a job in the flower market but was very disillusioned from his emigration experience. His boss required him to stand still throughout the day, which physically exhausted him. He earned about 1,200€ a month after taxes, the minimum wage in the Netherlands yet much higher than any salary he ever had in Greece, but his living costs were much higher. Similarly to most newcomers, he could not afford renting an apartment on his own but could only rent a room for 400€. Elsa, on the other hand, a graduate in civil engineering, arrived as an intern in a start-up company via the Erasmus exchange scheme. She complained about long working days, way beyond those agreed in the contract, and a demand to perform activities that were irrelevant to the subject of her internship. At the end of the contract she was asked to continue working with a salary well below the minimum wage and for longer hours than is legally acceptable in the Netherlands.

Notably, exploitation at work is also reported by those working for Greek employers. Similarly to him, Andreas, for example, who had worked in several Greek taverns, claimed that "he will never work for Greeks in the Netherlands again." We also recorded instances of blatant exploitation. Such was the case of a group of people who were invited by a Netherlands-based Greek employer to come for temporary work in a renovation project in Volendam. When they finished their work, the employer had disappeared without having paid neither them, nor the landlord of the apartment where they stayed.

Lastly, exploitation and precarious employment are widespread among minority Muslims from Greece, as deriving from our survey results and the aforementioned meetings. Following earlier migration patterns, most appear to be spatially concentrated mostly in Rotterdam, Den Hague, but also Leeuwarden, where they are organised around local associations. According to estimations by community leaders more than 1,000 people live in the Netherlands, a large share of whom have not registered their stay in the country. This is because they may not be aware of this requirement, or because they are unable to do so, or finally because they deliberately choose not to. In addition to settled migrants, a considerable number of minority Muslims are coming and going on a seasonal basis. According to survey results, minority Muslims are on average older than most recent migrants from Greece and a large segment (40 per cent) has only primary education. They almost exclusively work in low status - low paid jobs, mostly in greenhouses, slaughterhouses and construction. One out of four does not have health insurance, as most work on hourly-paid contracts, while some are asked to register as free lancers and then given a zero hour contract so that employers do not have to pay for social and health contributions. Almost none speaks Dutch or English and many neither speak Greek, which is why many are dependent not only on their mostly Turkish-Dutch employers and employment brokers through whom they find work, but also from 'accountants' as they call the people who do their paperwork charging them very high fees.

CONCLUDING REMARKS

Some of the difficulties experienced by new migrants to the Netherlands as in most cases outlined above could perhaps have been smoother, if community structures and host society institutions were in place to support and provide orientation to newcomers. Although for minority Muslims community associations still play an important social role (even though this does seem to protect them against exploitative conditions and precarious living), this is not the case for most other recent migrants from Greece. The purpose and functions of community organizations set up by Greek immigrants of earlier decades have long faded away, while changes in Dutch integration policies have meanwhile led to decreasing (financial) support, depriving those surviving from the capacity to sustain a meeting place. Increasing arrivals of mostly younger migrants from Greece in recent years found hence no community infrastructure where they could seek information and support, while the image of existing associations as old-fashioned clubs for elderly 'guestworkers' makes contact problematic.

We are aware of just one organization with a meeting place in Amsterdam that a group of recent migrants try to transform into a center for newcomers, as well as of a number of initiatives aiming at specific purposes (news-gathering, organizing parties, a student society, a network for psychological support). But the range and scope of these initiatives is fairly limited, and most new migrants lean on family and friends/acquaintances, or even employers for basic information and help. The main attempts towards some sort of community networking are to be found on the internet with various Facebook groups mushrooming in recent years, on which newcomers share experiences and seek information on an impressive range of topics (from the criteria to receive unemployment benefit or finding a room to stay, to selling a sofa or sending a package to Greece); yet these seem to rest on the shoulders of a handful of people. Although the basic information a newcomer needs to know about life and work in the Netherlands can be found digitally quite easy, sometimes in Greek or at least in English, more detailed information can be only found in Dutch. Considering that most newcomers do not master the language, much of the information circulated in informal social and digital networks is not always reliable, and often generate situations of misinformation, indistinctness and confusion. Hence, as other EU migrants, recent arrivals from Greece make use of their basic right of free movement within the

European Union but are left in the dark about their rights and duties in the host country. The withdrawal of the state from providing minimum support shifts the responsibility for integration to the migrants themselves, and rests on the assumption that EU migrants do not have particular difficulties in their adaption pathways.

Of the multiplicity of individual pathways and migration experiences we have encountered, we hereby chose to highlight aspects that problematize idealistic perceptions of life and work 'in Europe' often depicted in Greek media. Not only have we showed how adaptation to a new life abroad is not as straightforward, but we also accounted for neglected components of contemporary outflows, including people in need from a diverse range of socio-economic, educational and ethnic backgrounds. By highlighting difficulties, we do not intend to overlook the many positive experiences of Greeks in the Netherlands or other EU countries (and beyond), but rather to deconstruct conventional assumptions of emigration as a monolithic project and lifetime decision, of 'successes' and 'failures' as definite outcomes, of the youngest and brightest who are valued abroad but are doomed at home. People like those we have talked to may be 'pioneers of European integration' in that they promote it in practice from below (Favell/Recchi 2009), yet they are at the same time product of its present-day shortcomings.

The Greek crisis has amplified pre-existing mobility patterns of young graduates, but also impacted on the mobility practices of people of other socio-economic backgrounds. Emigration turns into a survival strategy for many who are finding it hard to make ends meet, while, at the same time, it emerges as an increasingly appealing option for others in less pressing need who see their career potentials critically reduced. Outflows since 2009 appear to be comparable in size with those of post-war decades, but they take place alongside ongoing immigration to or through Greece. Moreover, there are significant differences in the socio-economic, educational and demographic profiles of today's 'crisis' migrants, while the macro-structural causes triggering emigration at present are radically different, as is its context and infrastructure. New migrants are not supported by state institutions and migration trajectories are shaped by their socio-economic background and social capital. People specialized in fields for which there is high demand can easily secure employment abroad in many cases even before they actually emigrate. People with lower education or skills that are not valued in the labor market of their destinations find it more difficult to find employment that matches their qualifications, as do those with poor language skills and lack of social networks. On the other hand, free movement within the European Union makes emigration an easier mobility strategy to pursue, reducing its economic and psychological costs. Emigration is no longer seen as a once-in-a-life-time decision, as people increasingly move spontaneously and provisionally, looking for potential opportunities mostly in Northern Europe. This not only suggests the multiplicity of mobility pathways, but also the open and dynamic character of migration projects and processes, rather than simply the relocation from one place to another.

REFERENCES

Booi, Hester/Slot, Jeroen/Lindenman, Ellen (2014): Monitor EU-migranten 2013, Amsterdam: Gemeente Amsterdam, Bureau Onderzoek en Statistiek.

Cavounides, Jennifer (2014): "The emigration of Greeks and related policies." In: Greek Economy: Monthly Bulletin on Economic Developments, 12/12, Athens: Centre of Planning & Economic Research, pp. 28-32, [In Greek].

Damanakis, Michael (2014): "Greek New emigration to Germany." In: Michael Damanakis/Stefanos Konstantinidis/Anastasios Tamis (eds.), New Migration to and from Greece, Rethymnon: University of Crete, pp. 139-177, [in Greek].

Dimou, Thaleia (2013): "Shocking testimony of a Greek migrant in Germany." In: enikos.gr, May 22. April 05, 2016 (http://www.enikos.gr/society/146194,Martyria-sok-Ellhna-metanasth-sth-Germania.html).

Ethnos (2012) "New emigration wave: the Greeks, the crisis, and the routes of flight." In Ethnos, January 28. April 05, 2016 (http://www.ethnos.gr/entheta.asp?catid=25810&subid=2&pubid=63608646).

European Commission (2010): Geographical and Labour Market Mobility. Special Eurobarometer 337, Wave 72.5, TNS Opinion & Social. June 22, 2016 (ec.europa.eu/public_opinion/archives/ebs/ebs_337_en.pdf).

European Commission (2006): Internal Market: Opinions and Experiences of Citizens in EU-25. Special Eurobarometer 254, Wave 65.1, TNS Opinion & Social June 22, 2016 (http://ec.europa.eu/internal_market/strategy/docs/eurobarometer/eb_254_analytical_report_en.pdf).

Fakiolas, Rossetos/King, Russell (1996): "Emigration, Return, Immigration: A Review and Evaluation of Greece's Experience of International Migration." In: International Journal of Population Geography 2, pp. 171-190.

Favell, Andrian/Recchi, Ettore (eds.) (2009): Pioneers of European Integration: Citizenship and Mobility in the EU. Cheltenham: Edward Elgar.

Fotiadi, Ioanna (2014): "Neomigrants are victims of exploitation." In: Kathimerini, December 28. April 05, 2016 (http://www.kathimerini.gr/797439/article/epikairothta/ereynes/8ymata-ekmetalleyshs-oi-neometanastes).

Galanis, Dimitris (2012): "Greeks exploit Greeks in Germany." In: To Vima, May 20. April 05, 2016 (http://www.tovima.gr/society/article/?aid=458528).

Gemi, Eda (2014): "Transnational practices of Albanian families during the Greek crisis: unemployment, de-regularization and return." In: International Review of Sociology, 24/3, pp. 406-421.

Georgiou, M./Paschali, Ilectra/Papataxiarchis, Efthymios/Pechlivanos, M./Bami, Nefeli/Labrianidis, Lois (2013): New Greek emigration to Germany in times of crisis: the significance of social and cultural capital in emigration and integration, IKYDA report.

Huberts, Daan (2015): Internationalisering in beeld, Den Haag: EP Nuffic. June 22, 2016 (https://www.epnuffic.nl/documentatie/publicaties/internationalisering-in-beeld-2015.pdf).

Imerisia (2011): "139,000 scientists out of Greece." In: Imerisia June 24. April 05, 2016 (http://www.imerisia.gr/article.asp?catid=26510&subid=2&pubid=111455282).

Imerisia (2015): "The crime of emigration of 200.000 young talented Greeks." In: Imerisia January 19. June 22, 2016 (http://www.imerisia.gr/article.asp?catid=34291&subid=2&pubid=113436545).

In.gr (2012): "Unemployment banishes the young: almost half Greeks of productive age look for work abroad." In: in.gr December 19. April 05, 2016 (http://news.in.gr/economy/article/?aid=1231227353).

Kambouris, Nikos (2015): "The slow-burning bomb of brain drain." In: The Huffington Post, November 02. April 05, 2016 (http://www.huffingtonpost.gr/nicos-campouris/-brain-drain_b_8450864.html).

Karamessini, Maria (2010): "Life stage transitions and the still-critical role of the family in Greece." In: Dominique Anxo/Gerhard Bosch/Jill Rubery (eds.), The Welfare State and Life Transitions. A European Perspective, Cheltenham: Edward Elgar, pp. 257-283.

Kathimerini (2013): "A flow of Greek doctors, as Germans emigrate." In: Kathimerini October 12. April 05, 2016 (http://www.kathimerini.gr/56216/article/epikairothta/kosmos/roh-ellhnwn-giatrwn-ka8ws-metanasteyoyn-oi-germanoi).

King, Russell (2000): "Southern Europe in the changing global map of migration." In: Russell King/Gabriela Lazaridis/Charalambos Tsardanidis (eds.), Eldorado or Fortress? Migration in Southern Europe, London: Macmillan Press, pp. 1-26.

Konstandinidis, Stefanos (2014): "New Greek migration: The case of Canada." In: Michael Damanakis/Stefanos Konstantinidis/Anastasios Tamis (eds.), New Migration to and from Greece, Rethymnon: University of Crete, pp. 83-115, [in Greek].

Labrianidis, Lois (2011): Investing in leaving: The Greek case of international migration of professionals in the globalization era, Athens: Kritiki, [in Greek].

Labrianidis, Lois (2014): "Investing in leaving: The Greek case of international migration of professionals." In: Mobilities 9/2, pp. 314-335.

Labrianidis Lois/Pratsinakis, Manolis (2016): "Greece's new emigration at times of Crisis", GreeSE: Hellenic Observatory Papers on Greece and Southeast Europe, paper 99, Hellenic Observatory, LSE (http://eprints.lse.ac.uk/66811/1/GreeSE-No.99.pdf).

Lifo (2013): "A young Greek doctor in Germany." In: Lifo, July 15, 2016 (http://www.lifo.gr/confessions/view/78107).

Lifo (2015): "More than 7000 Greek doctors have left abroad due to the crisis." In: Lifo, December 21. April 05, 2016 (http://www.lifo.gr/now/greece/84500).

Lindo, Flip (2000): "The silent success: the social advancement of Southern European labour migrants in the Netherlands". In: Hans Vermeulen/Rinnus Penninx (eds.), Immigrant integration: The Dutch case, Amsterdam: Het Spinhuis, pp. 123-152.

Macedonia (2014): "Greece drives her children away: youth unemployment at 58 per cent." In: Macedonia, January 9. April 05, 2016 (http://www.makthes.gr/news/GR/reportage_S/reportage_C/Diohnei_ta_paidia_tis_i_Ellada_Sto_58_i_anergia_ton_neon?mode=archives).

Martinou, Anna (2015): "I have come back to Greece, but what for?" In: Popaganda, September 26. April 05, 2016 (http://popaganda.gr/ke-pou-girisa-stin-ellada-ti-katalava/).

Mihopoulos, Aris (2014): "Greek migration to the US: yesterday and today." In: Michael Damanakis/Stefanos Konstantinidis/Anastasios Tamis (eds.), New Migration to and from Greece, Rethymnon: University of Crete, pp. 115-139, [in Greek].

Ooijevaar, Jeroen/Verkooijen, Lona (2015): Expat, Wanneer ben je Het?, tabellenset Den Haag: Centraal Bureau voor de Statistiek (https://www.cbs.nl/nl-nl/achtergrond/2015/03/expat-wanneer-ben-je-het-).

Papadopoulos, Yiannis. (2015): "Return in crisis-ridden Greece." In: Kathimerini October 18. April 05, 2016 (http://www.kathimerini.gr/835404/gallery/epikairothta/ellada/epistrofh-sthn-ellada-ths-krishs).

Pelliccia, Andrea (2013): "Greece: education and brain drain in times of crisis." In: IRPPS Working Paper Series 54, Roma: Consiglio Nazionale delle Ricerche - Istituto di Ricerche sulla Popolazione e le Politiche Sociali.

Pratsinakis, Manolis (2002): National Minorities and Emigration (BA dissertation). Mytilene: University of Aegean, [in Greek].

Pratsinakis, Manolis (2013): Contesting National Belonging: An Established-Outsider Figuration on the Margins of Thessaloniki, Greece (PhD thesis). Amsterdam: University of Amsterdam.

Protagon.gr (2014): "Looking for a job in London." In: Protagon July 27. April 05, 2016 (http://www.protagon.gr/anagnwstes/psaxnontas-douleia-sto-londino-35567000000).

Rovva, Katerina (2015): "Berlin's psychic clinics getting full of Greeks." In: Ethnos October 22. July 07, 2016 (http://www.ethnos.gr/koinonia/arthro/ta_psyxiatreia_tou_berolinou_gemizoun_apo_tous_ellines_metanastes_tis_krisis-64274385).

Stathopoulou, Elizabeth (2015): "A Greek woman leaves abroad. Her family's reactions: Where the hell are you going?" In: news247.gr, July 23. July 07, 2016 (http://news247.gr/eidiseis/diaspora/mia-ellhnida-feugei-gia-ta-ksena-h-antidrash-ths-oikogeneias-ths-pou-sto-diavolo-pas.3543386.html).

Tamis, Anastasios (2014): "Return Migration of Greek-Australians and Emigration of Greeks to Australia." In: Michael Damanakis/Stefanos Konstantinidis/Anastasios Tamis (eds.), New Migration to and from Greece, Rethymnon: University of Crete, pp. 45-83, [in Greek].

Triandafyllidou, Anna/Gropas, Ruby (2014): "'Voting with their Feet': Highly Skilled Emigrants from Southern Europe." In: American Behavioral Scientist 58, pp. 1614-1633.

Tsakiri, Tonia (2014): "Greeks leave abroad for work: big increases in the flow towards Britain, Germany, Norway and Belgium." In: To Vima, January 16. May 17, 2016 (http://www.tovima.gr/finance/article/?aid=557343).

Tsiros, Thanos (2014): "Economic migrants fleeing Greece massively." In: Kathimerini, August 15, 2014 (http://www.kathimerini.gr/780032/article/oikonomia/ellhnikh-oikonomia/egkataleipoyn-mazika-thn-ellada-oi-oikonomikoi-metanastes).

TVXS (2014): "Record-high migration of graduates towards Germany: new wave." In: TVXS, January 18. July 07, 2016 (http://tvxs.gr/news/ellada/metanasteysi-rekor-ptyxioyxon-pros-germania).

TVXS (2015): "Which countries are Greek scientists-migrants heading to: brain drain." In: TVXS, October 19. April 29, 2016 (http://tvxs.gr/news/ellada/se-poies-xores-pigainoyn-oi-ellines-epistimones-metanastes).

Vermeulen, Hans/Van Attekum, Mariëtta/Lindo, Flip/Pennings, Toon (1985): De Grieken, Muiderberg: Coutinho.

Part II: Structure and agency in European crisis migration

5. Study German to shape your future? – Motives for foreign language acquisition among Spaniards

BIRGIT GLORIUS

ABSTRACT

In the context of the global financial and economic crisis, the mobility of Spaniards changed considerably, not only in quantitative terms but also referring to motives and socio-demographic characteristics of migrants. In the light of increasing mobility intentions and practices especially of the younger Spaniards, this chapter draws the attention to language proficiency as an important prerequisite for both, mobility and destination decisions. It reports from an online survey among language students at German language schools in Spain. The main research goal was to explore the motivation of language acquisition and possible linkages to mobility intentions. A further research aim was to analyze perceptions of Germany as a possible migratory destination, compared to perceptions of Spain.

The results show clearly the effects of an ongoing internationalization process in Spain, which results in a new generation of well trained, internationally experienced and transnationally oriented Spaniards. Among those receiving German language training, there is a high mobility affinity and high level of mobility experiences and social networks in Germany. Digging deeper into the motives and aspirations of those interviewees, it turns out that mobility cannot solely be interpreted as an escape from the domestic crisis, but that it represents one (among various) possible options of professional and personal development.

Keywords: Germany, Language Schools, Migration, Spatial Perceptions

INTRODUCTION

The financial crisis which hit Spain in 2008 brought economic hardship and increased difficulties of labor market access especially for the Spanish youth. From 2007 to 2010, unemployment numbers for Spaniards aged 16-19 years almost doubled and resulted in an unemployment rate of over 50 per cent, while the unemployment rate for those aged 20-24 increased by 125 per cent and reached 33.4 per cent in 2010 (INE 2011). Youth unemployment rates at those levels are observed in most South European countries, and they are not only due to economic recession, but also to various system failures that especially hit young people at the life-cycle passage from education towards labor market entry. For Spain, reasons have to be sought in the rapid change of labor market structures since the 1990s, in mismatches between education, vocational training and the requirements of the labor market as well as in changes in the composition of the labor force, which is mainly due to a large increase in female employment and rising numbers of working immigrants. All those groups – young adults, women and immigrants – are disproportionately affected by unemployment (Bernecker 2006: 276).

While former periods of high unemployment did not influence emigration numbers, we observe an increasing mobility of Spaniards during the recent crisis (cf. Domínguez-Mujica/Pérez-García in this volume). For example Germany, which until 2008 had a slightly negative migration balance with Spain, recorded rising immigration numbers from 7,778 in 2008 to over 36,000 in the peak-year 2013, which resulted in a positive migration balance with Spain as of 22,360 in 2013 (figure 5.1).

Figure 5.1: Movements of non-German nationals between Spain and Germany, 1996-2014

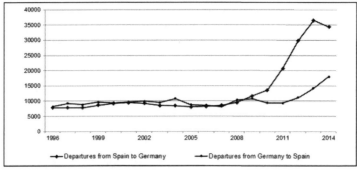

Source: BMI 2013; StBA 2013, 2014, 2015

Likewise, we can observe an increasing labor market participation of Spaniards in Germany. Whereas before 2010, the number of regularly employed Spaniards was continuingly decreasing – among other reasons, due to many former Spanish immigrants reaching retirement age – , occupation numbers almost doubled from 34,625 in December 2010 to 62,480 in December 2015 (BA 2016). Also the inflow of Spanish students to Germany increased significantly. While before 2008, the number of Spanish first degree students used to be around 2.600, numbers escalated after 2008 until 5,895 in 2014 (DAAD/DZHW 2014, 2015). Thus, we can conclude that immigration of Spaniards to Germany has increased significantly since the onset of the economic crisis, and that a large part of this immigration was targeted on the labor market and the higher education system.

Considering those recent changes of mobility development for example to Germany, we have to ask the question which prerequisites are necessary until a young Spaniard actually moves to Germany. Surveys like the Eurobarometer survey regularly displayed rather low mobility intentions of Spaniards, compared to other Europeans, and revealed strong local ties and lacking language capacities as major reasons (European Commission 2010, 2012, 2013). However, the effects of societal change and internationalization of the Spanish society may have produced a new generation of young Spaniards, who are well trained, multilingual and pursue transnational career strategies. For them mobility may be an option to secure the job position or even improve their career. In order to achieve this, language proficiency is the key determinant.

With the purpose to gain exploratory insight into the mobility intentions of Spaniards, their motivations and preparatory steps, the author launched an online survey among language students at German language schools in Spain. The main research goal was to explore the motivation of language acquisition and possible linkages to mobility intentions. A further research focus was to analyze perceptions of Germany as a possible migratory destination, compared to perceptions of Spain.

The chapter is organized in four parts: Following the introduction, the author will discuss conceptual approaches and empirical data that deal with the question *if, how*, and *under which circumstances* mobility intentions are put into practice. Furthermore this second part will deal with the development of spatial perceptions and their influences on the structuration of migratory decisions. Part three will present the results of the online survey among Spanish language students with respect to the research questions raised above. Part four will summarize the results and will discuss possible implications for science and policy makers.

THE NEXUS BETWEEN MOBILITY INTENTIONS AND ACTION: CONCEPTUAL THOUGHTS

The question to what extent mobility intentions are put into practice is of great interest for state authorities in source and destination countries of migration, as those questions touch various fields of governance like labor market, social welfare, housing or education. Especially if it comes to changes of crucial framing features of a migration system (such as migration and residence policies), there is rising interest for questions of migration potentials in quantitative and qualitative terms. However, research on mobility or stay intentions and their realization have to deal with various constraints, as decision making processes on the microlevel are influenced by multiple determinants that are located both on the macro- and the micro-level. Thus, not only the economic and political situation of possible source and destination countries plays a role in the decision making process, but also the perception of life quality, individual career chances and job opportunities, and personal constraints that may influence the decision making process and determine if migration plans are put into practice or not.

Macro- and micro-level approaches for mobility scenarios

While estimations of migration flows are usually constructed on the macro-level in the context of neoclassical approaches, we have to analyze individual profiles on the micro-level in order to learn more about the decision making process and the determinants of putting a plan into practice. When in 2004 and 2007 ten Central and Eastern European countries with a population of 105 million people joined the European Union, there were severe concerns of mass migration from East to West and possible negative consequences for West European labor markets and social systems. Several economic research institutes provided estimations of the migration potential from Central and Eastern European countries, assuming the economic disparities and income differentials as major pull factors. Those studies were usually based on neoclassical approaches that modelled the income variance between Western European and Central and Eastern European countries as main variable. On this basis, estimations varied between 63,000 and 157,000 migrants per year, with a maximum scenario of 1.18 million persons per year who would permanently move from Central and Eastern European countries to Western European countries (Straubhaar 2001; Weise et al. 1997). The variances in the estimations already signal that calculations solely based on economic factors may face serious shortcomings regarding the likelihood that these predictions actually come true.

Other studies were developed on the basis of population surveys, asking for general mobility intentions and preparatory steps towards emigration. Fassmann and Hintermann (1997) for example calculated the migration potential of citizens from four Central and Eastern European countries on the basis of population surveys, asking for general mobility intentions and preparatory steps towards emigration. They differentiated three stages, starting from the mere articulation of mobility intentions, reaching further to the collection of information until tangible preparatory steps such as looking for housing or signing a labor contract. The study revealed that between 16 (Poland) and 30 (Slovakia) per cent of a country's population had already considered moving abroad. About half of those interviewees had already taken some preparatory steps. However, only between 0.7 and 2.2 per cent were actually ready to move in the moment of the survey (Fassmann/Hintermann 1997: 13). These findings confirm theoretical considerations on migration decisions based on psychological theories about decision-making (Heckhausen 1991; Gollwitzer 1996) as multi-step-projects, starting from a vague desire to move, continued with the development of migration intentions and finalized with a migration decision and the subsequent planning and realization of a migratory move (Kalter 1997; Kley 2011).

The role of human capital and its implementation

In the context of societal development, there is increasing attention towards the availability and utilization of human capital. Studies that analyze the gain of human capital through migration mostly make use of Bourdieu's (1986) expanded concept of human capital, distinguishing between economic (e.g., savings, remittances), social (personal networks, institutionalized relations) and cultural (knowledge, skills, qualifications) capital. Empirical studies frequently reveal not only the impact of human capital loss through emigration (brain drain), but also the waste of human capital due to difficulties to adequately apply it in the destination country. In this context, also the question of social integration comes to the fore.

The aforementioned study of Fassmann and Hintermann (1997) also integrated considerations on the personal profile of the potential migrants and asked the question to what extent the migration project will pay off. They assumed that those at younger age will have a higher probability to migrate than someone who is in the final stages of working life. Also, only those persons would migrate who have a realistic chance of being employed in the destination country. Crucial issues identified in this context are foreign language proficiency and the question how professional qualifications can be transferred. Furthermore, Fassmann and Hintermann considered integration costs as relevant variable, which depend on age, sex, marital status, education, distance, and the presence of an "ethnic community" in the destination country (Fassmann/Hintermann 1997: 9f).

Transnational social networks and transnational biographical projects

The transnational perspective in migration and integration research reaches further in the analysis and evaluation of social networks, proposing that the continuous exchange of ideas, money, products, symbols and cultural practices leads to the development of transnational social spaces as basic reference frame for migrants' daily life (Pries 1997: 16). Being embedded into a transnational social space, migrants have greater biographical resources than non-migrants from which they can profit, making them more flexible towards further mobility and life cycle steps (Nowicka 2013). Transnational migrants or persons with transnational biographies thus have the ability to compare labor market situations and aspects of daily life on a transnational basis. Given their transnational social capital, they are easily ready to take off for another country if their current living circumstances are not satisfying and if they assume that they will do better abroad. Those decisions are especially likely at specific life cycle passages, such as the passage from education to work life.

Spatial perceptions and their role in the structuration of migration

A further aspect we have to consider is the subjective perception of geographical locations and the impact those perceptions may have on mobility decisions. Understanding the process of cognition as result of subjectivity and selectivity, individual perceptions may have tangible effects on the subjective appearance of a geographical location and on actual spatial behavior. In geographical research, there is a long lasting research tradition on the nexus of perception and spatial behavior. Most studies in this context focus on urban spaces and daily mobility processes, such as the seminal studies of Lynch (1960) and Downs and Stea (1982), who developed a template for mental mapping processes and the interpretation of mental maps.

But also in the context of migration studies, the subjective perception of place utility is considered as important factor for mobility decisions. Wolpert (1965: 162) defines place utility as the "net composite of utilities which are derived from the individual's integration at some position in space." Individual perceptions of space can develop from direct experience and indirect influences. Personal perceptions of space derive largely from the level of satisfaction or dissatisfaction and thus are densely connected to personal aspirations and life cycle steps (De Jong/Fawcett 1981; Lindenberg 1996). Therefore, critical re-evaluation of spatial features and consecutive migration decisions are especially likely during life-course transitions (Kley 2011: 470).

Even though the influence of spatial perceptions on migration decisions and locational choice is theoretically sound, until today empirical evidence is rare, especially in the context of international migration. Mostly, studies are addressing relocation decisions within a country and either stress differing preferences concerning urban or rural destinations or lifecycle considerations, or a combination of both (Benson/O'Reilly 2009; Davies 2008; Halfacree 2007; Stockdale 2014). In the context of international migration, perceptions of place utility are rather studied as one decisive factor among many others; frequently, empirical studies state an affinity of younger migrants for large urban agglomerations, as they perceive better opportunities to pursue individual goals regarding education, career or personality development. Fielding (1992, 1995) introduced the notion of "escalator regions" in this context, which are regions that propose a well-developed opportunity structure for personal development and thus experience a high fluctuation of especially highly-skilled young (internal) migrants. Likewise, Favell's (2006, 2008) notion of "Eurocities" point to the effects of global cities on the European scale for specific life stages and for the realization of individual goals during those specific life stages.

It is important to point out that, if it comes to possible future destination, many people will have to draw their spatial perceptions from secondary sources, such as experiences of friends or relatives, but also media reports. Thus, perceptions based on secondary sources can strongly depend on the public image of a certain geographical location and the way those images are produced and reproduced. As an actual example we can mention the city of Berlin, where we can easily draw a connection between its recent image as "Eurocity" and meeting point of the global youth and the rising numbers of Spanish migrants who move to Berlin (Montero 2014: 82).[1]

---

1   Between 31 December 2010 and 30 June 2013, the number of Spaniards in Berlin increased by 60%, from 7.670 to 12.262.

Empirical evidence: motives and consequences of foreign language acquisition

In the following paragraphs, the conceptual considerations from above will be integrated into a concise research frame. Thus, the mobility intentions of Spanish language students will be explored considering their cultural and social capital, former mobility experiences, perceptions of migration destinations and socio-demographic factors that might influence the decision making process prior to the mobility decision.

Study aims, methodology and characterization of the sample

In order to assess the likelihood of mobility in connection with the necessary language skills and language acquisition in more detail, the author launched a survey among language students at the Madrid Goethe Institute and other German language schools in Spain. The questionnaire was developed in cooperation with the Madrid Goethe Institute and contained 42 mostly closed or semi-closed questions, starting with questions on motives of language acquisition. A set of filtering questions explored migration intentions in detail: We asked for international experiences, the existence of social networks abroad, motives for an eventual stay abroad as well as preparatory steps that had already been taken. Furthermore, we integrated questions on perceptions of Germany and Spain, which were partly taken from Eurobarometer-surveys in order to have a level of comparison. Finally, we asked for general expectations for the future and socio-demographic information. In the end of the questionnaire, we provided space for comments, which were vividly used in order to express personal opinions and concerns and to tell own migratory experiences or accounts of difficult living situations.

The survey was launched online on the survey platform *Soscisurvey*; the link to the survey was distributed via social media and a mailing list of the Madrid Goethe Institute. Furthermore, the Madrid Goethe Institute offered two scholarships for free language classes that were raffled among all survey participants. This offer raised the attention considerably. Already during the first week of the survey, 95 persons accessed it online. The survey ran between September 18 and December 18 2013 and delivered 564 completed questionnaires, mainly from students of Madrid Goethe Institute (490 out of 564 completed questionnaires). Even though the sample is not representative for the Spanish population, it represents the typical clientele of Goethe Institutes with a strong selectivity regarding age and education: The survey participants (57 per cent female) were mostly young adults, the largest age group (40 per cent) were those aged between 25 and 34 (table 5.1). About 28 per cent were younger than 25 years, and rounded 20 per cent between 35 and 44 years. Only a small share was older than 45 years.

The majority of respondents were single (66 per cent) and without children (88 per cent). They were mostly well educated, about 70 per cent held a tertiary degree. About half of the respondents were employed at the time of the survey, 29 per cent were students and 13 per cent were unemployed. There were some respondents who were still attending secondary school (3 per cent), who were retired (2 per cent) or at maternity leave (1 per cent).

Table 5.1: Main characteristics of survey participants

Characteristics (number of valid answers)	Percentage of respondents
Gender (n=542)	
male	43.0
female	57.0
Age groups (n=538)	
14-24	28.3
25-34	40.5
35-44	19.5
45-54	7.6
55 and older	4.0
Marital status (n=538)	
single	65.6
living in partnership	14.7
married	17.1
divorced/widowed	2.6
Parenthood (n=538)	
no children	88.5
one or more children	11.5
Highest Educational Degree (n=493)	
no degree (attending high school)	11.3
high school degree (*Bachillerato*)	3.7
university entry degree (*PAU/Selectividad*)	11.9
undergraduate degree (*Titulo de Grado/diplomado/ Ingeniero/Superior*)	23.6
master degree (*Titulo de Master/Licenciado*)	46.8
PhD (*Doctor*)	2.6
Highest Professional Degree (n=493)	
no professional degree	46.5
medium vocational training degree (*Técnico/auxiliar*)	6.9
higher vocational training degree (*Técnico Superior/ Especialista*)	46.7

Labor Market Position (n=548)	
employed	52.7
student	29.0
unemployed	13.0
attending school/traineeship	2.6
retired	2.0
parental leave/housewife	0.7

Source: own survey

Among the survey participants, one tenth held a foreign citizenship, mainly from Latin American and European countries. Most survey participants were located in the province of Madrid, further smaller sub-centers were the provinces of Granada, Navarra, Zaragoza and Vizcaya/Bilbao. Even though most of the survey participants took their language class at a Goethe Institute, the total response shows the variety of opportunities for language acquisition, containing language schools of the Autonomous Communities (Escuela Oficial de Idioma/EOI), university language centers or initiatives like "language-tandems". Most of the language courses had a general character (92 per cent), rounded four per cent of the respondents attended a job oriented language class and two per cent learned German as part of their university education. Roughly half of the respondents planned to acquire a language certificate, mostly on the level B1 and B2.[2] Generally, the internationally accepted certificates were preferred (figure 5.2). Rounded 70 per cent of our respondents had repeatedly taken German language classes.

---

[2] The *Common European Framework of Reference for Languages* differentiates six levels of foreign language proficiency from A1 (Beginner) to C2 (expert). Level B1 is considered as minimum requirement for university entrance and for employment; for qualified professionals or those with a high proportion of communication (for example medical staff), level B2 is considered necessary (Council of Europe).

Figure 5.2: Type of language certificate pursued

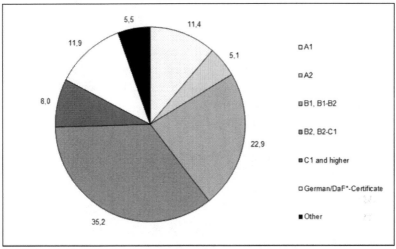

Source: own survey; n=236; *DaF = Deutsch als Fremdsprache (German as foreign language)

Motives for studying German

Motives for studying German were manifold; we recorded 1,511 answers of 560 respondents, which is an average of 2.7 responses per person. More than three quarters of respondents study German for job related reasons (table 5.2). Almost every second respondent studied German to be prepared for a possible labor migration to Germany or another German speaking country, and 21 per cent can imagine studying in one of those countries. But besides those economically rational reasons of language acquisition, two thirds also mentioned a general interest in German language and culture as a motive for studying German, one third of respondents prepared for touristic travel, and 18 per cent wanted to improve their German communication skills because they had German friends or relatives. Some comments in our survey give further explanations concerning motives of language acquisition:

"I hope that by learning German I can improve my professional development, but I am not interested in working in Germany. Rather I want to have a job where I can deal with Germans." (female respondent, 25 years)

"The main reason why I study German is that I can move freely through Europe as a European citizen. As soon as I know German well, I would like to study French." (male, 33 years)

Especially among students of so-called MINT[3]-subjects, the good reputation of German universities as environment for study and research promotes the intention to study the German language. Some respondents express the intention to boost their career by studying in Germany:

"For me, personally, experience in Germany would be of high significance, especially for my career. I am biologist and pursue a Master program of physical anthropology. I know that there are excellent research environments in Germany, where I could extremely expand my professional knowledge." (female, 22 years)

"I study mechanical engineering, therefore I want to finalize my studies in Germany." (University of Aachen)

"Germany is an interesting country for me, because there are many opportunities. I would like to live and work in Germany for four or five years." (male, 23 years)

Table 5.2: Reasons for studying German

Reasons for studying German	Share of Respondents
I think that German is important for my future in the job	77.3
I am interested in German language and culture	66.6
I'd like to work in a German speaking country	46.6
I'd like to travel in a German speaking country	35.4
I'd like to study in a German speaking country	21.1
I'd like to communicate with German friends/relatives	18.0
Other reasons	4.8

Source: own survey; n = 560, multiple answer set with 1,511 answers

---

3   MINT is a collective term for subjects of study or professions in the fields of mathematics, computer science, natural science and technology. Since these subjects are said to have a high innovation potential, workers with these qualifications are especially sought-after.

Migration-specific cultural and social capital

The probability to perform a stay abroad depends largely on the individual cultural and social capital. Cultural capital includes qualifications and language skills which enable migrants to integrate in the target country of their migration. Social capital comprises friends and relatives who – due to their own migration experience – can support migratory moves and ease the first steps of integration significantly. Also, own mobility experiences are of value for the implementation of migration projects. In sum, these aspects are considered to be crucial for the realization of migration intentions. Therefore, these aspects were integrated in our survey, as presented below.

First, we examined the language proficiency of our survey respondents. In their self-estimation, 46 per cent reported to be able to understand German while their active language competence is rather low, and 38 per cent stated they could not express themselves but understand some German. One tenth was at the beginner level. Most of the interviewees were competent in other foreign languages, especially English, which 73 per cent estimated to have very good or perfect knowledge, followed by French, where 40 per cent stated a good knowledge. Also other romance languages such as Italian or Portuguese were part of the interviewees' language profiles (figure 5.3). This shows the increasing importance of language skills in working life, but is also an indication of the cosmopolitanism of the respondents.

Figure 5.3: Foreign language proficiency, self-estimation, in per cent of cases

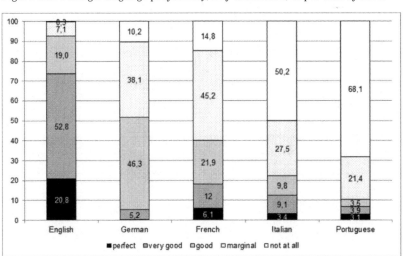

Source: own survey; n=562

Prior migration experiences and transnational social networks

The majority of respondents already had prior migration experiences: 54.6 had already stayed abroad for at least three months. Prior migration locations were often English speaking countries as well as various European countries. About one fifth of respondents had already been in Germany for at least three months (figure 5.4).

Figure 5.4: Experiences staying abroad (more than three months), in per cent of cases

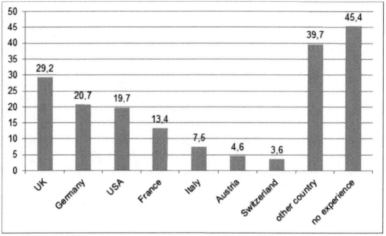

Source: own survey; n=535

Generally, the survey respondents showed a high level of internationalization, having access to social networks abroad, having foreign friends or foreign relatives in Spain, or – as already mentioned – having own migration experiences or a good foreign language proficiency (table 5.3).

Table 5.3: Level of internationalization of respondents

Aspect of internationalization	Share in per cent
Friends/relatives abroad	88,6
Foreign friends/relatives in Spain	72,8
Experience abroad of more than three months	54,6
Very good/perfect proficiency of a foreign language	24,3

Source: own survey; n=535

Mobility intentions and level of preparedness

Considering the high share of mobility intentions that were mentioned as reason for language acquisition, we wanted to find out more about the probability that those plans are put into practice. Therefore we added a set of filtered questions referring to general mobility intentions, the concretization of mobility plans (displayed for example by gathering information on possible migration destinations) and mobility preparations (displayed for example by looking for housing or signing a labor contract).

Figure 5.5 shows the general attitude towards moving abroad and main motives for this step. The results display a very high proportion of career oriented intentions (more than 70 per cent of respondents), while labor market oriented motives such as the wish to acquire a higher income or to avoid unemployment were mentioned by roughly half of the respondents. Further frequent motives were to gain new experiences and to develop one's personality and thus were not coupled to economic necessity. A similar variety of motives was displayed in the open answers of our survey:

"I have my job in Spain and I would like to stay in a German city for a while, to develop a better understanding of German language, customs, labor market situation, social relationships and so forth." (female, 48 years)

"The employment opportunities in Spain are very bad for specialized doctors such as me, except in specialized hospitals, depending on the field of expertise. We have the option to rotate to abroad, and many people are taking this option in order to find out possible future employment opportunities abroad. This phenomenon is very common." (female, 28 years)

Practically none of the respondents would generally refuse a migratory stay.

Figure 5.5: "Could you imagine living abroad? Which possible reasons could you imagine?", in per cent of cases

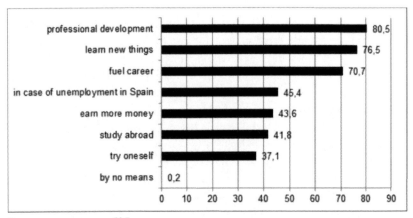

Source: own survey; n=535

Considering the estimated duration of a migratory stay, respondents neither prefer short-term stays of less than one year, nor permanent emigration. Roughly one quarter of respondents would estimate sojourns between one and three years as preferable, 14 per cent opted for sojourns between three and five years. Every second respondent would not decide the duration of a migratory stay in advance. This underlines the rather low concreteness of emigration plans at the time of the survey. But it also displays the awareness that the length of a migratory stay will depend on a successful integration into the labor market and on social factors, both of which are difficult to estimate in advance. A further set of questions detailed labor market oriented expectations and considerations, such as the probability to search for work abroad during the next two years. The results display a high pressure for action among the unemployed, but also a clear determination among the students not to rely on the domestic labor market regarding their professional career (figure 5.6).

Figure 5.6: Probability of job search abroad within the following two years, in per cent of cases

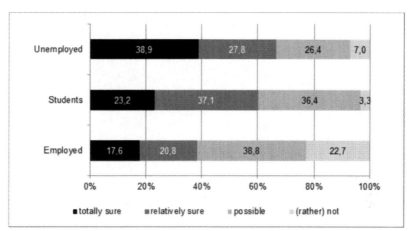

Source: own survey; n=497

In order to get a more precise picture on migration intentions and probability, we designed a set of filter-questions, starting with the analysis of motives for language learning (table 5.2). As a follow-up from this question, we filtered out those respondents who reported the preparation of work or study related migrations as major motive for learning German (n=240 and 154), and asked them for further preparations. It turned out that a significant share of those respondents was already involved in further preparations for a professional or study-related stay abroad (figure 5.7/5.8). Among those respondents who learned German for labor migration related reasons (240 respondents or 46.6 per cent of the whole sample), four fifths have already gathered general information on the labor markets in Germany, Austria or Switzerland. More than two fifths had received advice, 14.6 per cent have already applied for jobs abroad and five per cent are nearing the realization of their plans. They have either signed a job contract or are currently searching for housing in a German-speaking country.

Figure 5.7: Level of preparation for a job related migratory stay in a German-speaking country, in per cent of respondents

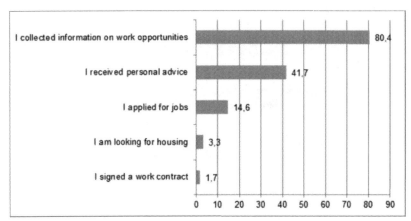

Source: own survey; n=240, multiple answer set with 340 answers

Also among the students there is a significant share preparing for a stay abroad, with 78.6 per cent collecting information about studying in a German speaking country and 35.1 per cent receiving personal advice. About one fifth of the responding students already applied for a study program or an Erasmus scholarship abroad, and 3.2 per cent were looking for housing abroad at the time the survey was carried out.

Figure 5.8: Level of preparation for a study related migratory stay in a German-speaking country, in per cent of respondents

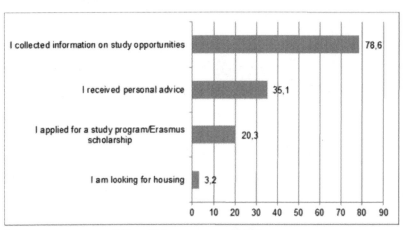

Source: own survey; n = 154, multiple answer set with 211 answers

For collecting information on German-speaking countries as possible migratory destination, the respondents used a broad variety of sources. As an average, 2.6 sources were mentioned; while the internet was the most frequently used source of information, more than half of the respondents relied on personal information from people who already lived in Germany and over two fifths consulted friends and relatives. Those personal and socially reliable contacts were much more common than advice from professional consultants, social media or printed media. In this respect, also the German language course itself and the opportunity to talk to teachers or fellow students might be an important reference point for those planning a migratory move.

Table 5.4: Which means of information are you using for collecting information on study and job opportunities in a German speaking country?

Information source	Share of respondents, in per cent
Internet	84,1
Social Media	29,0
Newspaper	15,2
TV/Radio	8,3
Personal contact to friends/relatives	42,4
Personal contact with people who already lived in Germany/Austria/Switzerland	56,9
Personal advice from professional consultants	30,1

Source: own survey; n=276, multiple answer set with 734 responses

Perceptions of Germany and Spain

Exploring perceptions and geographical knowledge of Germany, it turned out that the survey participants have a fairly differentiated geographical knowledge. For most of them, Germany represents a well ordered and economically strong country with relatively good opportunities on the labor market and attractive cities and landscapes. The majority of respondents are aware of the fact, that there is considerable regional differentiation and thus living conditions vary throughout the country. The German population is characterized as diligent and profound and partially as friendly and open minded. The majority of respondents perceived Germany as a country with good income opportunities and a high standard of living (figure 5.9). Many of our respondents draw these perceptions from personal experience, as 84 per cent already visited Germany, mostly for holidays, but also for visiting friends and relatives or for study and job related reasons.

Figure 5.9: Perceptions of Germany, in per cent of respondents

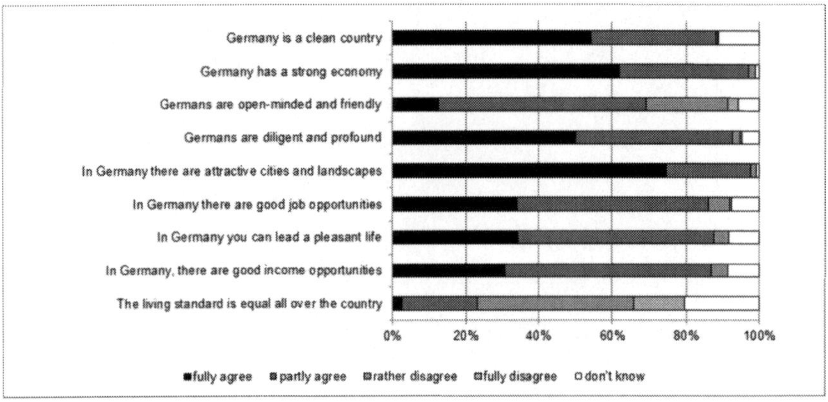

Source: own survey; n=542

A comparison of the perceptions of Germany between those who have already visited Germany and those who have never been to Germany reveals some interesting differences (figure 5.10). For example, those with personal experiences in Germany chose negative or neutral categories significantly less often than those without personal experiences. This is particularly evident in categories that can only be assesses by personal experience, such as the statements regarding the cleanliness, the German mentality, the quality of life and the regional disparities within Germany. By contrast, those without personal experiences more often agree to those statements that are related to the economic power and the labor market in Germany. Obviously, those with own experiences have made their own minds about their opportunities on the German labor market, so that their assessment is a little less optimistic.

These findings seem particularly relevant in light of the current ongoing initiatives to recruit Spanish professionals for the German labor market. The opportunity to gain personal insight into aspects of daily life and regional specifics in Germany can prevent later disappointment and is therefore an important prerequisite for the long-term success of recruitment initiatives.

Figure 5.10: Perceptions of Germany in relation to personal experiences, in per cent of cases

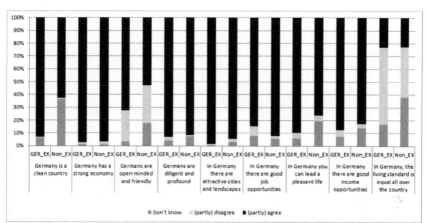

Source: own survey; n = 560; GER_EX = Persons with experience in Germany; Non_EX: Persons without experience in Germany

As a contrast to perceptions of Germany as possible migratory destination, we asked for perceptions of the home country, Spain (figure 5.11). The items we asked are partly equivalent to the Eurobarometer-surveys, which are carried out by the European Commission on a regular basis, so that they give a valuable picture of the public climate of a nation and its changes over time (cf. European Commission 2010, 2011, 2012).

Our respondents display a rather critical view on their own country, especially when it came to labor market related questions. In their view, in Spain there are rather bad job opportunities, poor income and instable living conditions. Even though a majority thought, that Spain would have passed the peak of the economic crisis, the vast majority thinks that reforms are urgently needed. EU-membership is rather evaluated positively in terms of dealing with the economic crisis.

Figure 5.11: Perceptions of Spain, in per cent of respondents

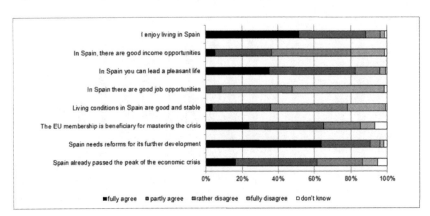

Source: own survey; n=542

Some very critical comments in our survey further underline the critical assessment of our interviewees:

"When I am asked for my current job and if I am happy, my answer is that I didn't get paid since July (written December 2013). I am a manager, and, yes, I would be happy." (female, 30 years).

"We need a thorough review of the current economic system, which needs to set limits, instead of promoting poor management. We need an equal and open electoral law. Political corruption must be put to an end, and we need mandatory programs to provide for a reduction in tax rates, to encourage spendings." (male, 27 years)

"I'd like to say that I like Spain as a country, such as landscape and climate. But today, I would be happy if I could run away, because it's embarrassing. Be it the political landscape, the widespread corruption and the high level of taxation, which is passed on to ordinary citizens." (female, 44 years)

Nevertheless we can state that Spain is assessed very positive considering its life quality.

DISCUSSION AND CONCLUSION

In contrast to earlier periods of high unemployment, during the current economic crisis there is a considerable increase of international mobility among Spaniards. We hypothesized that mobility is used as possible strategy to avoid economic hardship, and that rising levels of education, language proficiency and transnational social capital set the basis for mobility as strategical option. With the purpose to gain exploratory insight into the mobility intentions of Spaniards, their motivations and preparatory steps, an online survey was implemented focusing on language students at German language schools in Spain. The main research goal was to explore the motivation of language acquisition and possible linkages to mobility intentions. A further focus was on the influence of subjective perceptions of Germany as a possible migratory destination, compared to perceptions of Spain.

The survey revealed that language students at Goethe Institutes and other language schools have a considerably high educational level and a high level of transnationalisation, combining multiple language skills with transnational social networks and own experiences living abroad. Even though only a small proportion of our respondents actually suffered economic hardship such as unemployment, there was a common notion that migration would be a possible strategy to avoid unemployment, poor labor conditions and bad payment. While only a small proportion of respondents actually prepared for migration, no-one would refuse migration and most of the respondents connected migration with personal and career development. Following the perceptions on home and possible destination country, we could observe a high level of dissatisfaction with the economic and political situation in Spain, with negative effects for the functioning of the labor market and work ethics. On the contrary, Germany was assessed as preferential place concerning economic stability, fair working conditions and high living standards. There was a clear distinction in the perceptions of those who had personal experiences in Germany and those who developed an imagination of Germany from secondary sources, such as media reports. While the latter integrated personal dreams and positive future scenarios in their spatial perception, the first group showed a more differentiated and thus realistic approach towards Germany as possible migratory destination. Irrespective of the spatial representation, however, the majority would choose a temporary option, as after all, life in Spain is preferred.

Even though these results are not representative for the whole of Spain and taking into account the difference between intention and execution of actions, we can state a high affinity towards mobility among students in language classes.

The probability for transforming the intention into action is supported by a high level of international experiences, a transnational social network, high education level and a good knowledge of foreign languages. At the same time it becomes evident that migration cannot solely be interpreted as an escape from the domestic crisis, but that it represents one (among various) possible options of professional and personal development.

REFERENCES

Bundesagentur für Arbeit (BA) (2016): Arbeitsmarkt in Zahlen. Beschäftigungsstatistik. Beschäftigte nach Staatsangehörigkeit in Deutschland, December 12, 2015, Nürnberg: Bundesagentur für Arbeit.

Bundesministerium des Innern (BMI) (ed.) 2013: Migrationsbericht des Bundesamtes für Migration und Flüchtlinge im Auftrag der Bundesregierung. Nürnberg: Bamf.

Benson, Michaela/O'Reilly, Karen (2009): "Migration and the search for a better way of life: a critical exploration of lifestyle migration." In: Sociological Review 57/4, pp. 608-625.

Bernecker, Walther (2006): Spanien-Handbuch. Geschichte und Gegenwart. Tübingen: UTB.

Bourdieu, Pierre (1986): "The forms of capital." In: John G. Richardson (ed.), Handbook of Theory and Research for the Sociology of Education, New York: Greenwood, pp. 241-258.

Council of Europe (ed.) (without year): Common European Framework of Reference for Languages: Learning, Teaching, Assessment. Strasbourg: Language Policy Unit. September 13, 2016 (http://www.coe.int/t/dg4/linguistic/Source/Framework_EN.pdf).

Davies, Amanda (2008): "Declining Youth In-migration in Rural Western Australia: The Role of Perceptions of Rural Employment and Lifestyle Opportunities." In: Geographical Research 46/2, pp. 162-171.

De Jong, Gordon F./Fawcett, James (1981): "Motivations for migration: an assessment and a value-expectancy research model." In: Gordon F. De Jong/Robert W. Gardner (eds.), Migration decision making: Multidisciplinary Approaches to Microlevel Studies in Developed and Developing Countries. New York: Pergamon, pp. 13-58.

Deutscher Akademischer Austauschdienst (DAAD), Deutsches Zentrum für Hochschul- und Wissenschaftsforschung GmbH (DZHW) (2014): Wissenschaft Weltoffen 2014. Facts and Figures on the International Nature of

Studies and Research in Germany. Bielefeld: W. Bertelsmann Verlag GmbH & Co. KG.

Deutscher Akademischer Austauschdienst (DAAD), Deutsches Zentrum für Hochschul- und Wissenschaftsforschung GmbH (DZHW) (2015): Wissenschaft Weltoffen 2015. Facts and Figures on the International Nature of Studies and Research in Germany. Bielefeld: W. Bertelsmann Verlag GmbH & Co. KG.

Downs, Roger/Stea, David (1982): Kognitive Karten: Die Welt in unseren Köpfen. New York: Harper & Row.

European Commission (2010): Geographical and labour market mobility. Report. Brussels (= Special Eurobarometer 337). February 12, 2015 (http://ec.europa.eu/public_opinion/archives/ebs/ebs_337_en.pdf).

European Commission (2011): Employment and Social Policy. Report. Brussels (= Special Eurobarometer 377). February 12, 2015 (https://webcache.googleusercontent.com/search?q=cache:SCjUQxuXh7MJ:https://www.consilium.europa.eu/uedocs/cms_data/docs/pressdata/en/lsa/119656.pdf+&cd=3&hl=de&ct=clnk&gl=de&client=firefox-b).

European Commission (2012): European Citizenship. Report. Brussels (Standard Eurobarometer 77). February 12, 2015 (http://ec.europa.eu/public_opinion/archives/eb/eb77/eb77_citizen_en.pdf).

Fassmann, Heinz/Hintermann, Christiane (1997): Migrationspotential Ostmitteleuropa (ISR-Forschungsberichte, 15), Wien: ISR.

Favell, Adrian (2006): "London as Eurocity: French Free Movers in the Economic Capital of London." In: Michael P. Smith/Adrian Favell (eds.), The Human Face of Global Mobility: International Highly Skilled Migration in Europe, North America and the Asia-Pacific, New Brunswick NJ: Transaction Publishers, pp. 247-274.

Favell, Adrian (2008): Eurostars and Eurocities: Free Movement and Mobility in an Integrating Europe, Oxford: Blackwell.

Fielding, Anthony J. (1992): "Migration and social mobility: South East England as an escalator region." In: Regional Studies 26/1, pp. 1-15.

Fielding, Anthony J. (1995): "Migration and social change - a longitudinal study of the social mobility of immigrants in England and Wales." In: European Journal of Population 11/2, pp. 107-121.

Gollwitzer, Peter M. (1996): "The volitional benefits of planning." In: Peter M. Gollwitzer/John A. Bargh (eds.), The Psychology of Action: Linking Cognition and Motivation to Behavior, New York: Guilford Press, pp. 287-312.

Halfacree, Keith (2007): "Back-to-the-land in the twenty-first century – making connections with rurality." In: Tijdschrift voor economische en social geografie 98/1, pp. 3-8.

Heckhausen, Heinz (1991): Motivation and Action. New York: Springer.

Instituto Nacional de Estadística (INE) (2011): Indicadores Sociales 2011. Trabajo. Tablas nacionales. February 12, 2015 (http://www.ine.es/daco/daco42/sociales11/sociales.htm).

Kalter, Frank (1997): Wohnortwechsel in Deutschland. Ein Beitrag zur Migrationstheorie und zur empirischen Anwendung von Rational-Choice-Modellen, Opladen: Leske & Budrich.

Kley, Stefanie (2011): "Explaining the Stages of Migration within a Life-course Framework." In: European Sociological Review 27/4, pp. 469-486.

Lindenberg, Siegwart (1996): "Continuities in the theory of social production functions." In: Harry Ganzeboom/Siegwart Lindenberg (eds.), Verklarende Sociologie. Opstellen voor Reinhard Wippler, Amsterdam: Thela Thesis, pp. 167-184.

Lynch, Kevin (1960): The Image of the City, Cambridge MA: MIT Press.

Montero Lange, Miguel (2014): "Innereuropäische Mobilität am Beispiel der neuen spanischen Arbeitsmigration nach Deutschland. " In: Christian Pfeffer-Hoffmann (ed.), Arbeitsmigration nach Deutschland. Analysen zur Neuen Arbeitsmigration aus Spanien vor dem Hintergrund der Migrationsprozesse seit 1960, Berlin: Mensch & Buch Verlag, pp. 12-105.

Nowicka, Magdalena (2013): "Successful Earners and Failing Others: Transnational Orientation as Biographical Resource in the Context of Labor Migration." In: International Migration, 52, 1, pp. 74-86.

Pries, Ludger (1997): "Neue Migration im transnationalen Raum." In: Ludger Pries (ed.), Transnationale Migration (Soziale Welt, Sonderband 12), Baden-Baden, pp. 15-44.

Statistisches Bundesamt (StBA) (2013): Bevölkerung und Erwerbstätigkeit. Vorläufige Wanderungsergebnisse 2012. Wiesbaden: Statistisches Bundesamt.

Statistisches Bundesamt (StBA) (2014): Bevölkerung und Erwerbstätigkeit. Vorläufige Wanderungsergebnisse 2013. Wiesbaden: Statistisches Bundesamt.

Statistisches Bundesamt (StBA) (2015): Bevölkerung und Erwerbstätigkeit. Vorläufige Wanderungsergebnisse 2014. Wiesbaden: Statistisches Bundesamt.

Straubhaar, Thomas (2001): Ost-West-Migrationspotential – Wie groß ist es? (HWWA Discussion Paper 137). Hamburg.

Stockdale, Aileen (2014): "Unravelling the migration decision-making process: English early retirees moving to rural mid-Wales." In: Journal of Rural Studies 34, pp. 161-171.

Weise, Christian/Brücker, Herbert/Franzmeyer, Fritz/Lodahl, Maria/Möbius, Uta/Schultz, Siegfried/Schumacher, Dieter/Trabold, Harald (1997): Ostmitteleuropa auf dem Weg in die EU. Transformation, Verflechtung, Reformbedarf (Beiträge zur Strukturforschung, 167). Berlin: DIW.

Wolpert, Julian (1965): "Behavioral aspects of the decision to migrate." In: Papers of the Regional Science Association 15, pp. 159-169.

6. The changing migration projects of Spaniards in the UK
The case of Brighton[1]

PABLO PUMARES

ABSTRACT

Several years of deep economic crisis with a devastating impact on youth employment have had important repercussions on the Spanish migration flows. The expectations that Spanish society had after a long period of growth have surprisingly been cut short. Young people unable to find their place in the labour market feel especially deceived with a sense of anger and anomy towards their country and unfairly forced to move abroad. Traditionally quite reluctant to migrate, now the idea of emigrating prowls around their minds. This chapter intends to contribute to knowledge of the reasons for the new Spanish emigration and determine the influence the crisis has had, based on analysis of interviews held with young Spaniards in the Brighton and Hove area (Sussex, UK). This study reveals that the dominant project is a short term one which produces intense movements of people going and returning. But at the same time it is open and subject to changes following the logic of post-industrial liquid migration. For many young Spaniards migrating to the UK fits perfectly with the idea of doing something useful while the crisis limits severely the access to employment in Spain: it is easy to find a job and learn or improve the English language, which has become a very demanded quality in Spain and it is essential to get promoted

---

1 Research done as a guest researcher at the Sussex Centre for Migration Research, partly funded by the University of Almería's Own Research Plan, the Centre for Migration and Intercultural Relations (CEMyRI) and the 37th Parallel Research Group.

in the UK. But since only a few of them get a job according to their skills, there is a big uncertainty about what to do in the following years.

Keywords: Economic crisis, Liquid migration, Migration motivations, Migration project, Spanish emigration

Introduction

The profound economic crisis and unequal impact in different European countries has caused a radical change in migratory flows on the continent. The countries in the South and Ireland, which have become great receivers of immigration, after a long period of growth, sustained by pillars which are not always solid, have returned to decade-old positions in which the net migration rates are negative, both for foreign and national flows. In contrast to this are those countries which have undergone the most migratory pressure, as the few destinations possible for a growing demand.

In Spain, the crisis has had two stages (which is why Oliver 2013, and other authors discuss a double recession): a first (2008-2010) tied to the financial crisis (shared by most of the developed world), which in some countries like Spain is complicated terribly by the explosion of the real estate bubble; the second stage of the crisis (2011-2014) is linked to the adjustment policies established in response to it, policies to which some authors (Méndez/Abad/Echaves 2015; Fontana 2013) attribute an attempt to widen social and territorial differences as Keynesian redistributive policies weaken, generating a recessive spiral in countries in Southern Europe, which has a strong social impact. The first stage had a strong impact on industry and construction that led to a drop in gross employment, and eventually to a loss of two thirds of the jobs in the construction industry from 2007 to 2013 (Quarterly Spanish National Accounts, INE). Nevertheless, during this first stage, there was hardly any Spanish emigration. The second stage, however, was characterized by stagnation in the administration, technical and professional sectors related to cuts in government spending, the extended crisis itself and reduction in associated consumption. This second stage clearly affected young people who had finished their studies and were entering the market, but had no jobs to go to, as well as young people who had begun to work, but because they had been with their companies a short time, were the cheapest to dismiss when adjustments were made. The unemployment rates among young people from 20 to 24 years of age rose to 52 per cent, and to 32 per cent in the 25 to 29 age group in the first quarter of 2014 (EAPS, INE). This is when Spanish emigration took a leap, beginning a clear trend which has not yet ended, even though the country has been on the path to economic growth again since 2014.

Becoming a country of emigration again, in spite of the enormous differences from emigration in the seventies, has generated concern about the consequences, controversy due to its dimensions and anger and deception about the causes. Díaz-Hernández et al. (2015) reviewed the numerous and varied repercussions which the new Spanish emigration has had in the communications media[2], in blogs and social networks, research articles and audio-visual productions, from reports to films. The rapidity with which it has emerged, its extent and the intensity of its manifestations go much further than emigration figures, and are indicative of a phenomenon which Spanish society in general and emigrants in particular, have experienced traumatically, reflecting a society in which the family still exerts strong pressure, its orientation is protective and little value is given to migration which is dispersing its members. Domingo et al. (2014) believes this deployment in the media has itself become a factor stimulating emigration in a sort of "self-fulfilling prophecy".

Apart from this psychosocial dimension, to adequately evaluate the consequences of Spanish emigration, it would be essential to find out the number of emigrants, their sociodemographic characteristics (age, education) and their migratory projects (whether they plan on returning or not). Unfortunately, the statistics that would be the best tools for estimating emigration volume and characteristics are subject to margins of error over which there is hardly any control. The immediate consequence is that there is a long path open to speculation, and leading to, like almost everything else in these convulsive times, Spanish emigration not being able to drag itself out of controversy. At the height of the crisis it became one of the elements stirred up by media and politics, and was presented in a very negative spotlight. It was a clear indication of economic failure retrospective of a recent period of Spanish history associated with lack of development. It was an undesirable process and was feared because of the multiple negative effects it could have in the short and mid-term, especially loss of well-educated youth. The lack of sensitivity in governmental responses and its tendency to trivialize the phenomenon contributed to inflaming spirits, especially in those who had been forced to emigrate.

The issue also arose in the academic environment. Some (González-Enríquez 2013a, 2013b; Garrido-Medina 2013; Domingo et al. 2013), covered by some

---

2 For example, *El País*, the largest Spanish newspaper, devoted a long series of reports covering most of the main destinations entitled "Expatriados por la crisis" [*Expats because of the Crisis*].

very modest figures in the beginning, underlined precisely how unwilling young Spaniards seemed to be to emigrate, in spite of the chilling unemployment rates confronting them. Others (González-Ferrer 2012, 2013a, 2013b; Navarrete 2013), on the contrary, insisted on the strong underestimation of overseas migration in national resources, in contrast to the entries in some host countries, such as the United Kingdom or Germany. The enormous limitations of statistical resources for measuring emigration, which is normally not declared, as, of course, neither are the returns, as well as the few variables included and the short time series covered, impede any reliable overall evaluation of the phenomenon.

There is, however, a consensus that most young Spanish emigrants have a higher education, which would fit the theory of human capital (Sjastaad 1962). Online surveys done by the Real Instituto Elcano (Gonzalez-Enriquez/Martínez-Romera 2014) of 1.082 Spaniards born in Spain who emigrated between 2007-2013 and by Aparicio (2014) of 1.173 Spaniards born in Spain and residing in five large cities on three continents, who also emigrated after 2007, show 91 per cent and 86 per cent of Spaniards with university degrees. Although due to the survey method, they are subject to possible biases, the percentages are still overwhelming. On a more solid statistical basis, the Labour Force Survey, Kaczmarczyk and Stanek (2015) observed that from 60 to 70 per cent of Spanish women (which could include those born abroad), who had recently emigrated (in the past three years) to EU member countries during the crisis were university graduates (double the Polish figure).

This fact added concern on the loss of human capital which has led to generalisation in the communications media of the term 'lost generation', due to the slow perspectives of employment recovering. Among scholars, the question is approached from positions found. Several authors emphasize the role this emigration has as a labour market regulating mechanism (Elsner/Zimmermann 2013; Holland/Paluchowski 2013; Kahanec et al. 2014; Krause et al. 2014; Kaczmarczyk/Stanek 2015), which lightens the pressure on the labour market and unemployment subsidies by sending part of the workforce overseas. Aparicio (2014: 23) underlines the positive aspect of training which allows them to "seek a better life and not be resigned to rivalry for poor jobs with others here in Spain." Domingo et al. (2014) do not perceive dramatics either because of its modest dimensions, and González-Enríquez (2014) thinks brain dripping would be more appropriate than brain drain. Kaczmarczyk/Stanek (2015) on observing that the intensity in the case of Spain (unlike Poland) is relatively low and seems to respond to a short and mid-term strategy, while the unfavourable conditions at home continue. Cachón (2014) believes the accent should be placed on circulation. The question would not be so much whether qualified youth are emigrating abroad, but whether Spain is able to recover a good part of those young people with the experience they have acquired and then attract others in turn. In this sense, Pumares (2015) observes the predominance of a short term migration project, but a satisfactory labour insertion is still difficult for those who return. This may deter especially those with higher qualification (Pumares/González-Martín 2016).

On the contrary, Alba et al. (2013) stress the brain waste derived from the unqualified jobs they hold, and Cortés-Maisonave et al. (2015) point out that many enter in the rising category of poor workers. González-Ferrer (2012, 2013a) is concerned about the increase in the intention of degree-holders to emigrate shown by the 2011 Flash Eurobarometer, which placed young Spaniards and in particular those 30-34 years of age at the head of Europe. This could be indicative of greater convergence with European patterns, but might also be a deep-felt disenchantment with the country which Bygnes (2015: 3) describes in her study on qualified Spaniards in Norway. She applies the concept of anomy, "which refers to a breakdown of purpose and ideals in society", and which leads one to think of a set of noneconomic factors reflected in a discontent with ways of doing things and lack of hope that they will improve, an aspect that could be more important than the quantitative dimensions of the phenomenon. Domínguez-Mujica et al. (2016) also observe the "annoyance" of Spanish emigrants "with political leaders and business community".

This chapter intends to contribute to knowledge of the reasons for the new Spanish emigration and determine the influence the crisis has had based on analysis of interviews held with young Spaniards in the Brighton and Hove area (Sussex, UK). Starting out from the testimonies of these young people on their emigration experience, their lives abroad and their projects for the future, some of the consequences this process may have for Spain and its young emigrants are suggested.

The case of Brighton may be considered representative of Spanish emigration to the United Kingdom, which has been the main destination of Spanish migratory flows for over a decade. The existence of emigration prior to the crisis, and the considerable attraction of some British cities beyond the purely economic (King et al. 2014), invite to an in-depth analysis of any possible changes and continuities experienced because of the crisis. British statistics show 172.809 new Spanish allocations in the National Insurance from 2008/2009 to 2013/2014, of which 5.261 were in this city (outside of Greater London, the second after Edinburgh). Brighton is a middle-size city located on the southern coast of England, which enjoys a more benign climate than other more northern localities and is very well connected to the Gatwick Airport (half an hour by train) and to London itself (one hour). It is also characterized by great vitality derived from summer tourism and the multitude of students, many of them foreign students, who attend its two large universities (Sussex and Brighton), or English language courses, and it has an environment appropriate to artistic expression, especially music.

METHOD

This study is based on 27 in-depth interviews and numerous contacts which took place from September to December 2014 and the first week of February 2015. The interviews were held with young Spaniards from 22 to 37 years of age, brought up in Spanish families in Spain and who reside and/or work in Brighton. Except for one, who emigrated somewhat earlier, all of them emigrated after 2008. With the exception of one, who had only been in the city for five weeks, all of them had been residing there for over six months at the time of the interview. Of those interviewed, 16 were women and eleven men, seven had a partner, but no children, and one had children, but was divorced. Sixteen of them had university degrees, another was taking distance courses and nine had diplomas from vocational schools. For the purposes of official statistical evaluation, all of them had a British social security number, but only seven were registered with the Spanish Consulate, which resulted in a nearly traumatic experience due to poor organisation and treatment received. All except two of them were working, mostly in the hotel and restaurant sector or as salespersons in shops, others were self-employed and working in web design or as sound technicians, but four held highly qualified positions. There were also a nurse, a singer, a secretary, a social educator, and a maintenance technician (table 6.1 for more details).

Contact was incidental, either purposely looking for and asking about them, mainly in clothing shops, restaurants and hotels, either by starting up a conversation when Spanish was heard to be spoken (rather frequently), especially at the Jubilee Library in Brighton, at the basketball court on the beach, or at meetings for English and Spanish exchange. Some of those interviewed provided other new contacts, thereby enabling this many interviews to be collected. The interviews usually took place in cafes and were recorded and transcribed. They lasted an average of 100 minutes. The discussion established parallels with the categories applied by Trevena (2013) for qualified Polish young people in London: career seekers, whose priority is to impulse their professional career; drifters, who search for vital experiences and live the moment; and target earners who aim to maximize savings for their return. An adaptation of it, substituting the objective of maximizing savings (not found in the Spanish migrants) for other concrete objectives like learning English or finding a job, will be used as a typology for the migration project of young Spaniards in Brighton.

The interview followed a script which began with the situation in Spain before they emigrated (employment, education, family) and decisive elements that influenced their decision to emigrate (including attitudes toward emigration perceived in their family and social setting), and continued with the reasons that led them to decide on Brighton as their destination. It ended with what they had planned as their short and mid-term migratory projects. These points are going to be developed in this communication. In between, we asked about their whole migratory trajectory and their employment, residential and social insertion.

THE DECISION TO MIGRATE AND THE INFLUENCE OF THE CRISIS

Emigration to the United Kingdom is not new. Before the crisis it was already the main destination of Spanish emigrants, particularly youth, as shown by the Residential Variations Statistics. The reasons are usually complicated and combine several factors, but the classic reasons are learning English (by studying or working) and a career with a better future. Nor should we omit a certain element of adventure and personal growth from the foreign experience that would be open to better educated young people with more possibilities for travelling. Our interviewees also noted these were aspects basic to emigrating, showing that there is some continuation. However, the jump in numbers in the British National Insurance from 2011[3], and extending into the following years, leads us to believe that it was not limited only to a somewhat more accentuated continuation of what had been occurring up until then. One consequence is the increase in the number of Spaniards whose main goal is to find employment and the importance of their being sick and tired of the state the country is in and corruption going on in it. Thus, based on the testimonies collected, the crisis would have influenced not only the increase in outward flows, but also how they are confronted: The reasons may be similar when summarized, but the experience, the approach, the consequences, change. The process is sometimes traumatic and undesired, while

---

3   2002 to 2008 NINo data on Spanish enrolment show 10.000-11.000 per year, with no clear trend. In fiscal year 2008/09, there was a slight rise, but it was in 2010/11 when the figure shot up to 24.377, which and over 45.000 new enrolments in 2012/13 and following years.

in others it is a secretly longed for opportunity of seeing other places or simply starting a new, more independent life, free of family and social pressures.

Career seekers: A discrete influence of the crisis

It seems clear that some had emigrated regardless of the crisis. They would fit in with the type Trevena (2013) classified as career seekers. The crisis influenced them in the sense that it made it harder for them to achieve professional goals in Spain and therefore drove more people to seek them abroad, but in fact, this group would probably be predisposed to go wherever those interests took them. They formed two distinct groups, the first with people with strong professional ambitions and a clearly highflyer profile (Favell 2008; King et al. 2014) who were very clear about wanting to leave Spain for a better future and more stimulating employment settings, as Javier:

"I am very motivated by the work I do. If there is challenge that interests me, then I take the job and I move again. Salary is another variable [...] and the people you work with [...] to create something innovative or something that can change people's life." (Javier, engineer working as an engineer)

And a second group those with more modest goals, but difficult to achieve in Spain even before the crisis. This group was made up of artists (five of those interviewed), in fine arts and audio visual techniques who hoped to find better opportunities in a more diversified setting, and who would have emigrated anyway. The peculiarity in this case is that some even gave up a stable job with good conditions, but of no interest to them, to pursue their dream. In general, there are hardly any complaints about Spain in this group; they simply left to go where there were better professional opportunities for them.

The obsession to learn English

Learning English has always been a reason that had to be taken into consideration in emigration to the United Kingdom. It existed before, and several of the interviewees had also come with that idea. However, starting with the crisis, this reason acquired a new dimension. Van Dalen/Henkens (2012) mentioned that one of the reasons influencing the low mobility of Dutch youths was that they did not think employers in their country valued foreign experience. Something similar probably occurred in Spain before the crisis. However, one of the strong effects of the crisis has been the definitive push into Spanish awareness of the importance of learning other languages, or rather, of speaking English. In a country that combines a huge touristic potential with poor fluency in foreign languages, it is paradoxical how little it was appreciated or valued when selecting personnel, with few exceptions. In the new context of the crisis, speaking English is finally being perceived as a useful skill, both for being able to get a job overseas, and for working inside Spain. With rocketing unemployment rates, the requirements of employers looking for potential personnel for hire are becoming limitless and have gone on irredeemably to include English, whether necessary or not, if only as a way of clearing out CVs piling up on their desks. Associated with this is the fever unleashed for private and public bilingual schools, triggering language requirements for teaching staff[4] (at least B2, in most regions, although in the region of Madrid, C1 is required). Obviously, this means that many more people are involved in becoming competent and earning degrees that will give them a greater advantage. Furthermore, it has become one of the useful things (now even more useful) that one can do in times of crisis.

And, after so many unfruitful years of learning English at school, there is a widespread idea in Spain that almost the only way to learn it is to go to a country where English is spoken. This impression is corroborated in most cases when they get to the country. Again and again, the persons interviewed spoke of their difficulties in understanding relatively simple expressions. Only a few, who had had additional training, were free of that feeling. The result was that the number of people interested in going to the United Kingdom to learn English multiplied. Throughout my stay in Brighton, I found many young people (interviews aside) who had come for that specific purpose, normally associated with achieving a given level. Many of them returned home after a few months, as soon as they had reached it, and did not leave a mark on the statistics. However, others decided to stay longer because they realized that that level of English was not really good enough and preferred to improve it, now by working, which would maintain them in the beginning, so later they could hope for more. The most extreme cases were mothers who moved to the United Kingdom with their school-age children for a couple of years, so they would be enrolled in school there and learn English as natives.

---

4 For example, in the region of Madrid, the number of teachers qualified to teach in English increased 60% from academic year 2011/12 to 2014/15, and tripled in high schools (Regional Ministry of Education, Youth and Sports based on the General Directorate for Improving the Quality of Teaching and the General Directorate of Human Resources).

Find a job

It should be kept in mind that learning English in the United Kingdom is often combined with a job opportunity (au pair, waiter, etc.), which is where people with fewer resources start. Therefore, finding a job is nothing new, in principle, but again the crisis introduces important elements. In the first place, the volume increases, not only because it generates worse conditions for more people, but also because it encourages them to flirt with an idea of how to go from theory to practice. In the second place, finding a job becomes an end in itself, and not only a way to learn English. However, we did not find the classic typology of economic migration, which Trevena (2013) defines as target earners, where the main goal is to maximize savings for their return. If they are able (which is not always possible), improving their living conditions and social relations is their priority. What these people expect to take home with them is not savings, but experience and knowledge. Finally, the crisis caused a change in approach, which acquired a bitter tint, especially for those who felt forced to emigrate when they did not want to. This feeling, characterized by frustration and deception with the country, leads to a virulence which has become one of the differential traits of this emigration.

One common feeling in young people with university degrees is that there was nowhere for them to go when they got their degree, or else, they saw working conditions deteriorate, or directly lost their job because of the crisis. Contrary to what might be thought at first, a direct transition from studies to emigration is not so frequent, perhaps because most of those who have finished their studies prefer to further their training first (indeed, some with English courses). What was most common among the interviewees was that they had had prior job experience in Spain (all but two) and had been living on their own without their families before (sometimes because they had studied in a different city).

These young people had either lost their job due to the crisis or were very unhappy with it, sometimes because the working conditions were worsening, in others due to the poor working climate or even because it was not what they had hoped for. Faced with absence of any hope of finding a satisfactory job in Spain at that time, they felt obligated to emigrate. They were in that situation after having "done things right" and having had a work experience which, far from progressing, was deteriorating, leading them to emigrate. This coincided with many cases of corruption coming to light and accentuation of company abuse rooted in the crisis, and gave rise to a storm of ferocious criticism, with references loaded with indignation for offers to work "for free", or salaries of 600€ per month for engineers and messages from the boss that they could "take it or leave it [...]".

In fact these reactions have to do with the concept of anomy observed by Bygnes (2014) in Spaniards in Norway. This disillusionment can also be found in qualified Italian (Conti 2014; King et al. 2014), Greek (Triandafyllidou/Gropas 2014) or Irish (Ryan/Kurdi 2014) emigrants. However, while in testimonies collected by these authors, deception led to a loss of confidence in the country they had given up on as a lost cause, in Spaniards in Brighton, it often led to enormous indignation and belligerent anger. Such active anger shows that they had not fallen into disinterest, but wanted to fight to change the situation in Spain and had blossomed in movements such as the *Marea Granate* (the Crimson Tide) or the initiative "We are not leaving, they are throwing us out" of the 'Youth Without a Future' Platform (cf. López-Sala in this volume).

Adventure, personal growth

For those who most valued the foreign experience factor, the crisis also provided a shove, the perfect excuse to take the leap, especially since the social setting did not usually promote it. In several interviews there was a desire for a change of atmosphere, to try something else, to live in another environment. However, if things had gone well in Spain, many of them would not have decided to take the step. Indeed, it seems that this component is gaining in weight and could be influencing the growing numbers of departures of Spaniards even though the recession has now been left behind. As some of those interviewed commented, "Lately it seems like migrating to the United Kingdom has become fashionable", a certain commonplaceness of the phenomenon on observing young people excited about having an experience, compared to those who had been there longer. In line with the experiences of the older migrants, the significant amount of information now available (nothing to do with the first arrivals), the feeling of support from the social networks and with the panorama in Spain still clearing up, it seems that this option is starting to be popular among young Spaniards who feel safer when they leave.

Perhaps, as Glorius (2016) notes, it is an indicator of the mobility that is beginning to gain acceptance among Spanish youth, like a rite of passage in a process of convergence with countries in central and northern Europe. Whether they emigrate or not, what is true is that the possibility is more and more present in the minds of the young, as noted by Ros (2014) and corroborated by surveys taken in 2014 by The Institute for Society and Vodaphone Communications which showed that 55 per cent of young Spaniards from 18 to 30 years of age posed the possibility of moving to another country to seek employment opportunities.

Emancipation and transitions in life

Emigration may also be understood as mediating, or being part of life's transitions (Corijn/Klijzing 2001), from youth to adult life, from study to employment, from unemployment to employment. In Spain, these transitions have traditionally been slow. The difficulties of young people in becoming independent have been high and fraught with difficulties in finding a decent job, lack of housing, lack of public aid and thanks dependent on family support (Observatorio de Emancipación del Consejo de la Juventud de España [Observatory of Emancipation, Spanish Council on Youth] 2013). With the crisis, all those factors have become aggravated (Moreno-Mínguez et al. 2012), and it is becoming harder for young people to become emancipated, and some had even had to go back and live with their parents, which is not easy.

With the growing popularity of emigration, it may also be observed that emigration is posed as a more and more plausible option for achieving some of those goals, in particular, the transition from study or unemployment to work and emancipation from the family and being able to make their own decisions. The possibility of living with a partner may be another attraction. However, in general, it is observed that emigration delays forming a family. The temporariness that is often coupled with it does not favour stable relationships much less children. Of everyone we interviewed, only one had children. Among the others, we found only seven with a partner (two of them British, and one French). Furthermore, most of the people we interviewed had already lived independently before emigrating, and that seemed to be something they were not willing to sacrifice, and that tipped the balance in favour of emigration if placed at risk by deterioration of employment. This return to the parental home was considered intolerable and was one of the weighty factors driving to emigration, although just to end up in a room in a shared flat. This situation has continued, even for those for who have had a better time of it, because of the scarcity of housing.

On the other hand, the social setting did not help them much. The attitude of their parents was not usually one of encouragement for their children to emigrate. In general, they would rather have them close. However, except for counted exceptions, once they had made their decision, the parents went along with it, because they could see their children's personal suffering with the situation in Spain, and to a good extent, shared their perception of lack of any good expectations if they stayed. In any case, the family relationships were kept up in spite of the distance, and even in some cases, improved there, where precisely because of employment problems, they had deteriorated. Parents saw that their children were more mature and felt proud that they were able to get along abroad. However, unlike what was observed in other economic migrations, among the Spanish emigrants, I did not find any case in which they sent money to the family. On the contrary, they were emigrants who generally felt supported by the family and felt they could go to them in case of need, and have sometimes been offered cash to help them out, especially at first when it was hardest to settle in.

To summarize, the decision to emigrate is the result of a combination of factors, so any of the main reasons may be reinforced by others. The case of Spaniards in the United Kingdom is particularly eloquent: the tandem of working and learning or improving English is very powerful, and it combines with possibilities of professional progress on one hand and the component of experience and personal growth on the other, favoured by the multiculturalism and tolerance in Brighton.

THOSE WHO EMIGRATE AND THOSE WHO DO NOT

As attractive as this position may seem, in fact, in spite of the increase in emigration to the United Kingdom, it is still moderate. That is, there is a choice to emigrate not determined only by the employment situation, but by personal and social factors which influence those who leave and those who stay. Many of those interviewed said that friends or acquaintances had been in a similar employment situation and decided to stay (because they had a family or simply did not dare) and their decision to emigrate was not very common in their environment. The reasons repeated most often were fear of leaving their setting, in which they felt protected, especially to go abroad where they did not know the language, or already having formed a family, or were at least living with a partner. They get used to the situation and prefer to get along on help from family and stick it out with precarious jobs.

This is a concept that came up with some frequency, both in these interviews and in a discussion group held previously with Spanish emigrants in London. Those who stayed were referred to as being "comfortable", or claiming that they did not want to leave their "comfort zone". On the contrary, our interviewees could no longer stand by and watch, with no hope of getting a job, or while their working conditions gradually deteriorated, or their economic independence was threatened. This reflects the importance of sociocultural factors or factors related to the personality of each, such as risk aversion (Williams/Baláž 2005), self-efficacy (Van Dalen/Henkens 2012), or the inclination to search for sensations, which could be more important than the target employment situation.

Similarly, as mentioned in the introduction, the data available show a much stronger trend among university students, who following the theory of human capital would be those who would have the most to gain and those who would have the most skills for emigration. Even though unemployment has hit the segments with the least qualifications hardest, among our interviewees, almost two thirds had a higher education, which would be in consonance with this theory. However, among these, there is a noticeable variety of ambitions and degrees (six were engineers or architects or had a Master's degree) with a different fit in the British labour market. Only a couple of them could clearly respond to the higher Eurostar profile (cf. Favell 2008) with high qualifications and strong professional ambitions, which direct their steps to a great extent. More frequently Spanish migrants could be classified as middling transnationals (a more middle-range occupational status such as teachers, nurses etc.) (Conradson/Latham 2005; King et al. 2014).

UNCERTAINTY: A PROJECT IN THE AIR

The migratory project is dynamic and evolves over time, depending on what the experience is like, achievements, changes in expectations, and so forth, so it was hard to get a handle on it, because it depended on the situation the interviewees were in when the interview took place. Although there was a prior plan, the project had a strong component of uncertainty and was subject to change, sometimes unexpected, even for that person. When this question was approached during the interview, there were moments of silence, of looking into space and finding themselves confronted with a crucial question, which was always going around in their head, but was very hard to find an answer to.

For what we have called career seekers, the migratory project was long-term, although not always limited to Brighton. The most ambitious were open to flying wherever their professional opportunities would take them. For those who were fighting for employment in their profession, it depended partly on whether they achieved it or not, which was not always possible. They tended to persevere, but if they were unsuccessful, time was wearing them away and they had not entirely abandoned the idea of going home. In any case, that will to stay also favoured development of more stable relationships, so life with a partner was more frequent among them and more of them had settled down in the city.

However, the predominant tone was probably thinking about returning in a not too distant future, but not yet decided either, and subject to certain conditions, which would fit in with the new tendencies of liquid mobility observed by

Engbersen/Snel (2013) and Grabowska-Lusinska (2013) in migrations within Europe by Central Eastern Europeans. The majority of starting projects had to do with doing something useful that contributed to their training and experience while waiting out the crisis. In this sense, Brighton could be a special destination, hardly ever planned for the long term. There were many projects that started out with very clear time limits: getting a certain certificate in English or working for a summer, which usually lead to returning quickly, although in some cases they lead to a longer stay, in particular, to improve and consolidate the level of English acquired. This combined with those who were unable to adapt, who came without really being convinced and could only hold out a few months before they were overwhelmed by loneliness, distance from family and friends, the anxiety of not understanding, hard work and poor living conditions. Almost all of those interviewed mentioned the large number of Spanish emigrants (or even other nationalities) whom they met during their stays there but were no longer in the city.

However, Brighton is a city full of life, which generates extraordinary experiences and can be fascinating for a young person. One of the characteristics of the Spanish emigrants interviewed is the importance that sociability and the search for quality of life had for them, more than savings. And in this sense, Brighton is full of opportunities to relate to other Spaniards or foreigners and for the most diverse activities. Another of the factors that hooks them on Brighton and invites them to stay there is tolerance. In some cases, this is decisive, as it was for one of the interviewees who was black (and who found that there were other black people there in any job position and he always felt like he was treated normally) or for another of the interviewees who was gay. Even though Spain is a country with legislation among the most advanced with regard to the rights of homosexuals, not only in this interview but in others, the city's tolerance was mentioned, and how undoubtedly, their social acceptance was much greater there than in Spain. This tolerance extends to many areas, such as where people are from, how they dress, etc., and that is in general highly valued by the interviewees. That tolerance and the possibility of recreating new surroundings from zero made them feel freer than in Spain.

From the point of view of employment, emigration has a bright side and another darker one. Almost all of them had to go through a period of disqualification, at least until they learned English. They had to work as waiters, cleaners, caretakers, and sometimes under very hard conditions. However, that was compensated for in the short term by the fact that they had a job, where they could learn the language and hope for more in the future. In general, they acknowledged better treatment in the companies, more recognition which made them feel more comfortable and contrasted constantly with the work climate in Spanish companies. In the highest spectrum of employment positions, the differences were even greater, and those who attained those positions especially valued how, unlike what happens in Spain, their dedication to the job not only enjoyed more recognition, but was compatible with free time for leisure or undertaking other projects. This is a key element for understanding some possible consequences of the Spanish emigration (and probably not only to the United Kingdom): those who improve professionally, which is usually the case for those who are more qualified, it becomes harder and harder to go back. Although some may miss Spain and want to return, they consider it really hard to find a job with the conditions of recognition, possibilities of promotion, flexibility and work hours similar to those they have found here. Political corruption may cause some of them to become detached from their country of origin, but usually, they keep up on the situation in Spain and still feel involved.

The experience marks a before and after, changes people, makes them mature, know themselves better and at the same time, opens a new world of possibilities to them. Some who probably would not have emigrated without the crisis, have seen how their view of the world took a Copernican turn and if they only left to try it out or avoid unemployment, now they have given up the idea of returning in the short term. They have become drifters as observed by Trevena among the young Polish graduates in London, "who get 'sucked in' by global city life" (2014:183), and change their perspective of life to focus on living for the moment, doing what they like to do best and enjoying freedom. Their migratory project is transformed and return is postponed indefinitely, and the possibility of going to live elsewhere as a way to continue increasing their accumulated experience is planned more seriously.

"Well, I think that my friends, my brother for instance, his life is on the right lines. There's little chance his life changes. But I don't know, I don't know how my life is going to be, I don't know my future, not even know what I'm gonna do in one week, but I love it. I love having that feeling of uncertainty." (Alicia, bachelor in Business Administration working at a hotel front desk)

And nevertheless, this may also just be a stage. Because after a certain time, that rhythm of life becomes exhausting and one has to move on. And part of that exhaustion is due to the difficulty of taking the leap to sectors more in agreement with the qualifications of the emigrant. In particular, university graduates who enter the hotel and restaurant sector without difficulty and progress somewhat there may find themselves trapped. And the conditions or treatment that may seem acceptable to a young person without work in Spain so he can gain experience or learn English, are still types of work within the gradually more precarious employment in the United Kingdom, and it is hard to think about settling down, and in particular, forming a family. The sensation of temporary relationships also influences them. People come and go constantly and the whole environment of Brighton is impregnated with its temporary nature. Very few dare to think about how long they will remain there, even those who have decided to stay in the United Kingdom. This affects the way they relate to each other: personal relationships are frequent and intense, fruit of the intensity of what they are living, but at the same time, marked by being provisional, because they do not know how long they will remain in Brighton. In contrast to the provisional personal relationships, virtual relationships are a hub that lasts over time. Somehow the term liquid relationships could also be applied to them.

The question is that in spite of everything, there is onwards migration to other places, and more often, return. Sometimes this is because their goals have been fulfilled, sometimes, as mentioned above, because they could not adapt and sometimes also because of that exhaustion commented on. Of the interviewees, at least six had already left Brighton, five after three or four years staying abroad and another after a year and a half. One person interviewed found employment in Spain where she was longing to return to and for which the experience in the United Kingdom and English were fundamental. Two others returned to Madrid to finish their studies and to begin new ones. In another case, the person left for a few months to travel around Asia and returned temporarily to Spain. A fifth had met his goal (learn enough English and do an internship there). In spite of having had a hard time there, and having a job offer on the table, he decided to go to France where his girlfriend lived in the hope of finding better opportunities and better working conditions.

Finally, the fourth case is especially significant. After three long years and having finally been able to get a job under conditions which could hardly be better (£7.50/hour, 8:00 a.m.-4:00 p.m., Monday to Friday), after a very hard beginning, he decided he could not take it anymore and went home. He was one of the first to be interviewed and curiously, the first time I spoke to him (at the beginning of September) he told me he was thinking of leaving by Christmas. The next time, ten days later, I had to hurry to make an appointment with him, because he was already leaving at end of month. The feeling was that, suddenly, return had become a need, one that could not be put off. When he left, he had no job waiting for him, but did have several ideas and was confident that he would get one.

Conclusion

As observed, the reasons to migrate are very similar to what they were before the crisis. However, its influence is undeniable, increasing the number of emigrants and somehow transforming the meanings of those reasons. In the first place, many of the migrations are perceived as forced and are wrought with frustration, disenchantment and anger with their home country. The intensity of that anger and its activism constitute one of the most specific characteristics of this new Spanish emigration. Emigration has also been revealed as important as a way of becoming independent, but perhaps more revealing than acquiring it is the fact that it may be the only way to maintain it, so those who had worked and begun to live independently would be more prone to emigration with clearly defined goals. Furthermore, the crisis has clearly boosted interested in learning English. And finally, the crisis may be said to have generated a more fertile environment for emigration, encouraging those most inclined to do so to take the step. For most, staying means unemployment or jobs with very poor conditions. Many people are resigned to that. For the most daring, active and restless, the feeling of not being able to do anything useful with their lives becomes unsupportable and drives them to take advantage of the moment, to take a step forward and do something of personal and professional interest while the economy recovers. A positive selection of Spanish emigrants is therefore observed, not only for their qualifications, but also their personality.

Thus emigration to Brighton (and by extension to other British cities with more Spanish immigrants) offers many options: English language courses, plentiful employment in hotels, restaurants and shops, possibilities for a diversity of other interesting jobs once they have learned English, and a very young, multicultural and highly tolerant atmosphere. These characteristics strengthen each other and explain the attraction of this city, by simultaneously responding to several of the main motivations of Spanish youth.

Of the migratory projects, there is a longer-term group, less dependent on the crisis, whose main goal is either to achieve a more ambitious professional career, or a specific vocational job. However, as mentioned above, the main theme is a short to mid-term project, without exact limits, which remains open depending on how things go, and fits in with the characteristics of liquid mobility. Many of these projects lead a priori to an early return, which materializes when the goal of having learned the language, or when employment goals pursued are not achieved. However, their migratory project is dynamic and sometimes transformed and extended over time depending on the circumstances.

Emigration itself usually changes the life of its actors and also their project. Some of those who thought they would return soon discovered a new world that gave their goals a radical turn, and chose another type of life, postponing the idea of returning indefinitely. Those who went there seeking employment in a certain vocation, may end up thinking about going back if after years, they have found that there is no way to achieve it. Similarly, if they cannot advance at work, it is hard to sustain living conditions that remain precarious, and which are accepted as an investment while still learning, and they still have hope, but not when they can no longer advance. Others who fared better and originally wanted to go home, now would not do so anyhow, and it would depend on the expectations offered in Spain. In any case, the relationships with family and friends in the home country are kept up through social networks and relatively frequent visits.

With regard to questions of gaining or losing talent (brain gain, brain drain), the emigration of Spanish youth seems to offer several lessons as well as questions. It is partly a loss of youth from a country in a rapid process of aging, and of talent, both because of their qualifications and character. However, it is also true that at this time, that talent cannot find a place on the Spanish labor market, nor a way of contributing by remaining in the county. Therefore, emigration is a form of adjustment and of lessoning internal tensions in the short term as mentioned by many authors (Kaczmarczyk/Stanek 2014). This perspective changes in the point of view of the individual emigrants. Often, especially at the beginning, they suffer from disqualification, but these situations should only be qualified as brain waste if they remain stagnant over time. In reality, those who have remained a certain time have acquired professional skills, have found other ways of organising work, have made international contacts, and especially, they have matured, they have become stronger and they know themselves better. It seems obvious that it would add to the wealth of the country if they could go back, not only because of their own human capital, but also for what they could contribute in a concept which Faist (2008) calls "social remittances", that is, bringing other, better ways of doing things with them. As several other authors have suggested (Camarero 2014; Cachón 2014), the problem with losing human capital is not so much in the departure of young qualified Spaniards as it is in the ability to recover them or attract others who are in circulation. One point in favor is that many of them have the desire to go back, and this could be made use of to develop policies favoring their return. However, three very negative points should be kept in mind. First, the feeling with which many of them left that their government, their country, has failed them, and an overwhelming loss of confidence due to the impact of the crisis and the succession of political corruption and scandals, which to date, continue appearing. Their moral and emotional effect is enormous and contributes to their putting off the idea of returning. Second, the disappointing messages sent during the crisis on the Spanish R&D system, in which the University has shrunk, the Spanish National Research Council is on the verge of starving and many Ramón y Cajal contracts (which brought researchers working abroad) were not continued as promised. Finally, the decision on whether to return is subject to comparisons between working conditions they have and those they could expect to achieve in Spain. For those who have not been able to make a niche for themselves in a high-qualification segment abroad, it may not make much difference, but for those who have (usually the most qualified and competitive), the comparisons in the testimonies collected are hateful. Development of policies sensitive to our youths and strengthening sectors where their knowledge and experience can be made use of has now become imperative.

References

Alba, Susana/Fernández, Ana/Martínez-Veiga, Ubaldo (2013): Crisis económica y nuevo panorama migratorio en España. Madrid: Colección Estudios, no. 65. Fundación Primero de Mayo.

Aparicio, Rosa (2014): Aproximación a la realidad de españoles emigrados: Realidad, proyecto, dificultades y retos. Madrid: OIM y Ministerio de Empleo y Seguridad Social.

Bygnes, Susanne (2015): "Are they leaving because of the Crisis? The Sociological Significance of Anomie as a Motivation for Migration." Sociology 49, DOI:10.1177/0038038515589300, pp. 1-16.

Cachón, Lorenzo (2014): "La nueva emigración desde España y Cataluña en la Gran Recesión (¿2007-2016?): unas reflexiones provisionales." In: Elena Sánchez-Montijano/Xavier Alonso-Calderón (eds.), Nuevos flujos y gran recesión. La emigración en Cataluña, España y la UE Barcelona: CIDOB, pp. 45-70.

Camarero, Mariam (March 9, 2014): ¿Tiene España una 'generación perdida'? Valencia.Plaza, September 23, 2016 (http://epoca1.valenciaplaza.com/ver/ 124285/-tiene-espa%C3%B1a-una-generacion-perdida-.html).

Conradson, David/Latham, Alan (2005): "Transnational urbanism: attending to everyday practices and mobilities." In: Journal of Ethnic and Migration Studies, 31/2, pp. 227-233.

Conti, Francesca (2012): Leaving or staying – an analysis of Italian graduates' migratory patterns. Doctoral thesis (DPhil), University of Sussex, September 23, 2016 (http://sro.sussex.ac.uk/id/eprint/39453).

Corijn, Martine/Klijzing, Erik (2001): Transitions to Adulthood in Europe. Dordrecht: Kluwer.

Cortés-Maisonave, Almudena/Moncó, Beatriz/Betrisey, Débora (2015): Movilidad trasnacional de jóvenes españoles y latinoamericanos: una comparación en contexto de crisis, Madrid: Centro Reina Sofía sobre Adolescencia y Juventud.

Díaz-Hernández, Ramón/Domínguez-Mujica, Josefina/Parreño-Castellano, Juan (2015): "Una aproximación a la emigración española durante la crisis económica: herramientas de estudio." Ar@cne. Revista electrónica de recursos en Internet sobre Geografía y Ciencias Sociales 198, Barcelona: Universidad de Barcelona, September 23, 2016 (http://www.ub.es/geocrit/aracne/aracne-198.pdf).

Domínguez-Mujica, Josefina/Díaz-Hernández, Ramón/Parreño-Castellano, Juan (2016): "Migrating Abroad to get Ahead. The Emigration of Young Spanish Adults during the Financial Crisis (2008-2013)." In: Josefina Domínguez-Mujica (ed.), Global Change and Human Mobility, Singapore: Springer, pp. 203-223.

Domingo, Andreu/Sabater, Albert/Ortega, Enrique (2013): "¿Vuelta a la España de la emigración? El impacto de la crisis económica en el fenómeno reemergente de la emigración española." In: X Congreso de la Asociación de Demografía Histórica: Universidad de Castilla La Mancha and ADEH.

Domingo, Andreu/Sabater, Albert/Ortega, Enrique (2014): "¿Migración neohispánica? El impacto de la crisis económica en la emigración española." Empiria. Revista de Metodología de las Ciencias Sociales 29, pp. 39-66.

El País (2013): "Expatriados por la crisis." In: El País, Special Report, September 23, 2016 (http://elpais.com/especiales/2013/expatriados-por-la-crisis/).

Elsner, Benjamin/Zimmermann, Klaus F. (2013): 10 Years after EU Enlargement, Closed Borders, and Migration to Germany, IZA Discussion Papers, No. 7130, Bonn: Institute for the Study of Labor.

Engbersen, Godfried/Snel, Erik (2013): "Liquid migration Dynamic and fluid patterns of post-accession migration flows." In: Birgit Glorius/Izabela Grabowska-Lusinska/Aimee Kuvik (eds.), Mobility in Transition. Migration Patterns after EU Enlargement, Amsterdam: Imiscoe Research, Amsterdam University Press, pp. 21-40.

European Commission (2011): Youth on the Move. Education and Training, Mobility, Employment and Entrepreneurship. Flash Eurobarometer 319b.

Faist, Thomas (2008): "Migrants as transnational development agents." Population, Space and Place 14/1, pp. 21-42.

Favell, Adrian (2008): Eurostars and Eurocities, Free Movement and Mobility in an Integrating Europe, Oxford: Blackwell.

Fontana, Josep (2013): El futuro es un país extraño. Una reflexión sobre la crisis social de comienzos del siglo XXI. Barcelona: Pasado & Presente.

Garrido-Medina, Luis (2013): "¿Quiénes se van de España y qué hacemos para que vuelvan?" In: El País, April 2, 2013 (http://elpais.com/elpais/2013/03/27/opinion/1364396658_219336.html).

Glorius, Birgit (2016): "New 'Guest Workers' from Spain. Exploring Migration to Germany in the Context of Economic and Societal Change." In: Josefina Domínguez-Mujica (ed.), Global Change and Human Mobility, Berlin: Springer, pp. 225-248.

Gonzalez-Enriquez, Carmen (2013a): Are Spaniards emigrating? Madrid: Análisis del Real Instituto Elcano (ARI), 39/2013, September 23, 2016 (http://www.realinstitutoelcano.org/wps/wcm/connect/2b7bc780416221b89b3fdb58f644a475/ARI39-2013-Gonzalez-Enriquez-Are-Spaniards-emigrating.pdf?MOD=AJPERES&CACHEID=2b7bc780416221b89b3fdb58f644a475).

González-Enríquez, Carmen (2013b): "Los nuevos emigrantes españoles." In: El País, October 9, 2013 (http://elpais.com/elpais/2013/10/09/opinion/1381317179_264625.html).

González-Enríquez, Carmen (2014): Fuga de cerebros, Madrid: Real Instituto Elcano, September 23, 2016 (http://www.realinstitutoelcano.org/wps/portal/rielcano/contenido?WCM_GLOBAL_CONTEXT=/elcano/elcano_es/zonas_es/comentario-gonzalezenriquez-fuga-de-cerebros-espana-braindrain-spain).

Gonzalez-Enriquez, Carmen/Martínez-Romera, José Pablo (2014): Country Focus. Migration of Spanish nationals during the crisis, Madrid: Real Instituto Elcano, September 23, 2016 (http://www.realinstitutoelcano.org/wps/wcm/connect/bb7ebe804469cb8daef9bee307648e49/GonzalezEnriquez-MartinezRomera-Spain-migration-crisis.pdf?MOD=AJPERES&CACHEID=bb7ebe804469cb8daef9bee307648e49).

González-Ferrer, Amparo (2012): "¿Se van los españoles? Sí. Y deberíamos preocuparnos." In: Blog "Piedras de Papel", October 8, 2012 (http://www.eldiario.es/piedrasdepapel/crisis-emigracion_6_55704437.html).

González-Ferrer, Amparo (2013a): "La emigración española contada desde fuera." In: Blog "Piedras de Papel", April 25, 2013 (http://www.eldiario.es/piedrasdepapel/emigracion-espanola-contada_6_125697430.html).

González-Ferrer, Amparo (2013b): La nueva emigración española. Lo que sabemos y lo que no. Zoom Político, no. 18, Madrid: Fundación Alternativas, September 23, 2016 (http://www.fundacionalternativas.org/las-publicaciones/libros/la-nueva-emigracion-espanola-lo-que-sabemos-y-lo-que-no).

Grabowska-Lusinska, Izabela (2013): "Anatomy of post-accession migration. How to measure 'liquidity' and other patterns of post-accession migration flows." In: Birgit Glorius/Izabela Grabowska-Lusinska/Aimee Kuvik (eds.), Mobility in Transition. Migration Patterns after EU Enlargement, Amsterdam: Imiscoe Research, Amsterdam University Press, pp. 41-64.

Holland, Dawn/Paluchowski, Pawel (2013): Geographical Labour Mobility in the Context of the Crisis. European Employment Observatory Ad hoc Request. Brussels: European Commission, September 23, 2016 (http://www.niesr.ac.uk/sites/default/files/publications/ESDE-SynthesisPaper-June2013-Final.pdf).

INE (National Institute for Statistics): Quarterly Spanish National Accounts, September 23, 2016 (http://www.ine.es/jaxi/menu.do?type=pcaxis&path=%2Ft35%2Fp009&file=inebase&L=1).

INE (National Institute for Statistics): Residential Variations Statistics, September 23, 2016 (http://www.ine.es/jaxi/menu.do?type=pcaxis&path=%2Ft20%2Fp307&file=inebase&L=1).

INE (National Institute for Statistics): Economically Active Population Survey, September 23, 2016 (http://www.ine.es/dyngs/INEbase/en/operacion.htm?c=Estadistica_C&cid=1254736176918&menu=ultiDatos&idp=1254735976595).

Kaczmarczyk, Pawel/Stanek, Mikolaj (2015): "Crisis and Beyond: Intra-EU Mobility of Polish and Spanish Migrants in a Comparative Perspective." In: Anna Triandafyllidou/Irina Isaakyan/Giuseppe Schiavone (eds.), High-skilled Migration and Recession: Gendered Perspectives, London: Palgrave McMillan, pp. 69-100.

Kahanec, Martin/Pytlikova, Mariola/Zimmermann, Klaus F. (2014): The Free Movement of Workers in an Enlarged European Union: Institutional Underpinnings of Economic Adjustment, IZA Discussion Papers, No. 8456, Bonn: Institute for the Study of Labor, September 23, 2016 (http://ftp.iza.org/dp8456.pdf).

King, Russell/Lulle, Aija/Conti, Francesca/Mueller, Dorothea/Scotto, Giuseppe (2014): The lure of London: A comparative study of recent graduate migration from Germany, Italy and Latvia,Working Paper no. 75, Sussex Centre for Migration Research, University of Sussex, September 23, 2016 (https://www.sussex.ac.uk/webteam/gateway/file.php?name=mwp75.pdf&site=252).

Krause, Annabelle/Rinne, Ulf/Zimmermann, Klaus F. (2014): How Far Away Is a Single European Labor Market? IZA Discussion Paper no. 8383, Bonn: Institute for the Study of Labor, September 23, 2016 (http://ftp.iza.org/dp 8383.pdf).

Méndez, Ricardo/Abad, Luis D./Echaves, Carlos (2015): Atlas de la crisis. Impactos socioeconómicos y territorios vulnerables en España, Valencia: Tirant Humanidades.

Moreno-Mínguez, Almudena/López-Peláez, Antonio/Segado, Sagrario (2012): La transición de los jóvenes a la vida adulta. Crisis económica y transición tardía, Barcelona: Fundación La Caixa. Colección Estudios Sociales no. 34.

Navarrete Moreno, Lorenzo (dir.) (2014): La emigración de los jóvenes españoles en el contexto de la crisis. Análisis y datos de un fenómeno difícil de cuantificar, Madrid: Observatorio de emancipación del Consejo de la Juventud de España, September 23, 2016 (http://www.injuve.es/sites/ default/files/2014/17/publicaciones/Emigracion%20jovenes_0.pdf).

Statistics on National Insurance number allocations (NINo) to adult overseas nationals entering the UK since January 2002 for NINo registrations to June 2014, September 23, 2016 (https://www.gov.uk/government/collections/ national-insurance-number-allocations-to-adult-overseas-nationals-entering-the-uk).

Observatorio del Consejo de la Juventud (2013): Informe periódico sobre la situación de la población joven en España. First Quarter 2013, Madrid: Observatorio de emancipación del Consejo de la Juventud de España, September 23, 2016 (http://www.cje.org/descargas/cje4261.pdf).

Oliver, Josep (2013): "La inmigración y la doble recesión del mercado de trabajo en España 2011-2012." In: Eliseo Aja/Joaquín Arango/Josep Oliver (eds.), Inmigración y crisis: entre la continuidad y el cambio. Anuario de Inmigración en España, Barcelona: CIDOB, pp. 28-58.

Pumares, Pablo (2015): "Cosas que hacer en Brighton mientras escampa la crisis. El atractivo de Brighton para los jóvenes españoles en tiempos de crisis." In: Francisco J. García-Castaño/Adelaida Megías-Megías/Jennifer Ortega-Torres (Eds.), Actas del VIII Congreso sobre Migraciones Internacionales en España, Granada: Instituto de Migraciones, pp. S33/13-S33/22.

Pumares, Pablo/González-Martin, Beatriz (2016): "Movilidad, migración y retorno de jóvenes españoles en el Reino Unido." In: Josefina Domínguez-Mujica/Ramón Díaz-Hernández (coords.), Población y Territorio en la encrucijada de las Ciencias Sociales, Las Palmas de Gran Canarias: Universidad de Las Palmas, pp. 275-290.

Ros, Adela (2014): "Los que se van: cuestiones en torno a una realidad incómoda." In: Elena Sánchez-Montijano/Xavier Alonso-Calderón (eds.), Nuevos flujos y gran recesión. La emigración en Cataluña, España y la UE Barcelona: CIDOB, pp. 109-128.

Ryan, Louise/Kurdi, Edina (2014): Young highly qualified migrants: The experiences and expectations of recently arrived Irish teachers in Britain. Social Policy Research Centre (SPRC) at Middlesex University.

Sjaastad L.A. (1962): "The costs and returns of human migration." In: Journal of Political Economy 70, pp. 80-93.

The Institute for Society and Vodaphone Communications (2014): Survey– "Talking about a Revolution." Europe's_Young_Generation_Spain, September 23, 2016 (http://www.vodafone-institut.de/wp-content/uploads/2015/09/ YouGov_Vodafone_Institute_Europe_s_Young_Generation_Spain.pdf).

Trevena, Paulina (2013): "Why do Highly Educated Migrants go for Low-skilled Jobs? A case study of Polish Graduates working in London." In: Birgit Glorius/Izabela Grabowska-Lusinska/Aimee Kuvik (eds.), Mobility in Transition. Migration Patterns after EU Enlargement, Amsterdam: Imiscoe Research, Amsterdam University Press, pp. 169-190.

Triandafyllidou, Anna/Gropas, Ruby (2014): "'Voting with their feet': Highly Skilled Emigrants from Southern Europe." In: American Behavioral Scientist, 2014 58/12, pp. 1614-1633.

Van Dalen, Henrik P./Henkens, Kene (2012): "Explaining low international labour mobility: The role of networks, personality, and perceived labour market opportunities." In: Population, Space and Place 18/1, pp. 31-44.

Williams, Allan.M./Baláž, Vladimir (2005): "What human capital, which migrants? Returned skilled migration to Slovakia from the UK." In: International Migration Review 39/2, pp. 439-468.

Table 6.1: Interviewees' profiles

Alias	Gender	Age	Time in Brighton	Education Level	Last occupation in Brighton	Family status
Ana	Female	27	19 months	Master of Arts	Waitress/Griller specialist	With couple (Spanish)
Rosa	Female	27	18 months	Master in Human Resources	Secretary in a consultancy	With couple (French)
Ramón	Male	32	5 years	Master in European Studies	Policy director	With couple (British)
Tania	Female	34	18 months	Architect	Surveyor	Single
María	Female	33	2 years	Industrial Engineer	Engineer	Single
Javier	Male	28	3 years	Software Engineer	Technical leader/Software architecture	Single
Meri	Female	26	17 months	Bachelor in Biology	Waitress/body trainer	Single
Nafka	Female	33	3 years	Master of Arts	Singer	Single
Antonio	Male	29	21 months	Bachelor in Journalism	Waiter/body trainer	Single
Fermín	Male	25	22 months	Bachelor in Philosophy	Waiter	Single
Alejandro	Male	32	8 months	Bachelor in Audiovisual Media	Freelance Sound technician	Single
José Luis	Male	36	15 months	Bachelor in Journalism	Freelance graphic and web designer	Divorced with children
Flora	Female	37	7 years	Bachelor in Economics	Freelance accountant (unemployed at the	With couple (British)

					time of the interview)	
Carmen	Female	29	22 months	Bachelor in Pedagogy	Teacher in a nursery	Single
Esther	Female	27	3 years	Bachelor in Business Administration	Hotel receptionist	Single
Alicia	Female	26	2 years	Bachelor in Business Administration	Hotel receptionist	Single
Dani	Male	36	6 years	Vocational training in Tourism and Cooking	Stores clerk in a warehouse	Single
Manuela	Female	28	3 years	Vocational training in Airhostess	Hotel Housekeeping supervision	With couple (Spanish)
Roger	Male	25	3 years	Vocational training in Tourism and Cooking	Waiter	With couple (Spanish
Ariadna	Female	33	6 years	Vocational training in Sound and Image Technology	Waiter and photographer	With couple (British)
Mariana	Female	31	19 months	Associate in Nursing	Nurse	Single
Lola	Female	22	5 weeks	Vocational training	Searching for a job	Single

				in Hairdressing		
Ramón	Male	30	12 months	Vocational training in Graphic Design	Hotel receptionist	Single
Miriam	Female	26	12 months	Vocational training in Airhostess	Hotel receptionist	Single
Gonzalo	Male	23	16 months	Vocational training in Business Administration	Building entertainment	Single
Ainara	Female	25	4 months	Student of Psychology	Waitress	Single
Juan	Male	28	5 months	Compulsory Secondary Education	Hotel housekeeper	Single

Source: own data

7. A psychological perspective on adjustment of recent immigrants from Southern Europe in Germany
The correlation of adjustment with return intentions and personality predispositions for successfull adjustment

MARIA WASSERMANN

ABSTRACT

Inspired by the recent increase of migration from southern Europe to Germany, an online study was conducted among immigrants from Spain, Italy and Greece in order to investigate their psychological, socio-cultural and economic adjustment. This paper presents the results of 506 participants who moved to Germany between 2009 and 2014. It aims to demonstrate how immigrant adjustment is related to return intentions as well as to personality predispositions (namely, cultural empathy, flexibility, social initiative, emotional stability and open-mindedness). Results show that poor psychological and socio-cultural adjustment (but not economic adjustment) are related to the intention to leave Germany, and that cultural empathy, social initiative, emotional stability and open-mindedness (but not flexibility) are positively related to most of the adjustment indicators. In considering the differences between Spanish, Italian and Greek participants, the study indicates that Italian participants are most representative of a new generation of immigrants that makes use of a transnational space of living, whereas Greek participants are most representative of traditional, economically driven migration. Finally, the paper outlines how the field of psychology can make important contributions towards better understanding the adjustment of southern European immigrants in Germany.

Keywords: Immigrant adjustment, Return intentions, Multicultural effectiveness

Introduction

The recent economic crisis has caused unemployment to increase dramatically in southern European countries. This has resulted in an increase in migration from Spain, Italy and Greece to Germany over the past few years (BAMF 2015). On the one hand, these migration flows are driven by immigrants' hopes to improve their job situations, career prospects and general life conditions (Amit/Riss 2014; Bonin et al. 2008; Hoppe/Fujishiro 2015). On the other hand, migration from southern European countries is actively encouraged by the German Government as a means to meet the demand for skilled workers (Brücker/Brunow/Fuchs/ Kubis/Mendolicchio/Weber 2013). This has the potential to be a win-win situation if immigrants can successfully adjust to life in Germany. Media reports, however, have called the adjustment of southern European immigrants into question, and fueled public debates about their situation in Germany (Bertoli/Brücker/Fernández-Huertas Moraga 2013). Furthermore, an OECD report (2013) shows that only one in three immigrants from Spain and one in two immigrants from Greece remains in Germany for more than a year.

Interdisciplinary effort is needed to describe, understand and predict recent migration flows between southern European countries and Germany. As part of this effort, the field of psychology can shed light on issues such as the adjustment of immigrants by investigating personality predispositions that foster success in international environments. Migration is likely to be a stressful life event (Schwarzer/Schulz 2003) and personality characteristics are known to affect how individuals face and cope with stressors and challenges (e.g., Carver/Connor-Smith 2010).

This paper presents the results of an online study of immigrants to Germany from Spain, Italy and Greece regarding psychological, socio-cultural and economic adjustment. The main goal of the paper is to show how these forms of adjustment are related to return intentions[1] and personality predispositions for successful adjustment (namely, cultural empathy, flexibility, social initiative, emotional stability and open-mindedness). Furthermore, it considers differences between Spanish, Italian and Greek participants regarding adjustment, return intentions and personality predispositions.

---

1 *Return intentions* in this work not only refers to intentions to move back to the country of origin but also to intentions for further migration to a third country.

STUDY BACKGROUND

Adjustment

Moving to a foreign country brings with it a variety of challenges (e.g., finding an apartment, a job and friends or dealing with a foreign language). In order to meet these challenges and adjust to the host country, changes in individual behavior and attitudes have to take place (Berry 2003). Successful adjustment is characterized by functioning well in everyday life and finding a good fit between immigrant and host society (Berry 1997; Ward/Bochner/Furnham 2001). The literature on the subject distinguishes between psychological, socio-cultural and economic adjustment (Aycan/Berry 1996: 242). *Psychological adjustment* refers to internal psychological outcomes, including general life satisfaction and a sense of belonging to the host society. *Socio-cultural adjustment* refers to the ability to deal with the challenges of adapting to the social life of the host country, including language acquisition and building up a supportive social network. *Economic adjustment* refers to the degree to which participation in the labor market is achieved.

These forms of adjustment are interrelated (Aycan/Berry 1996: 241-242). For example, in terms of stronger identification with the host country, research has shown that language competence, social contacts with host nationals and being employed are all conditions that contribute to better psychological adjustment (Vroome/Verkuyten/Martinovic 2014). In terms of adequate inclusion in the labor market, likewise, social contact with, and informational support from, host nationals were also shown to be valuable resources for economic adjustment (Amason/Allen/Holmes 1999; Mahajan/Toh 2014). A lack of language competence, on the other hand, limits job prospects in the host country, and is therefore associated with poor economic adjustment (Chiswick/Miller 2002; Dustmann/Fabbri 2003; Selmer/Lauring 2015).

The present study examines the adjustment of recent Spanish, Italian and Greek immigrants in Germany by considering indicators of psychological adjustment (life satisfaction and identification with Germany), socio-cultural adjustment (language competence, number of German friends and perceived social support from German friends), and economic adjustment (employment status, job satisfaction and perceived overqualification). Further, it aims to explore whether Spanish, Italian and Greek participants differ regarding these adjustment indicators.

Return intentions

Reduced barriers to mobility facilitate migration, but they are also conducive to migration patterns that do not result in permanent settlement (Favell 2008). Within the European Union, temporary migration is common and characterized by rather short-term, circular movements backwards and forwards across borders (Wallace 2002: 604). Preexisting intentions to leave the host country (either to return to the country of origin or to another country) are widely considered to be predictors of actual emigration behavior (Ajzen 1991), even though the correlation between return intentions and actual emigration can be rather small (Dustmann 1996; Waldorf 1995). Many immigrants are rather uncertain about how long they want to stay in the host country (Luthra/Platt/Salamońska 2014; Waldorf 1995). It is common that immigrants postpone their return in opposition to their initial intention (Mehrländer 1981; Waldorf 1995), and the propensity to return decreases in accordance with the number of years of residence (Dustmann 1996).

It is widely assumed that adjustment and return intentions are associated. Language competence, social ties in the host country and identification with the host nation (e.g., feeling German) decrease the likelihood of return migration (Constant/Massey 2003: 39-40; Haug 2008), whereas being unemployed, inadequately employed or dissatisfied with one's current job increases the likelihood of return migration (Constant/Massey 2003; Waldorf 1995).

However, the relationship between return intentions and adjustment is likely to be reciprocal. Return intentions are also considered to impact immigrants' attitudes towards adjustment as well as their adjustment outcomes (Ajzen 1991; Luthra/Platt/Salamońska 2014). Immigrants who intend to stay for a short term may put less effort into building social networks (Dustmann 1999) and may have lower expectations regarding their job situation. Immigrants who intend to stay for a longer term may invest more in social relationships and try to find a job that matches their qualifications, rather than taking any job they find (Luthra/Platt/Salamońska 2014; Parutis 2014).

The present study examines the return intentions of recent Spanish, Italian and Greek immigrants in Germany, with regard to *whether* and *when* they intend to leave Germany and, if they do intend to leave, *where* they intend to go to. It aims to determine how their psychological, socio-cultural and economic adjustment is related to their return intentions. The following hypothesis is derived from the findings mentioned above:

Hypothesis 1: Successful adjustment is negatively related to return intentions: the higher the level of psychological, socio-cultural and economic adjustment, the less likely it is that an immigrant intends to leave Germany.

Furthermore, the present study aims to explore whether Spanish, Italian and Greek participants differ regarding their return intentions.

Personality predispositions for successful adjustment

Psychological research has put effort into identifying personality characteristics that help to successfully deal with intercultural situations (known as multicultural effectiveness) and can therefore function as personality predispositions for psychological, socio-cultural and economic adjustment (Van der Zee/Van Oudenhoven 2000). Van der Zee and Van Oudenhoven postulate that five personality characteristics are relevant for the multicultural effectiveness of a person: cultural empathy (the ability to empathize with the feelings, thoughts and behaviors of individuals from different cultural backgrounds), flexibility (the ability to adjust behavioral strategies to the different circumstances within a foreign culture), social initiative (the tendency to actively approach social situations and to take the initiative), emotional stability (the tendency to remain calm in stressful situations) and open-mindedness (the extent to which people have an open and unprejudiced attitude toward different groups, cultural norms and values; Van Oudenhoven/Van der Zee 2002: 680–681). These personality characteristics are assumed to buffer against stress and make individuals feel challenged by the social and cognitive opportunities of intercultural situations. They also appear to be important as predictors of health, well-being, social support and performance in an international context – as well as successful adjustment in general (Leong 2007; Van Oudenhoven/Van der Zee 2002).

The present study examines the cultural empathy, flexibility, social initiative, emotional stability and open-mindedness of recent Spanish, Italian and Greek immigrants in Germany. It aims to answer the question of how these personality characteristics are related to the adjustment of immigrants. The following is hypothesized:

Hypothesis 2: Cultural empathy, flexibility, social initiative, emotional stability and open-mindedness are positively related to psychological, socio-cultural and economic adjustment.

Furthermore, the present study aims to explore whether Spanish, Italian and Greek participants differ regarding the value of these personality characteristics.

METHOD

Survey procedure and sample

The survey was conducted among Spanish, Italian and Greek immigrants in Germany between February and October 2014. Data was collected using a standardized online questionnaire. The link to the questionnaire was spread over online social networks via posts in more than 100 different groups. In total, 2,303 clicks to open the survey were registered, and 615 people finished the survey. The questionnaire was provided in Spanish, Italian and Greek and took an average time of 23 minutes to complete. Three prizes of 50€ were raffled off among participants as an incentive.

In order to capture *recent* migration from Spain, Italy and Greece, the analyses only included people who migrated in 2009 or later ($n = 506$). The sample contains 189 Spanish nationals (37.3 per cent), 183 Italian nationals (36.2 per cent) and 134 Greek nationals (26.5 per cent). The basic characteristics of the sample are described below.

Gender and age: 313 (61.9 per cent) of the study participants were female. The participants were between 18 and 59 years old ($M = 30.9$; $SD = 7.1$). On average, Spanish participants ($M = 29.6$ years; $SD = 6.9$) were younger than Italian participants ($M = 31.4$ years; $SD = 7.1$) and Greek participants ($M = 32.2$ years; $SD = 7.2$). Figure 7.1 shows the percentage of participants across age groups.

Figure 7.1: Age of study participants (n=506)

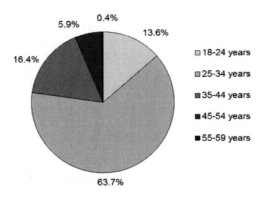

Source: own survey

Level of education: In terms of the highest level of education achieved, the respondents can be considered highly qualified. Among the participants, 70 (13.8 per cent) had a high school or college degree, 227 (44.9 per cent) had a bachelor's degree or equivalent, or a professional qualification obtained through professional training, 153 (30.2 per cent) had a master's degree or equivalent, and 49 (9.7 per cent) had a PhD. Only six participants (1.2 per cent) did not have any of the degrees mentioned above.[2]

Partnership and children: 336 study participants (66.4 per cent) had a partner, and most partners lived in the same city (247; 74.2 per cent).[3] Some lived in a different country (74; 22.2 per cent) or a different German city (12; 2.4 per cent). The majority of the participants had no children (422; 83.4 per cent).

Time of migration: Figure 7.2 shows the year of migration to Germany for the study participants. Data collection was completed in April 2014 for Spanish and Italian participants (and in October 2014 for Greek participants), which accounts for the relatively low number of participants that migrated in 2014. The average duration of residence in Germany at the time of participation in this study was one year and ten months ($M = 22.1$ months; $SD = 16.1$). On average, Greek participants lived longer in Germany ($M = 26.6$ months; $SD = 16.5$) than Spaniards ($M = 19.3$ months; $SD = 15.3$) and Italians ($M = 21.9$ months; $SD = 15.9$).

Figure 7.2: Year of migration (n=506)

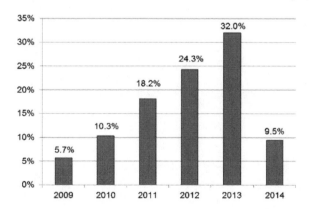

Source: own survey

---

2 $n = 503$. Numbers do not add up to 100% due to missing data.
3 $n = 505$. Numbers do not add up to 100% due to missing data.

Reason for migration: The majority of study participants migrated for job reasons (302; 59.7 per cent; cf. figure 7.3). However, 33.7 per cent of the participants mentioned reasons that were not job related as the most important for their migration. These included social reasons (e.g., to live together with partner or friends), lifestyle or cultural reasons (e.g., to explore a new city), personal reasons (e.g., to get to know themselves better/for personal growth), or language reasons (e.g., to learn German). Among the participants who stated "other reasons" (6.6 per cent), studies and Erasmus were primarily indicated as the main reason. Among Greek participants, a higher percentage of people migrated for job reasons (101; 75.4 per cent) than was the case for Italians (101; 55.2 per cent) and Spaniards (100; 52.9 per cent).

Figure 7.3: Main reason for migration (n=506)

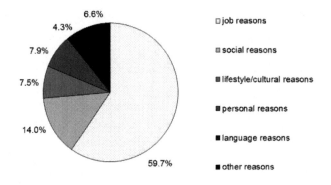

Source: own survey

Place of residence in Germany: Participants of this study lived in 85 different German cities. The majority resided in one of the three biggest German cities, Berlin (163; 32.2 per cent), Hamburg (44; 8.7 per cent) or Munich (49; 9.7 per cent). Berlin (163; 32.2 per cent), North Rhine-Westphalia (81; 16.0 per cent) and Bavaria (65; 12.8 per cent) were the most common German federal states of residence among the study participants. No participants were sampled in the East German states Thuringia, Brandenburg and Mecklenburg-West Pomerania.

Place of residence before migration to Germany: The majority of Spanish, Italian and Greek participants lived in their native country before moving to Germany (444, 87.7 per cent). A smaller proportion of participants had previously been living in another European country (45; 8.9 per cent), or in another non-

European country (5; 1.0 per cent).[4] Moving to Germany from a country other than the country of origin was more common for Italians (24; 13.1 per cent) than for Spaniards (16; 8.5 per cent) and Greeks (10; 7.5 per cent).

Measures

Measures to assess indicators of psychological adjustment

Life satisfaction was assessed with the five-item Satisfaction with Life Scale (e.g., "In most ways, my life is close to my ideal"; Diener/Emmons/Larsen/Griffin 1985: 72). Answers were given on a Likert scale ranging from 1 (strongly disagree) to 5 (strongly agree). Internal consistency reliability[5] (Cronbach's alpha) for this scale was 0.89.

Identification with Germany was measured using three items (Fuller-Rowell/Ong/Phinney 2013: 413) that assess the sense of belonging to the host country, as well as endorsement of the values of the host national society and culture (e.g., "I have a strong feeling of belonging to, or being part of, German culture"). Each item was measured on a scale from 1 (strongly disagree) to 5 (strongly agree). Cronbach's alpha was 0.83.

Measures to assess indicators of socio-cultural adjustment

Language competence was measured with three questions (Yeh/Inose 2003: 13): "What is your present level of German fluency?" (1 = "very low", 5 = "very high"), "How comfortable are you communicating in German?" (1 = "very uncomfortable"; 5 = "very comfortable"), and "How often do you communicate in German?" (1 = "never", 5 = "every day"). Cronbach's alpha was 0.90.

The *number of German friends* was assessed. Participants answered the question, "How many close German friends living in Germany do you have?" (cf. Jasinskaja-Lahti/Yijälä 2011: 505) by choosing one of five response categories ("none", "1-3", "4-6", "7-9" and "more than 9").

For those who stated that they had at least one German friend, *social support* from German friends was assessed by means of the adaptation of four items from

---

4 $n = 494$. Numbers do not add up to 100% due to missing data.
5 Internal consistency indicates whether several items are suitable to consistently measure the same general construct. Internal consistency is measured with Cronbach's alpha, a statistic calculated from the pairwise correlations between items. A Cronbach's alpha coefficient of at least 0.7 indicates an acceptable reliability of the measurement.

the Multidimensional Scale of Perceived Social Support (e.g., "I can count on my German friends when things go wrong"; cf. Zimet/Dahlem/Zimet/Farley 1988: 35). Items were scored on a Likert scale from 1 (strongly disagree) to 5 (strongly agree). Cronbach's alpha was 0.93.

Measures to assess indicators of economic adjustment

The current *employment status* of participants was assessed with the help of ten categories (1 = "full-time employed", 2 = "part-time employed", 3 = "self-employed", 4 = "in internship", 5 = "registered as unemployed", 6 = "in re-employment program", 7 = "on maternity leave/sabbatical", 8 = "not employed (e.g., homemaker)", 9 = "student", 10 = "in vocational training") or the category "other". The item was dichotomized by subsuming employed and self-employed participants (category 1, 2 and 3) into one group and all others into a second group. Accordingly, only participants of the first group answered further questions regarding their job satisfaction and perceived overqualification.

Job satisfaction was measured with one item ("All in all, I am satisfied with my current job"). The item was answered on a Likert scale ranging from 1 (strongly disagree) to 5 (strongly agree).

Perceived overqualification was measured using nine items from the Scale of Perceived Overqualification (Maynard/Joseph/Maynard 2006: 536). Items indicate the extent to which a person has more education, experience, knowledge, skills and abilities than required by his or her job (e.g., "My job requires less education than I have") on a Likert scale ranging from 1 (strongly disagree) to 7 (strongly agree). Cronbach's alpha was 0.95.

Measures to assess return intentions

Return intentions were assessed by posing the question, "How long do you intend to stay in Germany?" (Dustmann 1996: 227-228). Three possible answer categories were given (1 = "I intend to leave Germany within the next 12 months"; 2 = "I would like to stay in Germany for a few more years"; 3 = "I can imagine staying in Germany forever"). The item was dichotomized by subsuming participants with return intentions (category 1 and 2) into one group.

Those who indicated that they would like to stay "a few more years" specified the number of years they would like to stay in Germany. If estimates were given by time ranges, means were calculated. Participants with return intentions were further asked where they intend to go when they leave Germany. The four response categories for that question were "back to Spain [Italy/Greece]", "to another European country", "to another non-European country", and "uncertain".

Measures to assess personality predispositions for successful adjustment

Personality predispositions for successful adjustment were assessed with the short version of the Multicultural Personality Questionnaire (Van der Zee/Van Oudenhoven/Ponterotto/Fietzer 2013) that contains 40 items to assess *cultural empathy* (e.g., "I am a person that usually pays attention to the emotions of others"), *flexibility* (e.g., "I am a person that usually looks for regularity in life"; reverse coded), *social initiative* (e.g., "I am a person that usually finds it difficult to make contacts"; reverse coded), *emotional stability* (e.g., "I am a person that usually keeps calm when things don't go well"), and *open-mindedness* (e.g., "I am a person that usually has broad range of interests"). Each dimension was measured with eight items. Items were answered on a Likert scale ranging from 1 (totally not applicable) to 5 (totally applicable). Cronbach's alpha was 0.83 for cultural empathy, 0.82 for flexibility, 0.80 for social initiative, 0.78 for emotional stability and 0.76 for open-mindedness.

Data analysis

Data analyses were performed using the statistics program SPSS 22. Distribution of frequencies, means and standard deviations were calculated. The scale median score was used in order to discriminate high and low manifestations of continuous variables.

One-way analyses of variance on ranks (Kruskal-Wallis H-test) and post-hoc analyses (Mann-Whitney-U-test) have been performed to detect differences between the subsamples for continuous and ordinal outcome variables. The decision to use this non-parametric test approach is justified because the variables within groups mostly do not have normal distributions in this study (Field 2009). χ^2-tests are used to detect differences in the distribution of binominal outcome variables between subsamples. Pearson correlation coefficients between study variables were calculated and are presented in table 7.1. In terms of the magnitude of effect size, correlation coefficients in the order of 0.10 are regarded as "small", those of 0.30 are regarded as "medium" and those of 0.50 or higher as "large" (Cohen 1988).

Results

First, the results section provides an overview of the manifestation of each study variable within the sample and reports significant relationships between the study variables and basic sample characteristics. Additionally, significant differences between Spanish, Italian and Greek subsamples will be addressed (sections 4.1-4.3). Second, the results section reports correlations between study variables in order to answer Hypotheses 1 and 2 (section 4.4).

Adjustment

Psychological adjustment

Life satisfaction: Mean life satisfaction among the total sample was $M = 3.43$ ($SD = 0.97$). Overall, 66.0 per cent of the participants were rather satisfied with their life in general. Having a partner was significantly related to higher levels of life satisfaction. There is a significant difference between the subsamples ($H(2) = 10.07, p < 0.01$)[6]: Greek participants showed lower life satisfaction ($M = 3.21$; $SD = 0.96$) than Spaniards ($M = 3.49$; $SD = 1.00$) and Italians ($M = 3.54$; $SD = 0.91$).

Identification with Germany: Mean score for identification with Germany among the total sample was $M = 2.61$ ($SD = 0.90$). 28.3 per cent of the participants indicated a rather strong sense of belonging to, and endorsement of, German society and culture. Older age and longer duration of residence were positively related to identification with Germany. There is a significant difference between subsamples ($H(2) = 17.10, p < 0.01$): Spanish participants showed lower levels of identification with Germany ($M = 2.41$; $SD = 0.77$) than Greeks ($M = 2.66$; $SD = 0.93$) and Italians ($M = 2.79$; $SD = 0.96$).

Socio-cultural adjustment

Language competence: Mean score for self-rated German language competence was $M = 3.43$ ($SD = 1.09$). A total of 63.0 per cent of the participants indicated that they perceive their German fluency as quite high, feel quite comfortable

---

6   H = test statistic of Kruskal-Wallis H-Test, that indicates whether responses differ between subsamples. If the test statistic is significant on a level of 5% ($p < 0.05$), it is regarded as unlikely that an observed difference between the subsamples arose by chance.

speaking German and/or speak German often or every day. Women showed higher levels of German language competence, as did people who lived in Germany for a longer time. There is a significant difference between subsamples ($H(2) = 20.90$, $p < 0.01$): Greek participants ($M = 3.76$; $SD = 1.03$) rated their German language competence significantly higher than Spanish ($M = 3.40$; $SD = 1.01$) and Italian participants ($M = 3.21$; $SD = 1.16$).

Number of German friends: Figure 7.4 shows the amount of close German friends living in Germany among the total sample.

Figure 7.4: Number of close German friends in Germany (n=506)

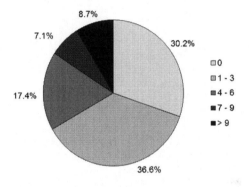

Source: own survey

153 participants (30.2 per cent) indicated that they do not have a single close German friend, while 185 (36.6 per cent) had one to three close German friends and 168 (33.2 per cent) had four or more German friends living in Germany. Larger number of children and longer duration of residence in Germany were positively related to the number of German friends. There is no difference between the subsamples regarding the number of close German friends. Those who stated they had at least one German friend ($n = 353$) were asked about the social support they derive from these contacts.

Social support from German friends: The mean score for social support from German friends was $M = 3.69$ ($SD = 1.08$). 69.7 per cent of the participants perceived their German friends as rather supportive. There is no difference between the subsamples regarding the perceived social support from German friends.

Economic adjustment

Employment status: The majority of participants were employed either full-time (217; 42.9 per cent) or part-time (59; 11.7 per cent) and 32 participants (6.3 per cent) were self-employed (dark grey bars, figure 7.5). 69 participants (13.6 per cent) were unemployed or not employed. Older age, male gender and longer duration of residence in Germany were significantly related to being employed or self-employed. There is no significant difference between the subsamples regarding the proportions of employed and self-employed participants.

Figure 7.5: Employment status (n=506)

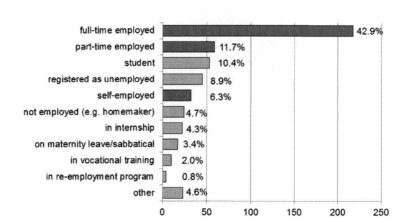

Source: own survey

Only the 308 participants who were full-time, part-time or self-employed answered the questions regarding their job satisfaction and perceived overqualification.

Job satisfaction: The mean score for job satisfaction was $M = 3.71$ ($SD = 1.21$). Overall, 63.9 per cent of the participants were slightly or highly satisfied with their current job. There is no significant difference between subsamples regarding job satisfaction.

Perceived overqualification: The mean score for perceived overqualification was $M = 4.02$ ($SD = 1.96$). 48.1 per cent of the participants indicated that they perceive having rather more skills, abilities and/or qualifications than required by their job. Participants that mainly migrated for job-related reasons perceived being overqualified to a lesser extent than participants that migrated for other reasons. Participants who had a partner perceived less overqualification. There is a significant difference between subsamples ($H(2) = 17.19$, $p < 0.01$): Italian participants ($M = 3.40$; $SD = 1.79$) perceived lower levels of overqualification than Spanish ($M = 4.39$; $SD = 1.99$) and Greek participants ($M = 4.37$; $SD = 1.97$).

Return intentions

Among all participants, 148 (29.2 per cent) could imagine staying in Germany forever. The majority of the participants wanted to leave Germany (358; 70.8 per cent), with 57 participants (11.3 per cent) even wanting to leave within twelve months. A larger number of children was positively related to higher intentions to stay in Germany. Furthermore, participants who could imagine staying in Germany forever were significantly older and had lived in Germany for a longer time. Among Italian participants, there is a significantly higher proportion of people who could imagine staying in Germany forever (70; 38.3 per cent), than was the case for Spaniards (41; 21.7 per cent; $\chi^2 (1) = 12.18$, $p < 0.01$) and Greeks (37; 27.6 per cent; $\chi^2 (1) = 3.92, p < 0.05$).[7]

Among participants who intended to leave Germany, the average duration they wanted to remain in Germany was about four and a half years ($M = 4.58$; $SD = 3.96$). In this regard, there is a significant difference between subsamples ($H(2) = 39.90$, $p < 0.01$): Greek participants ($M = 6.44$; $SD = 4.56$) intended to stay longer before leaving Germany than did Spanish ($M = 3.78$; $SD = 6.61$) and Italian participants ($M = 4.03$; $SD = 3.33$). Figure 7.6 provides an overview of the remaining duration that study participants intended to reside in Germany.

---

7   χ^2 = test statistic of Chi-Square Test, which indicates whether responses differ between subsamples. If the test statistic is significant on a level of 5% ($p < 0.05$), it is regarded as unlikely that an observed difference between the subsamples arose by chance.

Figure 7.6: Intended duration of residence in Germany (n=506)

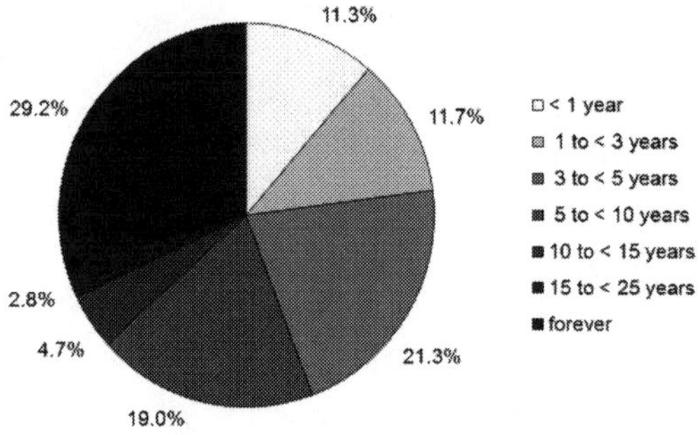

- < 1 year: 11.3%
- 1 to < 3 years: 11.7%
- 3 to < 5 years: 21.3%
- 5 to < 10 years: 19.0%
- 10 to < 15 years: 4.7%
- 15 to < 25 years: 2.8%
- forever: 29.2%

Source: own survey

Of the participants who intended to leave Germany, 154 participants (43.0 per cent) wanted to return to their country of origin, 50 participants (14.0 per cent) wanted to move to another European country, and 37 participants (10.3 per cent) wanted to move to another non-European country. 117 participants (32.7 per cent) were rather uncertain where they wanted to go when leaving Germany. Among Italian participants, there is a significantly lower percentage of people who intended to return to Italy when leaving Germany (35; 31.0 per cent), than for Spaniards who wanted to return to Spain (67; 45.5 per cent; χ^2 (1) = 5.50, $p <$ 0.05) and Greeks who wanted to return to Greece (52; 53.6 per cent; χ^2 (1) = 11.02, $p < 0.01$).

Personality predispositions for successful adjustment

The mean score for *cultural empathy* was $M = 4.05$ ($SD = 0.55$). 95.5 per cent of the participants showed quite high levels of cultural empathy. Female gender and larger number of children were positively related to cultural empathy. The mean score for *flexibility* was $M = 2.84$ ($SD = 0.72$). 37.7 per cent of the participants obtained scores that indicate quite high levels of flexibility. A larger number of children was negatively related to flexibility. The mean score for *social initiative* was $M = 3.33$ ($SD = 0.67$). 66.0 per cent of the participants scored quite highly on social initiative. Having a partner and larger number of children were positively related to social initiative. The mean score for *emotional stability* was $M = 3.06$ ($SD = 0.67$). 51.4 per cent of the participants showed quite high levels of emotional stability. Older age and male gender were associated with higher levels of emotional stability. The mean score for *open-mindedness* was $M = 3.64$

(SD = 0.57). 83.6 per cent of the participants obtained scores that indicate quite high levels of open-mindedness. Older age and larger number of children were positively related to open-mindedness.

There is a significant difference between subsamples regarding cultural empathy ($H(2)$ = 18.17, $p < 0.01$) and flexibility ($H(2)$ = 16.50, $p < 0.01$): Spanish participants (M = 4.17; SD = 0.55) showed higher levels of cultural empathy than Italian (M = 3.95; SD = 0.57) and Greek participants (M = 4.00; SD = 0.55); Italian participants (M = 3.00; SD = 0.71) showed higher levels of flexibility than Spanish (M = 2.82; SD = 0.71) and Greek participants (M = 2.66; SD = 0.69). There is no significant difference between subsamples regarding social initiative, emotional stability and open-mindedness.

Table 7.1: Correlations between study variables

Variable	1	2	3	4	5	6	7	8	9	10	11	12	13	14	15	16	17	18	19
Age																			
Gender[a]	-0.17**																		
Partnership[b]	0.08	0.04																	
Number of Children	0.52**	-0.06	0.17**																
Duration of Residence[c]	0.26**	-0.03	0.02	0.08															
Reason for Migration[d]	0.05	-0.04	-0.07	0.06	-0.09														
Life Satisfaction	-0.05	0.07	0.20**	0.06	0.01	-0.05													
Identification with Germany	0.12**	-0.01	-0.06	0.08	0.09*	-0.02	0.21**												
Language Competence	-0.04	0.16**	0.01	0.04	0.38**	-0.01	0.10*	0.20**											
Number of German Friends	0.07	0.00	0.04	0.14**	0.31**	-0.05	0.19**	0.30**	0.37**										
Social Support	0.00	0.00	0.00	-0.04	0.10	-0.05	0.17**	0.25**	0.22**	0.30**									
Employment Status[e]	0.12**	-0.11*	0.05	0.00	0.22**	0.08	0.15**	0.01	0.07	0.04	0.00								
Job Satisfaction	0.08	-0.02	0.05	0.08	0.04	0.08	0.45**	0.23**	0.08	0.18**	0.13*	0.13*							
Perceived Overqualification	-0.08	-0.01	-0.16**	-0.09	-0.03	-0.18**	-0.34**	-0.10*	0.02	0.04	0.01	0.04	-0.31**						
Return Intentions[f]	-0.18**	-0.02	-0.02	-0.16**	-0.13**	0.02	-0.07	-0.37**	-0.10*	-0.13**	-0.14**	0.04	-0.10	-0.08					
Cultural Empathy	-0.03	0.20**	-0.05	0.12**	0.00	-0.08	0.18**	0.12**	0.10*	0.16**	0.23**	-0.01	0.00	0.12*	-0.07				
Flexibility	-0.00	0.04	-0.06	-0.09*	0.02	-0.18**	-0.05	-0.12**	-0.06	0.01	0.02	-0.11*	-0.02	0.05	0.14**	-0.13**			
Social Initiative	0.06	0.02	0.13**	0.10*	0.04	-0.01	0.26**	0.18**	0.16**	0.14**	0.13*	0.05	0.17**	-0.01	-0.06	0.31**	-0.04		
Emotional Stability	0.11*	-0.18**	0.06	0.02	0.03	-0.03	0.35**	0.12**	0.06	0.06	0.20**	0.04	0.22**	-0.07	-0.02	0.09	0.11*	0.33**	
Open-Mindedness	0.09*	-0.01	0.01	0.17**	-0.01	-0.05	0.16**	0.22**	0.09*	0.17**	0.19**	-0.03	0.10*	0.08	-0.11*	0.44**	-0.05	0.48**	0.19**

Source: own survey; Note: n = 261-506, a: 0 = male, 1 = female; b: 0 = no, 1 = yes; c: in months; d: 0 = no job-related reasons, 1 = job-related reasons; e: 0 = not employed, 1 = employed; f: 0 = no, 1 = yes; *p > 0.05, **p > 0.01

Relationship between adjustment, return intentions and personality predispositions for successful adjustment

Correlations between adjustment and return intentions (Hypothesis 1)

Hypothesis 1 assumes that successful psychological, socio-cultural and economic adjustment is negatively related to return intentions.

Regarding psychological adjustment, a significant negative correlation was found between identification with Germany and return intentions ($r = -0.37$): the less a person felt a sense of belonging to German society and endorsed German culture and values, the more likely he or she was to intend to leave Germany. However, life satisfaction was not related to return intentions. Participants who intended to leave Germany showed lower levels of socio-cultural adjustment in terms of lower language competence ($r = -0.10$), fewer German friends ($r = -0.13$), and lower levels of perceived social support from German friends ($r = -0.14$). Regarding economic adjustment, neither employment status, job satisfaction nor overqualification was related to return intentions.

Taken together, results partly confirm Hypothesis 1. The most consistent support was found for the negative association between socio-cultural adjustment and return intentions; however, the correlation coefficients were quite small. The highest negative correlation was found between an indicator of psychological adjustment (namely, identification with Germany) and return intentions. There was no support for a negative association between economic adjustment and return intentions.

Correlations between adjustment and personal predispositions for successful adjustment (Hypothesis 2)

Hypothesis 2 assumes that cultural empathy, flexibility, social initiative, emotional stability and open-mindedness are positively related to successful psychological, socio-cultural and economic adjustment.

The strongest support for this hypothesis appeared with regard to psychological adjustment. Cultural empathy, social initiative, emotional stability and open-mindedness were significantly positively related to both indicators of psychological adjustment, namely life satisfaction and identification with Germany ($0.12 \leq r \geq 0.35$). However, flexibility was not associated with life satisfaction and was even negatively associated with identification with Germany ($r = -0.12$), indicating that people who are more flexible (in terms of adjusting their behavioral strategies to changing circumstances) identify less with Germany.

Regarding socio-cultural adjustment, Hypothesis 2 is consistently supported for cultural empathy, social initiative and open-mindedness: these personality predispositions were significantly positively related to language competence, number of German friends and social support from German friends ($0.09 \leq r \geq 0.23$). Emotional stability was only significantly related to perceived social support from German friends ($r = 0.20$). Flexibility was not associated with any of the indicators of socio-cultural adjustment.

Regarding economic adjustment, results provide rather inconsistent support for Hypothesis 2. Only flexibility showed a significant association with employment status, albeit in an unexpected direction: participants who were not employed showed higher levels of flexibility. Social initiative, emotional stability and open-mindedness were significantly positively related to job satisfaction ($0.10 \leq r \geq 0.22$). However, neither cultural empathy nor flexibility was related to job satisfaction. Only cultural empathy was significantly related to overqualification, again, however, in unexpected direction ($r = 0.12$), indicating that the higher the level of cultural empathy the higher the perceived mismatch of qualifications and job requirements.

DISCUSSION

Nowadays, EU citizens can make use of low mobility barriers within Europe that encourage migration for a broader variety of reasons, including lifestyle and culture. Traditional literature on migration has emphasized the economic motivations for migration (Borjas 1994; Massey/Arango/Hugo/Kouaouci/Pellegrino/Taylor 1999). However, as the barriers to migration within the European Union have been reduced, and the risks and costs of mobility have correspondingly decreased (Favell 2008), migration for non-economic reasons has also been encouraged (Favell/Recchi 2009). As a consequence, factors that drive migration flows and impact immigrant adjustment have become more complex, and knowledge from prior generations of immigrants cannot simply be transferred to recent immigrants. The present study investigates the adjustment of recent immigrants from southern European countries in Germany.

The study's results show, first, that various forms of adjustment (especially psychological and socio-cultural adjustment) are negatively related to return intentions. Second, results support the assumption that various personality characteristics (especially cultural empathy, social initiative, emotional stability and open-mindedness) are related to better adjustment among recent immigrants from southern Europe. Third, Spanish, Italian and Greek immigrants differ regarding various indicators of adjustment as well as their return intentions and personality predispositions for successful adjustment. In the following, the results will be discussed in this order.

Even though the majority of the study participants showed rather high levels of adjustment regarding most of the indicators considered, only a minority (29 per cent) could imagine staying in Germany forever. In this context, the results for identification with Germany are eye-catching: only 28 per cent felt a sense of belonging to German society and culture. This is noteworthy because the highest correlation of all adjustment indicators with return intentions was found for identification with Germany. Consequently, facilitating the identification with German society and culture might be one way to increase the desire of immigrants to stay in Germany over the long term. That can possibly be achieved by fostering socio-cultural adjustment by building up language skills and encouraging social contact with Germans in order to enlarge supportive social networks. The results of the present research indicate that these factors are related to both higher identification with Germany and lower levels of return intentions. However, a rather remarkable proportion of participants (30 per cent) did not have a single close German friend in Germany. Formal support to access a larger social network including Germans is needed and can be provided, for example, by groups in online social networks, organizational mentoring programs or language exchange programs offered by cultural organizations and language schools. Increasing social contact with Germans might be a good starting point to support adjustment in various ways, because it makes language acquisition easier and makes information about adequate, high-quality job offers more accessible.

Surprisingly, economic adjustment was not related to return intentions in this study. However, when calculating correlations between indicators of economic adjustment and return intentions only for those who migrated for job-related reasons, a significant positive correlation between job satisfaction and return intentions occurs. The proportion of registered unemployed people was higher in this study (8.9 per cent) than the average unemployment rate in Germany in 2014 (5.0 per cent; Eurostat 2015). Furthermore, results raise the question of whether those holding a job are actually adequately employed. Among the employed and self-employed participants in this study, every second person does not perceive his or her current job as a very good fit given their actual level of skills, education and training. Overqualification and job dissatisfaction were related to lower life satisfaction and lower identification with Germany in this study. The latter, in turn, was associated with return intentions. Consequently, measures and initiatives that promote finding a satisfying job that matches one's skills and qualifications are highly recommended and could have an indirect effect on return intentions by increasing psychological adjustment.

However, whether an immigrant finds an adequate job in Germany is likely to be at least partly influenced by the initial motivation to migrate to Germany. Correlation coefficients in this study show that people who migrated for reasons not related to employment are especially likely to perceive overqualification. Previous research also suggests that the initial motivation for migration is likely to have an impact on the adjustment to the host country (Campbell 2014; Cerdin/Diné/Brewster 2013), and that immigrants who move for job reasons are most successful in terms of employment and wages.

Overall, the correlation coefficients between various adjustment indicators and return intentions are rather small, suggesting that return intentions are likely to be influenced by multiple factors simultaneously.

A core purpose of psychological research into migration is to identify personality traits that facilitate adjustment. This study confirms that cultural empathy, social initiative, emotional stability and open-mindedness are related to better adjustment of Spanish, Italian and Greek immigrants in Germany. This is in line with previous research by Van Oudenhoven and Van der Zee (2002), who claim that these personality characteristics contribute to the multicultural effectiveness of a person. However, results depend on the adjustment indicator: whereas cultural empathy, social initiative, emotional stability and open-mindedness were related to all indicators of psychological adjustment and most of the indicators of socio-cultural adjustment in the present study, results were less consistent regarding economic adjustment. Unexpectedly, flexibility (another predictor of multicultural effectiveness proposed by Van Oudenhoven and Van der Zee 2002) was not related or even conversely related to better adjustment in this study.

Based on these findings, cultural empathy, social initiative, emotional stability and open-mindedness are personality predispositions worthy of consideration when selecting international employees (Van Oudenhoven/Van der Zee 2002). Furthermore, implementing trainings to increase these personality characteristics, for example, within inter-cultural training programs, can facilitate immigrant adjustment.

Last but not least, the study shows that there were ways in which Spanish, Italian and Greek participants differed regarding their adjustment, return intentions and personality predispositions for successful adjustment. *Spanish participants* showed the lowest levels of identification with Germany. Our data also contained questions about identification with the country of origin (which are not further considered in this paper) and post-hoc analyses revealed that Spaniards also showed the lowest levels of identification with their country of origin. It seems that this subsample was the least predisposed to identify with a national framework or think in cultural 'boxes'. This is further underpinned by the finding that Spaniards showed the highest levels of cultural empathy in this study.

Italian participants could most often imagine staying in Germany forever. When intending to leave Germany, they were most likely to move on to another country rather than return to Italy. Furthermore, moving to Germany from a country other than the country of origin was more common among Italians in this study than among Spaniards or Greeks. This adds up to the impression that Italian participants are most representative of the new "EU movers" (Favell/Recchi 2009: 9) and are most likely to use a transnational space of living. As a result of this spatial flexibility, one can speculate that Italian participants have created the possibility for broader access to jobs that match their qualifications, which might explain why they perceive less overqualification. *Greek participants* most often mentioned job-related reasons as the main reason for their migration, and they intended to stay longer in Germany before leaving than the Spanish and Italian participants. Also, they were the subgroup who most often expressed the intention to go back to their home country if they did intend to leave Germany. This leads to the conclusion that among the three subsamples in this study, Greek participants were most representative for the traditional, less dynamic and primarily economically driven migration (Favell 2008; Luthra/Platt/Salamońska 2014). Greek participants intended to stay over a longer term in Germany, and therefore may have invested more effort in learning the German language, which might contribute to their higher language competence in comparison to Spaniards and Italians. Furthermore, as they plan on residing for a longer time in Germany, they may have higher expectations regarding their adjustment and be at higher risk of being disappointed, which might partially explain their lesser level of life satisfaction. Finally, two major limitations of this study that could affect the interpretation of the results must be noted. First, the sample is highly self-selected. Assuming that people who are worse off, for example in terms of their job situation, are less likely to participate (Friedland/Price 2003), the variance in various indicators and the representativeness of results could be limited. Second, the results of this study give an overview of the status quo in the adjustment of recent Spanish, Italian and Greek immigrants in Germany, but causal explanations cannot be derived from cross-sectional data. Consequently, it remains unclear whether poor adjustment is to be seen as the cause or the effect of return intentions, or if instead a third variable is actually the explanation for both. Likewise, personality characteristics may affect adjustment, but the reverse could also be true.

Conclusion

The European Union actively facilitates intra-European mobility, enhancing the opportunity to counter discrepancies in labor demands within the European Union. The free movement of labor is seen by many Europeans as one of the most important accomplishments of the European Union (Eurobarometer 2010). Such possibilities for free movement result in new, more complex migration patterns, and our traditional migration paradigms that focus on long-term, economically driven migration fall short of the mark (Favell/Recchi, 2009). Interdisciplinary effort is needed to create a better understanding of recent intra-European migration. Research in the field of psychology can contribute to this understanding. This study has shown one way by examining personality characteristics as personal resources that help to master challenges in the context of migration and adjustment, but there are many more contributions that the field of psychology can make to our understanding of recent intra-European migration.

First, by exploring the anticipated benefits and challenges that immigrants will encounter prior to their migration, psychologists can increase the understanding of when and why immigrants will perceive their migration as a success or a disappointment (Hoppe/Fujishiro 2015). Expectations prior to migration set the course for adjustment after migration, and unmet expectations or negative surprises diminish the effort to adjust (Cerdin/Diné/Brewster 2013). Research that covers the whole process of migration, including the decision-making process to migrate prior to the actual migration (e.g., Jasinskaja-Lahti/Yijälä 2011), can lead to useful applications for migration preparation: for example, through training programs that foster realistic expectations and beneficial adjustment strategies.

Second, as typical structural barriers in the context of migration are reduced within the European Union, psychological and socio-cultural challenges after migration (e.g., learning the language or developing a sense of belonging) gain in importance. Likewise, in the context of work, taking up employment in another European country becomes easier and the focus shifts to the quality of available jobs and the working conditions of immigrants. Research in the field of occupational health psychology can help to identify and examine working conditions in the host country that positively impact the health and well-being of immigrants (e.g., Hoppe 2011; Hoppe/Heaney/Fujishiro/Gong/Baron 2015), and thereby facilitate adjustment. This knowledge can serve as the basis for designing working conditions that are beneficial for immigrant well-being and make the best use of the potentials that foreign professionals can add to organizations and the economy of host nations (Reid 2012).

Last but not least, research has shown that psychological, socio-cultural and economic adjustment are interrelated. Successful adjustment in one area is likely to foster adjustment in other areas, which can result in *adjustment spirals*. This assumption is in line with the Conservation of Resources Theory (Hobfoll 2001), which states that individuals seek to accumulate resources (e.g., social support, a satisfying job situation, high language competence or personal resources) and feel stressed when resources are threatened, lost, or wasted. Furthermore, it is assumed that a loss of resources increases the risk of losing even more resources (*loss spirals*), whereas gaining resources increases the chance that even more resources will be acquired (*gain spirals*; Hobfoll 2001: 354-355). Future research based on the Conservation of Resources Theory could determine the impact factor of various resources for *gain spirals* in reference to the adjustment of immigrants.

Taken altogether, an interdisciplinary perspective on this rather new form of migration from southern European countries to Germany is needed in order to understand the factors that determine and predict the successful adjustment of immigrants. With this knowledge we can help to create stories of success rather than stories of disappointment and exploitation concerning intra-European migration. The degree to which individuals, societies and organizations benefit from the free movement of persons within the European Union will, finally, have a significant impact on the success and sustainability of European integration.

REFERENCES

Ajzen, Icek (1991): "The theory of planned behavior." In: Organizational Behavior and Human Decision Processes 50/2, pp. 179-211.
Amason, Patricia/Allen, Myria Watkins/Holmes, Susan A. (1999): "Social support and acculturative stress in the multicultural workplace." In: Journal of Applied Communication Research, 27/4, pp. 310-334.
Amit, Karin/Riss, Ilan (2014): "The Subjective Well-Being of Immigrants: Pre- and Post-migration." In: Social Indicators Research, 119/1, pp. 247-264.
Aycan, Zeynep/Berry, John W. (1996): "Impact of employment-related experiences on immigrants' psychological well-being and adaptation to Canada."

In: Canadian Journal of Behavioural Science/Revue canadienne des sciences du comportement, 28/3, pp. 240-251.
BAMF (2015): Migrationsbericht des Bundesamtes für Migration und Flüchtlinge im Auftrag der Bundesregierung. Migrationsbericht 2013. [Migration report by the Federal Office for Migration and Refugees on behalf of the Federal Government of Germany. Migration report 2013], September 27, 2016 (http://www.bamf.de).
Berry, John W. (1997): "Immigration, acculturation and adaptation." In: Applied Psychology, 46/1, pp. 5-68.
Berry, John W. (2003): "Conceptual approaches to acculturation." In: Chun, Kevin/Balls-Organista, Pamela/Marin, Gerardo (Eds.), Acculturation: Advances in theory, measurement and applied research Washington, DC: APA Press, pp. 17-37.
Bertoli, Simone/Brücker, Herbert/Fernández-Huertas Moraga, Jesús (2013): "The European crisis and migration to Germany: Expectations and the diversion of migration flows." IZA Discussion Paper, No. 7170, Bonn: Institute for the Study of Labor.
Bonin, Holger/Eichhorst, Werner/Florman, Christer/Hansen, Mette Okkels/ Skiöld, Lena/Stuhler, Jan/Tatsiramos, Konstantinos/Thomasen, Henrik/ Zimmermann, Klaus F. (2008): "Geographic Mobility in the European Union: Optimising its Economic and Social Benefits." IZA Research report No. 19, Bonn: Institute for the Study of Labor.
Borjas, George J. (1994): "The Economics of Immigration." In: Journal of Economic Literature, 3274, pp. 1667-1717.
Brücker, Herbert/Brunow, Stephan/Fuchs, Johann/Kubis, Alexander/Mendolicchio, Concetta/Weber, Enzo (2013): "Fachkräftebedarf in Deutschland: Zur kurz- und langfristigen Entwicklung von Fachkräfteangebot und -nachfrage, Arbeitslosigkeit und Zuwanderung." [Demand for skilled workers in Germany: short- and long-term development of skilled workers supply and demand, unemployment and immigration]. In: IAB-Stellungnahme (1/2013). Nürnberg: Institut für Arbeitsmarkt- und Berufsforschung.
Campbell, Stuart (2014): Does it matter why immigrants came here? Original motives, the labour market, and national identity in the UK, No. 14, Department of Quantitative Social Science-UCL Institute of Education, University College London.
Carver, Charles S./Connor-Smith, Jennifer (2010): "Personality and coping." In: Annual Review of Psychology, 61, pp. 679-704.

Cerdin, Jean-Luc/Diné, Manel Abdeljalil/Brewster, Chris (2013): "Qualified immigrants' success: Exploring the motivation to migrate and to integrate." In: Journal of International Business Studies, 45/2, pp. 151-168.

Chiswick, Barry R./Miller, Paul W. (2002): "Immigrant earnings: Language skills, linguistic concentrations and the business cycle." In: Journal of Population Economics, 15/1, pp. 31-57.

Cohen, Jacob (1988): Statistical power analysis for the behavioral sciences (2nd ed.). Hillsdale, NJ: Erlbaum.

Constant, Amelie/Massey, Douglas S. (2003): "Self-selection, earnings, and out-migration: A longitudinal study of immigrants to Germany." In: Journal of Population Economics, 16/4, pp. 631-653.

Diener, Ed/Emmons, Robert A./Larsen, Randy J./Griffin, Sharon (1985): "The satisfaction with life scale." In: Journal of Personality Assessment, 49/1, pp. 71-75.

Dustmann, Christian (1999): "Temporary migration, human capital, and language fluency of migrants." In: The Scandinavian Journal of Economics, 101/2, pp. 297-314.

Dustmann, Christian (1996): "Return migration: the European experience." In: Economic Policy, 11/22, pp. 215-250.

Dustmann, Christian/Fabbri, Francesca (2003): "Language proficiency and labour market performance of immigrants in the UK." In: The Economic Journal, 113, pp. 695-717.

Eurobarometer (2010): European Citizenship: Cross-Border Mobility. Aggregate Report August 2010. Brussels: European Commission. September 27, 2016 (ec.europa.eu/public_opinion/archives/quali/5823_citizenship_en.pdf).

Eurostat (2015): Euro area unemployment rate at 11.5 per cent. European Commission. September 27, 2016 (http://ec.europa.eu/eurostat/en/web/products-press-releases/-/3-07012015-AP-EN).

Favell, Adrian (2008): "The new face of East–West migration in Europe." In: Journal of Ethnic and Migration Studies, 34/5, pp. 701-716.

Favell, Adrian/Recchi, Ettore (2009): Pioneers of European Union: Citizenship and mobility in the EU, Cheltenham, UK: Edward Elgar.

Field, Andy (2009): Discovering statistics using SPSS: And sex and drugs and rock'n'roll (3rd ed.), London: SAGE.

Friedland, Daniel S./Price, Richard H. (2003): "Underemployment: Consequences for the Health and Well-Being of Workers." In: American Journal of Community Psychology, 32(1-2), pp. 33-45.

Fuller-Rowell, Thomas E./Ong, Anthony D./Phinney, Jean S. (2013): "National identity and perceived discrimination predict changes in ethnic identity commitment: Evidence from a longitudinal study of Latino college students." In: Applied Psychology, 62/3, pp. 406-426.

Haug, Sonja (2008): "Migration networks and migration decision-making." In: Journal of Ethnic and Migration Studies, 34/4, pp. 585-605.

Hobfoll, Stevan E. (2001): "The influence of culture, community, and the nested-self in the stress process: advancing conservation of resources theory." In: Applied Psychology, 50/3, pp. 337-421.

Hoppe, Annekatrin (2011): "Psychosocial working conditions and well-being among immigrant and German low-wage workers." In: Journal of Occupational Health Psychology, 16/2, pp. 187-201.

Hoppe, Annekatrin/Fujishiro, Kaori (2015): "Anticipated job benefits, career aspiration, and generalized self-efficacy as predictors for migration decision-making." In: International Journal of Intercultural Relations, 47, pp. 13-27.

Hoppe, Annekatrin/Heaney, Catherine A./Fujishiro, Kaori/Gong, Fang/Baron, Sherry (2015): "Psychosocial work characteristics of personal care and service occupations: a process for developing meaningful measures for a multiethnic workforce." In: Ethnicity & Health, 20/5, pp. 474-492.

Jasinskaja-Lahti, Inga/Yijälä, Anu (2011): "The model of pre-acculturative stress – A pre-migration study of potential migrants from Russia to Finland." In: International Journal of Intercultural Relations, 35/4, pp. 499-510.

Leong, Chan-Hoong (2007): "Predictive validity of the Multicultural Personality Questionnaire: A longitudinal study on the socio-psychological adaptation of Asian undergraduates who took part in a study-abroad program." In: International Journal of Intercultural Relations, 31, pp. 545-559.

Luthra, Renee Reichl/Platt, Lucinda/Salamońska, Justyna (2014): Migrant Diversity, Migration Motivations and Early Integration: The Case of Poles in Germany, the Netherlands, London and Dublin. LEQS Paper No. 74/2014, Institute for Social and Economic Research: University of Essex.

Mahajan, Ashish/Toh, Soo Min (2014): "Facilitating expatriate adjustment: The role of advice-seeking from host country nationals." In: Journal of World Business, 49/4, pp. 476-487.

Massey, Douglas S./Arango, Joaquin/Hugo, Graeme/Kouaouci, Ali/Pellegrino, Adela/Taylor, J. Edward (1999): Worlds in Motion: Understanding International Migration at the End of the Millennium, Oxford: Oxford University Press.

Maynard, Douglas C./Joseph, Todd Allen/Maynard, Amanda M. (2006): "Underemployment, job attitudes, and turnover intentions." In: Journal of Organizational Behavior, 27/4, pp. 509-536.

Mehrländer, Ursula (1981): "Career aspirations of native and foreign born: Federal Republic of Germany." In: International Migration Review, 15/55, pp. 522-528.

Organisation for Economic Cooperation and Development (OECD) (2013): International Migration Outlook 2013, September 27, 2016 (http://static.pulso.cl/20130612/1768132.pdf).

Parutis, Violetta (2014): "'Economic migrants' or 'middling transnationals'? East European migrants' experiences of work in the UK." In: International Migration, 52/1, pp. 36-55.

Reid, Alison (2012): "Under-use of migrants' employment skills linked to poorer mental health." In: Australian and New Zealand Journal of Public Health, 36/2, pp. 120-125.

Schwarzer, Ralf/Schulz, Ute (2002): "The role of stressful life events." In: Nezu, Arthur. M./Nezu, Christine. M./Geller, Pamela. A. (Eds.), Comprehensive handbook of psychology, vol. 9: Health psychology, New York: Wiley, pp. 27-49.

Selmer, Jan/Lauring, Jakob (2015): "Host country language ability and expatriate adjustment: The moderating effect of language difficulty." In: The International Journal of Human Resource Management, 26/3, pp. 401-420.

Van der Zee, Karen I./Van Oudenhoven, Jan Pieter (2000): "The Multicultural Personality Questionnaire: A multidimensional instrument of multicultural effectiveness." In: European Journal of Personality, 14/4, pp. 291-309.

Van der Zee, Karen I./Van Oudenhoven, Jan Pieter (2001): "The Multicultural Personality Questionnaire: Reliability and validity of self-and other ratings of multicultural effectiveness." In: Journal of Research in Personality, 35/3, pp. 278-288.

Van Oudenhoven, Jan Pieter/Van der Zee, Karen I. (2002): "Predicting multicultural effectiveness of international students: The Multicultural Personality Questionnaire." In: International Journal of Intercultural Relations, 26/6, pp. 679-694.

Van der Zee, Karen/Van Oudenhoven, Jan Pieter/Ponterotto, Joseph G./Fietzer, Alexander W. (2013): "Multicultural Personality Questionnaire: Development of a short form." In: Journal of Personality Assessment, 95/1, pp. 118-124.

Vroome, Thomas/Verkuyten, Maykel/Martinovic, Borja (2014): "Host national identification of immigrants in the Netherlands." In: International Migration Review, 48/1, pp. 76-102.

Waldorf, Brigitte (1995): "Determinants of international return migration intentions." In: Professional Geographer, 47/2, pp. 125-136.

Wallace, Claire (2002): "Opening and closing borders: migration and mobility in East-Central Europe." In: Journal of Ethnic and Migration Studies, 28/4, pp. 603-625.

Ward, Colleen/Bochner, Stephen/Furnham, Adrian (2001): The psychology of culture shock (2nd ed.), Philadelphia, PA: Routledge.

Yeh, Christine J./Inose, Mayuko (2003): "International students' reported English fluency, social support satisfaction, and social connectedness as predictors of acculturative stress." In: Counselling Psychology Quarterly, 16/1, pp. 15-28.

Zimet, Gregory D./Dahlem, Nancy W./Zimet, Sara G./Farley, Gordon K. (1988): "The multidimensional scale of perceived social support." In: Journal of Personality Assessment, 52/1, pp. 30-41.

8. The role of intermediaries in Spanish emigration: past and present

DIRK GODENAU

ABSTRACT

This chapter focusses on the role of private and public intermediation in Spanish labor migration to Germany. It takes stock of the scarce empirical evidence available on migration intermediaries in the current wave of Spanish emigration to Germany and compares this profile of intermediation under conditions of free movement with the *Gastarbeiter* scheme used in the 1960s. Without the selective role of borders, intermediation along the migration process nowadays concentrates on the labor market and settlement, with the latter including housing, education (e.g., language), and other social services (e.g., health).

Most of these functions can be provided, in part at least, by private non-professional services and under conditions of free movement, the self-selection and self-organization of migrants through social networks is an outstanding feature of intermediation processes. As a consequence, the use of professional services tends to be sporadic and specific. In some specific matters institutionalized intermediaries are playing a major role, particularly if public services are involved (unemployment, social housing) or specific labor shortages in the host country lead to the implementation of publicly funded recruitment initiatives.

Keywords: Economic crisis, Labor migration, Migration industry, Migration intermediaries

INTRODUCTION

The impact of the international economic crisis in Spain triggered outmigration of both skilled and unskilled young workers. While the larger share of these emigrants are former immigrants, with foreign or Spanish nationalities, an increasing number of Spanish-born workers is also heading abroad looking to improve their professional qualification and/or find better job opportunities. Most of these migrants go to other EU countries, with Germany being one their preferred destinations, particularly when it comes to skilled workers (cf. Domínguez-Mujica/Pérez García in this volume; Montero 2014).

Although still relatively small in size, this labor migration flow is analytically relevant due to its high growth rates and its segmentation into different levels/niches of the human capital and occupational specialization of migrants in the host country. Furthermore, labor migration from Spain to Germany is an example of how and to what extent labor mobility responds to asymmetric economic shocks in the European Monetary Union (Bertoli et al. 2013: 3).

As in all international labor migration processes, it seems worthwhile to include in our analysis the organizational aspects of migration, and particularly the role of intermediaries. Do migrants travel with contracts already signed? Do they obtain specific information on employment opportunities before they migrate? What are their sources of information? To what degree is their decision based on social networking with friends and relatives? Are institutionalized information channels also relevant? Are German employers actively involved in channeling information on vacancies? Do they go to Spain in order to recruit migrants? Do intermediaries specialize in geographic areas or in occupational niches? All these questions relate to intermediation in the migration and settlement processes; most of the research on Spanish emigration to Germany includes some empirical evidence on intermediation, but the intermediation processes themselves are rarely at the center of their analysis (cf. Meinardus in this volume).

Although collective memory is usually weak, and many migrants might not be aware of the historic precedent, the Spanish-German migration link is not new, with the most relevant precursor being the migration of Spanish workers to Germany in the 1960s. Some lessons can be drawn from these earlier migration flows when analyzing the institutional frameworks and the activities of public and private employment agencies, companies, chambers of commerce, language schools, and real estate agents.

The chapter focuses on the role of private and public intermediation in Spanish labor migration to Germany, in the present and in comparison with the earlier migration in the 1960s. When comparing past and present intermediation, we will pay specific attention to the present context of free mobility in the European Common Market and its implications to intermediation profiles, their socio-economic stratification and forms of institutionalization. The chapter shows how the role of intermediaries and the actors in this field changed in the light of differing framing features and individual resources. We will draw on the empirical evidence made available by online surveys and fieldwork conducted by other researchers in Germany and Spain.

The chapter is structured as follows. First we will look at the context embeddedness of intermediation in migration processes. Then, the general determinants of intermediation will be set out and specified for the skilled international labor migration segment. The third section will focus on the empirical evidence available on young Spaniards who go to Germany for work-related reasons. The last section offers some conclusions.

CONTEXT EMBEDDEDNESS OF MIGRATION AND INTERMEDIATION

All migration is embedded in historical and geopolitical contexts. Spain and Germany have a limited but nevertheless important migration history. The last and most relevant precedent is Spanish labor migration to Germany in the 1960s. Additionally, although not directly related, we should also mention the flow of German migrants who go to Spain for work or leisure. Spanish migration to Germany and German migration to Spain are largely disconnected and not part of the same social networks. Therefore we will concentrate on the comparison and links between the past emigration episode (1955-1973) and the current incipient labor migration from Spain to Germany.

When comparing migration episodes, multiple criteria can be used in order to detect common and distinctive traits: the size of the migrant population, its age structure, sex ratio, cohabitation, education, labor motivation, occupational and professional distribution, expectations and plans (return), previous experience at the destination (tourism, Erasmus), how the trip and initial settlement is financed (language, studying), parental support (middle class parents in Spain), regional distribution at the origin and host countries, and the stage of the migration cycle.

Among these multiple criteria, the present Spanish emigration to Germany is said to be young and highly skilled, from urban areas, looking for education or their first job, and dependent on parental support. This flow seems to be triggered nearly exclusively by the bleak employment prospects in Spain (Alba et al. 2013; Montero Lange 2014: 20).

Social networks and path dependency are of crucial importance when analyzing the links between past and present migration flows and regions. Although both migration episodes from Spain to Germany are apparently different in composition and geographical distribution, we still have to ask whether the present emigration is influenced by the past. And it indeed is, for several reasons. First, collective memory in Spain sees the former Spanish emigration to Germany as a success; the message remains that when you work hard you can prosper, problems with cultural integration notwithstanding. Second, family networks of former migrants are rudimentary but can still play a role when it comes to obtaining and channeling information on job opportunities. They may be reactivated by new demands and opportunities.

But other contextual factors may be more important than the historical aspects: many young Spaniards have been to Germany before, as tourists or students. Although their knowledge of the country may be rather limited, it still makes a difference to have been there before as a student or tourist. Tourism has also created specific networks between Spanish regions (e.g., Balearic Islands, Canary Islands) and Germany, through business links, education (*Deutsche Schule*), and demographic links (children of German parents born in Spain). Furthermore, new communication technologies have increased the feasibility of staying in contact with people who live abroad and these contacts accelerate and multiply accumulative causation effects. Last but not least, young and highly skilled Spaniards have an open attitude towards spatial mobility and transcultural biographies; mobility may even have a positive spin ("ver mundo"; Santos 2013: 126).

Before we go into details on intermediation, we should identify some of the structural characteristics of the Spanish emigration flow to Germany, as well as some of the biases of academic work and discourses in the media, so as to have in mind when interpreting the intermediation mechanisms and processes.

One of the frequent – and often erroneous – perceptions is that all migrants who leave their home country do so because they are unemployed. The data available on Spanish emigration leaves little room for doubt that this supposition is wrong (Faraco 2014: 218). According to the digital survey conducted by González/Martínez (2014: 2), 52 per cent of respondents were employed prior to leaving and only 34 per cent cited unemployment as their reason for emigrating. Izquierdo et al. (2013: 223) go a bit further and underscore how the higher emigration rates of highly skilled workers may imply that "Spain might suffer a brain drain process with serious consequences on future potential growth".

In terms of human capital and education levels, some analyses focus explicitly, or implicitly through sample selection and selective return rates among respondents (digital surveys), on the emigration of young, highly skilled workers. In her online survey, Faraco (2014: 217) indicates that more than 50 per cent of migrants have university degrees. Consequently, the idea emerges that all migrants want to work in the destination country, nearly all of them as employees and not as entrepreneurs. Since information on other segments of migration is more difficult to obtain, the available data may be biased towards what researchers perceive as new and socially relevant about Spanish emigration: well educated, middle-class young people are seeing their professional careers under threat in Spain. Little attention is paid to other migration segments, such as students or less qualified migrants with weaker employment perspectives.

Concerning Germany as destination country, the media attention raised by Spanish emigration to Germany goes far beyond the quantitative weight of Germany as a host country (cf. Domínguez-Mujica/Pérez García et al. in this volume), and the attention focuses on migrants who went to large cities, and particularly to Berlin. It also seems all migrants were well informed before they left and they knew what to expect after arriving. Due to their youth they are supposed to use information and communication technologies for nearly everything. Once again little empirical information is available when we want to confirm these ideas. Maybe a larger than expected share of migrants improvise important decisions about where to go and how to tackle labor issues after arrival (cf. Glorius in this volume).

The need for intermediation and the preferred organization of intermediation processes are context-dependent. This embeddedness also includes the social stratification of intermediation processes, because differences in the resource endowments, social capital, and professional specialization of migrants will translate into different demands placed on intermediation, both from their side and from the side of the host country. The apparent contradiction may arise that those who are most in need of intermediation will be the ones who cannot afford the private services. And it is particularly in the segment of unsatisfied intermediation needs where public services should be more useful in integrating migrants.

DETERMINANTS OF INTERMEDIATION

The decision to migrate is an important one and as such, requires high ego-involvement, the search for information and a structured decision-making process. Consequently, somebody considering migrating from Spain to Germany will take the time to find out about potential benefits and risks. They will search for information, make plans, consider alternatives and look for resources. And this is where intermediaries come into play.

When it comes to explaining intermediation, we should be able to connect it to the theoretical frameworks in the field of migration. Every migration model that seeks to understand how migrants make their decisions will have to enter the debate between disciplines on how humans reach decisions in general. Are we rational beings? Are the *homo oeconomicus* assumptions realistic? To what extent do we depend on social networks and contexts when making decisions? Despite the significant differences in their basic assumptions, there are also some common elements we might point out: all approaches recognize the importance of information as a means to transform uncertainty into a known level of risk and admit that social networks are relevant information sources. Intermediation in migration processes is intrinsically linked to information asymmetries.

Migration modeling suffers from several blind spots. First, migration models are about explaining mobility, while immobility is what abounds. So we do not explain the normal, we explain the exception. Second, migration models normally assume migrants themselves make the decision; but frequently, it is others, such as the managers of the firm you work for, who decide. Third, models tend to assume revealed preferences; if you work in the host country then it seems you went there for a job. Maybe your motives and motivation had been completely unrelated to work – maybe you fell in love with somebody –, but since you have to make a living, you end up working there.

Particularly in highly skilled international labor migration, we see that intermediation is the rule, not the exception, due to the wide range of functions provided by intermediaries: a) intermediation is supposed to match supply and demand through information and negotiation; b) intermediation allows for simplifying transactional ties by interacting with a reduced number of parties; c) through intermediation, scale advantages and task specialization can be achieved; d) intermediation can include risk-sharing mechanisms; e) intermediation also may provide the functions of financing and payments; f) intermediaries can speed up matching processes when quick solutions are needed.

We may draw several conclusions from these general functions played by intermediation in migration. First, intermediaries are used once they become useful, not always and not in all types of migration. Second, their main function is to pool, transform and channel information about and between supply and demand. Third, their activities and added value may be focused on migration itself or on integration in the host society. Intermediaries specializing in migration itself are normally related to (irregular) international migration, while others center on job opportunities, housing or education. Fourth, intermediaries may target migrants as their only clients or may see migrants simply as one more market segment. For example, if we look at job portal web sites, nobody mentions migrants, although many of the users are or will be migrants. In these cases, migration is seen as nothing more than a mere spatial relocation derived from career decisions.

The role of intermediaries in migration processes is mainly related to one or several of these functions: as a source of information on destinations in general, information on job opportunities, handling transactions (such as work contracts, housing, etc.), and arranging for education and training. A typology of intermediaries would at least differentiate between worker organizations, State agencies (destination and origin), private recruitment agencies, migrant organizations, supra-national agencies, and private social networks (family and friends) (Nyberg/Gammeltoft 2013: 2; Xiang/Lindquist 2014: 132). In general terms, intermediaries are more useful for migrants if transaction costs are high (search for specialists), with the intermediation normally taking place under circumstances of asymmetrical information (Fernandez 2013: 815) and the need to make complex decisions. Intermediation is more probable when politicians decide to stimulate migration. Surprisingly, explicit references to intermediation in migration theory are scarce (although more frequent in migration history: indentured labor). This happens especially when microeconomic models (*homo oeconomicus*) and social network theory come into play: the former focus on the individual decision making process, while the latter mainly centers on private networks and is reluctant to admit the institutionalization of intermediation. As neither of these mainstream academic approaches deals explicitly with intermediation, this specific aspect is prone to be "lost in battle" (Massey et al. 1998; Hernández-León 2013).

Let us now turn to the specific functions of intermediaries in labor migration and job placement (Abella 2004). From the point of view of firms and their labor demand, intermediaries are specialized players who screen and select candidates for well-defined jobs on a global scale (headhunters). They channel information selectively and handle the paperwork (permits). They may also negotiate contracts. From the point of view of labor supply (including migrants), intermediaries pool and distribute information on applicants, facilitate information on job opportunities and may have a role in the travel and housing logistics. They inform migrants about the employability criteria used by firms for certain job categories and may offer related educational activities (career advice). Private intermediaries may also collaborate with public initiatives, like EURES in the EU market.

We should clarify some aspects of the intermediation process and its relation to the levels of aggregation (micro-meso-macro). Policies may be designed on a macro level (by the State, for example), but their implementation goes through meso structures (organizational group level) to micro environments (individual, family). Private and public opportunity and incentive structures may overlap and synchronize, but they can also diverge (as happened during the first phase of Spanish emigration to Germany in the late 1950s). Public should not be conflated with macro, nor private with micro, because private interests may be macro and public action is also micro. And the "crucial meso-level" (Faist, 2009: 59) is not limited to family and peer networks; also important are non-State players like trade unions, religious organizations, civil associations, etc. Private devices may be State-driven; and States may be governed by private interests.

What is different about intermediation in the case of highly skilled international labor migration? There are differences in how supply and demand act and interact. The internal labor markets of multinational companies are large and follow their own company-specific rules. Companies with international contracts also move personnel around the world. International recruitment agencies are salient in head-hunting activities. In an increasing share of high-skill activities, online labor flows have to be separated from migration (cf. the concept of "body shopping" in Aneesh 2001: 351), because labor migration is not always body migration; labor may flow internationally even if people do not.

Of indirect importance to the foreign labor supply are the stay rates of foreign-born graduate students, because after finishing their studies they may become part of the local labor supply. If student mobility is promoted, such as through the Erasmus program in the European Union, this international temporary mobility also increases subsequent migration probabilities. As Li et al. (1996: 51) put it, "migrating to learn might lead to learning to migrate". Universities might also have direct links to the business sector and increase the stay rates in foreign markets through their perceived role as a source of labor. Domínguez-Mujica et al. (2016) conducted an online survey with 170 respondents in 2013, which revealed that 46 per cent of these Spanish emigrants had moved abroad as students.

Additionally, immigration policies may have specific exceptions and devices for highly skilled migration, because most developed countries try to attract foreign talent through specific visa programs. Obviously this is not necessary in the case of free internal movement in the EU labor market, as the public initiatives are normally limited to introducing improved selective mobility into otherwise impermeable borders. Due to their importance in high-skilled migration, intermediaries grow and gain political weight and influence. As Bach (2001) exemplifies for the United States:

"A special feature of segmented transnational labor markets is the crucial role of middlemen, those who create and manage the connections between employers and potential foreign workers. [...] In the case of formal recruitments of professional and high-skilled specialty workers, as with H-1B visa petitioners, these middlemen often represent law firms or personnel management companies. [...] In the policy debates on H-1B workers, this 'middle sector' advocated fiercely for expansion of the visa category. [...] As a group, and in partnership with corporate sponsors, they organized and lobbied Congress for a dramatic increase in the numerical limits of H-1B workers [...]". (Bach 2001: 123)

The aspects that determine the likelihood of using intermediaries in migration and settlement are linked to higher transaction costs, and these in turn are conditioned by several factors:

- Border management and immigration policies determine the transaction costs for migrants, because they promote or hamper access to other geographical spaces. Furthermore, the institutional membership of the migrant's home country (e.g., whether it is part of the European Union or not) conditions these accessibility conditions.
- Economic specialization influences the structure and organization of firms and their labor demand. The gatekeeper structures in companies' recruitment policies (head-hunters, body-shopping) generate specific intermediation niches and activities. If the business sector is highly concentrated in huge companies (e.g., manufacturers), their recruitment mechanisms will be very different from those of a fragmented atomistic sector (like restaurants). On the supply side, workers seek to advertise their offers to the companies through these intermediaries.
- Labor supply shortages, as in the context of population aging, can stimulate the creation of international recruitment devices. These devices can be national initiatives or supra-national agreements (e.g., EU Blue Card). These pull factors reduce transaction costs for migrants and, as they tend to be selective, indirectly introduce asymmetrical migration probabilities in terms of nationalities and professions. These direct and indirect effects are embedded in the State's international relations (allies, enemies, securitization, etc.) and are not solely driven by migration or labor market forces.
- The cultural differences and distances between origin and destination countries, including language barriers, cause additional transaction costs for mi-

grants and host societies. These social and cultural integration costs vary widely among the multiple combinations of origin and destination countries. What is it like for a Spaniard to live in Germany? What aspects of social life will be more difficult to cope with? Are they enduring over time or simply adapting temporarily? Migration and settlement are contextualized in a complex web of related regulations, affecting both legal and cultural aspects. The way things are done in a new environment influences the need for specialized intermediaries (e.g., housing market).

Todays' Spanish labor migration to Germany takes place under a regime of free movement. Consequently, intermediation does not concentrate on overcoming restrictions imposed by international migration policies, such as visa constraints or even the organization of irregular transborder transportation. Instead, intermediation focuses on other aspects, particularly on the search for job opportunities, housing and language skills. In the process of matching labor demand in the destination country and labor supply from the origin country, intermediation under conditions of free movement between Spain and Germany attributes a salient role to companies and migrants themselves, supported by public financing and additional private initiatives for improving these matching processes.

In spite of free movement, the cultural barriers between Spain and Germany are still in place and the learning of the language is supposed to be a primordial task when migrants arrive. Intermediation is supposed to pay specific attention to cultural adaptation during the first stages of settlement and large cities, with their transnational social networks, are expected to be cultural adaptation hubs during the initial stages of integration. The next part will sum up the empirical evidence on these issues, drawing on the intermediation-related results of general surveys run by other researchers among migrants and participants in recruitment initiatives.

INTERMEDIARIES IN THE SPANISH LABOR MIGRATION TO GERMANY

What do we know about intermediation in Spanish-German labor migration? As a starting point we will use the comparison between the emigration wave in the 1960s and the current emigration to Germany to highlight the main differences in the field of intermediation.

Differences in the framing of Spanish-German emigration in the 1960s and today

Spanish emigration to Germany grew considerably in the 1960s as a consequence of a combination of push and pull factors. Although the Spanish economy was growing above five per cent, the employment rate was stagnating or even decreasing in a context of high productivity growth. With a young, growing population, Spain was facing considerable employment problems, even though rates of registered unemployment were low, due to the reduced levels of entitlements for the unemployed (Alba et al. 2013: 18). These problems of underemployment were affecting mainly young workers with low education levels. In contrast, Germany was also experiencing a positive growth cycle, but with high employment growth and a shortage of workers for less qualified manual jobs. The *Gastarbeiter* scheme was introduced as a way of attracting temporary immigrants, with Spain being one of the preferred countries in this specific immigration policy. Both States played a proactive role and coordinated promotion efforts through an agreement signed in 1960 (Muñoz 2012: 24). The Spanish government tried to control the selection of emigrants, but complaints from German companies concerning administrative delays and skill mismatches meant it was not able to fully implement these restrictions. As a consequence of the restrictions imposed on assisted emigration, a large share of Spanish migrants went to Germany as tourists, an irregular migration flow tolerated by both governments. Most of them had low skill levels and went to German regions with significant industrial growth (Petuya et al. 2014: 245).

Intermediation played an important role in the emigration itself and in the settlement and integration process in Germany. Public and private agencies were created to arrange for job placement and lodging. In these networks, the Catholic Church played an active role in the integration process and in consolidating the Spanish communities, particularly through educational support and stimulating parental self-organization in associations (e.g., sending periodic bulletins to parents, *Carta a los Padres*; Thränhardt 2014: 299). As Muñoz (2012: 40) points out, the success of Spanish emigrants in education and in the German labor market was partially due to this self-enclosure (*comunidad, colonia*) and social networking (Sevillano 2014; Montero 2014). This positive relation between social success and self-enclosure might be surprising, as integration seems to be the opposite of isolation, but Muñoz underlines that this community building was compatible with an extensive contact between migrants and German society, particularly as it related to work through the German trade unions (Martinez/Rohloff 2014: 332). The economic crisis of 1975-1985 resulted in high return migration, with around 80 per cent of the Spanish emigrants returning to Spain (Muñoz 2012: 31). For most, this return was not a sign of frustrated expectations but the culmination of a successful temporary migration project.

The current Spanish emigration to Germany is clearly different from this former episode. Now there are no border restrictions between the two countries, with both belonging to the European Common Market, a Monetary Union and the Schengen Space. This institutional integration process brought about free bilateral movement. As a consequence of this free movement, public intervention in migration processes is nowadays less proactive than in the 1960s and is focused on the access to job matching processes and the social services provided to all citizens. Free movement implies not needing middlemen to cross a border, but it does not mean States might not be interested in forging alliances to promote labor mobility between them. In fact, Chancellor Merkel's visits to Spain during the economic crisis, with explicit references to the needs of the German labor market (Fuchs et al. 2015), were interpreted as a sign of welcome for qualified Spanish migrants (Lester 2012: 24). In any event, free movement removed the States' role as gatekeepers at the borders, and nowadays they do not exert any selective influence on EU internal migration.

Another difference is that the Catholic Church does not play any significant role in the current emigration and integration in German society. The same is true for worker organizations and the transnational cooperation between them. Most of the labor intermediation is now in the hands of migrants themselves or is organized as private recruitment through the contracting companies or their externalized recruitment agencies. This tendency towards privatization can also be seen as an indirect consequence of free movement. The salient position of private actors does not necessarily imply that public support does not play a significant role in promoting networks and the structuring of labor matching processes. In fact, German public authorities like labor offices, chambers, and embassies do exert an influence on recruitment mechanisms, as do EU support programs like MobiPro-EU (Kraußlach/Stapf 2014: 134; cf. contribution of Meinardus in this volume).

Without the selective role of borders, intermediation along the migration process concentrates on the labor market and settlement, with the latter including housing, education (e.g., language), and other social services (e.g., health). Most of these functions can be at least partially covered by private non-professional services (social networks: family and friends, other migrants). As a consequence, the use of professional services tends to be sporadic and specific. In some specific matters, institutionalized intermediaries are playing a major role, particularly if public services are involved (unemployment, social housing). The online survey conducted by Aparicio (2014: 35) includes indicators on the search process migrants used to obtain information on the host countries. In general terms, the internet and personal networks are the most prominent sources of information. The specific profile of Germany is similar to that of the other countries analyzed, with the use of social media being slightly less important and employment agencies being more important in the destination country. The role of the Spanish embassy and consulates is less relevant in the German case compared to non-EU countries. Montero (2014: 75) points out that the new forms of self-organization of young Spanish migrants are not sufficiently taken into consideration by integration policies.

Since both Spain and Germany are part of the European Common Market, the transnational networks and internal labor markets in multinational companies are of growing importance.[1] Examples of industries like car manufacturing indicate the importance of internal vacancy chains and intra-firm international recruitment programs. For example, *BMW* has been actively recruiting personnel in the Spanish labor market through trainee programs linked to selection processes organized by Spanish universities (El País, May 6, 2015). Many of the trainees selected were already fluent in German, had been to Germany before (e.g., Erasmus program), and had parental links to Germany. Intra-firm recruitment and mobility also operates through those Spanish companies present abroad. For example, *Gamesa* is a major employer in Agreda (Soria, Spain) that specializes in manufacturing wind turbines. Due to the crisis and to cutbacks in subsidies for renewable energy sources in Spain, part of their personnel has been transferred to their production plant in Salvador de Bahia, Brazil, creating specific links between the two cities (Correo de Burgos, April 15, 2015).

Regional differentiation, perceptions and locational choice

Both in Spain and Germany there are considerable differences between local labor markets; thus, there may be significant supply shortages in some sectors and regions of Germany (Kraußlach/Stapf 2014: 124), while in others relatively high unemployment rates persist. Emigration pressure in Spain also is heterogeneous, with the South registering higher unemployment. The regional origin-destination patterns emerging from the scarce empirical evidence indicate only a moderate correlation between emigration rates and differentials in push factors in regions of origin (higher unemployment rates) and between immigration rates and dif-

---

1 Montero (2014: 67) reminds us that internal labor markets are still of limited quantitative relevance.

ferentials between pull factors in the regions of destination (lower unemployment rates). For example, Berlin is the most important destination for Spanish emigrants, although its unemployment rate is relatively high (Montero 2014: 89). And on the Spanish side, although the Southern regions of Spain have higher unemployment rates, their involvement in Spanish emigration is not higher than their proportion of the Spanish population.

The reason for this relative dissociation between labor market indicators and the self-selection of migrants is due to the information search process and to the non-labor amenities of destinations. The interviews conducted by Faraco et al. (2013) reveal a search process based on personal networks and a lack of institutional counselling. In the words of one interviewee, "I think that many people, many of those who are in Berlin now, if they had had sufficient information about what is going on in this city in economic terms, maybe they would have reoriented their search towards other places where they probably would find better opportunities" (Faraco et al. 2013: 225). In an interview we conducted in Berlin in May 2015 with the representatives of the *Marea Granate*[2] (Castillo 2014: 237), we asked them "Why Berlin?" and they answered with a big smile, *porque Berlín mola* ("because Berlin is really cool"), an expression which has nothing to do with labor market matching processes and takes us to the issue of amenities and culture.

Migrants' previous experience with other European cultures, the German culture included, is nowadays more extensive. Many migrants, especially those with higher education, have traveled to other European countries and have a more cosmopolitan view of (work) life. According to Navarrete et al. (2014: 172), 60 per cent of young Spanish emigrants knew the host country before migrating, due to tourism, scholarships, and having lived there before. Additionally, the considerable increase in the education and human capital of migrants has improved their employability (Ganau/Porsche 2014: 360), although specific language barriers (like not speaking German) still remain. These changes in the characteristics of migrants will influence their settlement, and therefore the use of intermediaries. In comparative terms the cultural differences between Spain and Germany are relatively large within the European context, and the language barrier in particular is a considerable obstacle when compared to English-speaking countries. Therefore, integrating into German society might be consid-

---

2   The "Maroon Wave" is a result of the civil activism crystalized in the 15-M (15 May) movement, with a "White Wave" in the health sector, "Green Wave" in education, and the "Maroon Wave" (due to the color of Spanish passports) for economic expatriates (cp. López-Sala in this issue, plus http://mareagranate.org/).

ered relatively difficult from the Spanish point of view. Looking at the migration motives of Spaniards living in Frankfurt, Aparicio's data (2014: 33) show that Germany is selected as a destination in spite of the language problems and of not having Spanish friends there.

In order to overcome these barriers, migrants might choose urban multicultural destinations not only because they have friends and relatives there, but also because of the advantages to acclimatization that major cities offer during the first stage of the settlement process (Kraußlach/Stapf 2014: 201). Additionally, larger urban areas produce a cultural diversity which also fosters the expansion and diversification of certain markets (like music, art, ethnic food, etc.) and their respective labor demands. Consequently, global cities like Berlin may serve as ports of entry with lower adaptation costs, leaving the optimization of one's labor career for a later stage, once the migrant speaks the language, accumulates social capital, and increases his/her employability. If migrants establish this kind of gradual sequence in their migration project, the urban hubs will host them for some years and afterwards watch them leave for other destinations in response to vertical labor market mobility. Anecdotal evidence published in the media (like the article "Ein Spanier in Deutschland"/["A Spaniard in Germany"], Frankfurter Allgemeine Zeitung, May 26, 2013; cf. also Alba and Fernández 2015: 12) seems to confirm the gradual accumulation of social and human capital in a step-by-step sequence (steps like au-pair → language → trainee → job → remigration to other countries).

In these cases, intermediation concentrates on initial settlement services (housing, permits, etc.), language competence (courses, translation/interpretation services), and job search (before leaving or at the destination). When they arrive, most of these migrants only have very limited financial resources (although they are better off than Spanish emigrants in the 1960s) and depend on parental support. For recent Spanish emigrants living in Frankfurt, Aparicio (2014: 26) estimates that 71.9 per cent relied on personal savings and 33.9 per cent had received money from their parents (multiple choice question); Faraco et al. (2014: 223) confirms the importance of parental support. Their demand for intermediation services will probably focus on cheap solutions, like gaining access to social housing through informal networks or learning German without having to pay language academies. Faraco et al. (2014: 223) highlights that housing is the main problem among Spanish migrants in Berlin and informal networks are the main instrument for finding a place to live. Institutionalized intermediation appeals to these migrants only if its cost is low, as in the case of public services involving housing, education, health and employment.

Labor market intermediation and skill stratification

Let us now turn to the specific aspect of intermediation in the labor market. A relatively large share (57.1 per cent) of the Spanish emigrants living in Frankfurt interviewed by Aparicio (2014: 33) had already traveled with a labor contract (intra-firm or inter-firm). Of this group, 23.3 per cent found a job by applying directly (sending CV), 22.4 per cent through the Spanish company they had been working with, and 21.6 per cent through on-line advertisements. Foreign agencies accounted for 7.8 per cent and government intermediation only for 6.0 per cent. The sum of friends, friends with businesses in Germany, and social media only accounted for a total of 11.3 per cent.

In the case of migrants who already have a job before they cross the border, no further labor market intermediation is required, because it took place beforehand. These international recruitment devices are positively correlated with firm size and the degree of skill specialization within the labor supply. It is larger companies looking for specialized workers that will invest more resources into their search processes. Additionally, these companies also look for talented trainees of diverse cultural origins for their internal training programs. Once employees and trainees are selected, the intermediation services in the host society might also include other non-labor aspects (like housing, language skills, and family needs; cf. Kraußlach/Stapf 2014: 204 on the *Kümmerer*, specific personnel dedicated to these tasks). In Aparicio's sample (2014: 36), 37.9 per cent of Spanish migrants living in Frankfurt had been received upon arrival by company representatives and 11.3 per cent by agency representatives; proportions considerably higher than in the case of Great Britain (London).

But many Spanish migrants heading to Germany do not travel with a contract in their hands and start looking for a job once they have arrived. According to Aparicio (2014: 41), of those migrants who find a job after arriving, the Internet is the main channel (47.3 per cent), followed by friends and relatives (21.6 per cent). Other channels are less relevant; for example, public and private employment agencies were only important for 10.8 per cent of these migrants and NGOs did not play a significant role.

Although public intermediation in Spanish migration to Germany is of limited importance when migrants are interviewed about their information sources, reception at destination and job search, some details concerning public initiatives should be added. In 2010, in response to the increasing demand for highly skilled immigrants in Germany (Hess 2009; Manpower Group 2014), Spain established a protocol called Bridges of Permanent Collaboration (Puentes de Colaboración Permanente, PCP), with the aim of matching professional supply and demand in the EU market, and linked it to EURES, a Common Market matching mechanism created in 1993 (Herrera 2014: 99). A large share of the relatively small amount of matches allocated through EURES is related to engineers, medical staff and architects. Most of the job searches by Spaniards who want to work abroad are characterized by low and selective coverage of public intervention.

Kraußlach/Stapf (2014) offer detailed results of an online survey conducted in 2013-2014 among German companies involved in recruitment initiatives. Their main findings reveal these initiatives are motivated by regional and branch-specific labor shortages, the importance of public funding (MobiPro-EU program; ESF-BAMF program[3] for supporting language skills), an increasing proportion of middle-sized companies participating in these recruitment initiatives, the focus on already skilled workers instead of recruiting trainees, the active cooperation with Spanish schools and universities, and the importance of language skills as a basic requirement for smooth and effective integration.

The actors participating in recruitment initiatives, according to Kraußlach/ Stapf (2014: 135), are employment agencies, educational institutions, commerce and industry chambers, and the companies themselves through their human resources staff. About half of the interviewees indicated they were directly in charge of the recruitment decisions, and among those who delegated recruitment to other partner organizations, the majority cooperated with partners in Spain, particularly with educational organizations and private recruitment companies. Spanish government agencies, chambers and companies were seen as less relevant (Kraußlach/Stapf 2014: 149-152).

Although most publications highlight the relevance of highly skilled Spanish emigrants to Germany (e.g., González-Ferrer 2013: 10), there are also public inter-state recruitment initiatives for less educated individuals. The German government promoted recruitment initiatives like "The job of my life", focusing on the recruitment of young trainees for vocational education in Germany, implemented by the German Employment Agency (Ganau/Porsche 2014: 10). Alba/Fernández (2015: 12) note the collaboration between the Andalusian and German employment agencies in programs for young, unemployed Spaniards who wanted to join the German *Ausbildung* and become butchers, office clerks, drivers, waiters, etc. Some of these initiatives raised concerns and media attention when the promised training and work conditions were not fulfilled (Alba/Fernández 2015: 16; Moreno 2013). The Program for Young Emigrants run

---

3   Language support program run by the Federal Office for Migration and Refugees (BAMF).

by the Ministerio de Empleo y Seguridad Social includes actions related to counseling, languages, employment, and return.[4]

As for the support received from the home country in the destination country, public Spanish support for emigrants living in Germany is perceived by migrants as rather limited, excessively bureaucratic and focused on the needs and interests of the community stemming from the earlier Spanish emigration to Germany. The representatives of the *Marea Granate* interviewed in Berlin in May 2015 clearly stated that their counseling of Spanish migrants was in place partly because there was no effective public alternative.

FINAL REMARKS

The economic crisis has intensified Spanish emigration to Germany in recent years. It is the first time that Spain is experiencing labor emigration to other EU countries under adverse economic circumstances and as a part of the Euro and Schengen zones. Consequently, it is Spain's first experience with labor emigration under conditions of free movement in the European Union and this chapter is focused on how public and private intermediation has unfolded under these conditions in the case of Spanish labor migration to Germany.

Does free movement imply more or less formal and institutionalized intermediation? On a general level of agency and context embeddedness, the interaction between institutional frameworks (structure) and intermediaries (agency) are noteworthy because the mobility restrictions create opportunity structures for intermediation (the so-called migration industry). In turn, free movement boosts self-selection of migrants and renders specific intermediation for border crossing useless. In light of the empirical evidence available, we find that self-organization of migrants in their mobility strategies seems to be an outstanding feature in a considerable proportion of todays' migration flows from Spain to Germany, particularly in the segment of migrants going to large cities like Berlin. Linked to self-organization, the informal networks within the migrant communities play a significant role in intermediation during the settlement process, especially in issues related to housing, language and bureaucratic procedures.

---

4 Budget data and legal conditions of this Program at http://www.boe.es/boe/dias/2015/05/14/pdfs/BOE-A-2015-5358.pdf. Examples of these subsidized initiatives for Germany are the "Picasso Project" (http://www.picassoproject.es/) and "Trabajo y oportunidades de negocio en Alemania para jóvenes españoles" (http://jovenesenalemania.fulp.es/).

Despite recognizing the relevance of self-organization and market mechanisms, public intermediation is still relevant and it is restricted basically to recruitment initiatives, oriented entirely by labor demand criteria, and has experienced a growing diversification in terms of the German host regions and business branches involved. The propelling force behind these initiatives implemented from the German side are regional and branch-specific labor shortages and, consequently, their design is meant to foster smooth and efficient recruitment in Spain in order to cover specific labor demands during the period of employment growth. These recruitment programs tend to establish active collaboration with educational organizations and private recruitment companies operating in Spain. Changes in the German business cycle and employment growth might have a profound impact on the recruitment schemes put into place during recent years.

The growing importance of transnational companies in the EU labor markets also has implications for intermediation processes in migration. In principle, internal labor markets do not need additional intermediaries but may outsource these functions due to the benefits of specialization. The large-scale multinational specialists hunting for talent are intertwined with company-specific recruitment and training programs. In the context of Spanish labor migration to Germany, these internal labor markets are not of outstanding quantitative relevance. In most cases these transnational initiatives are linked to German and not to Spanish multinational firms, as the geographical expansion of the latter is oriented towards other continents, especially South America.

Spanish labor migration to Germany is a socially and economically segmented phenomenon. This segmentation translates into specific profiles of intermediation needs and demands. Public intermediation is especially relevant if needs for intermediation go beyond labor demand issues and also involve social assistance, due to the lack of resources among migrants. Free movement implies public disintermediation in entry processes and if this disintermediation is extended to post-arrival settlement and social integration (EU citizens are not supposed to be immigrants in the European Union), less affluent EU migrants might suffer from a lack of public support in their integration processes. When facing these restrictions, intra-ethnic networks are an outstanding resource for compensation, but the introspective community solutions might be less effective in the long term and may restrict upward social mobility. The relatively high unemployment rates among Spanish migrants in Germany and their complaints about feeling abandoned by public institutions show that their integration is far from automatic and necessarily successful.

The migration of highly-skilled Spaniards to Germany is incipient and is expected to consolidate and diversify. Intermediation will develop alongside this migration flow and become more transnational, just as the EU labor market itself will integrate further through higher rates of international migration between Member States.

REFERENCES

Abella, Manolo (2004): "The Role of Recruiters in Labor Migration." In: Douglas. Massey/Edward Taylor (eds.), International Migration: Prospects and Policies in a Global Market, Oxford: Oxford University Press.

Alba, Susana/Fernández Asperilla, Ana (2015): Nueva emigración exterior y cuestión laboral. Fundación 1° de Mayo Colección Estudios núm 91, May 14, 2015 (www.1mayo.ccoo.es).

Alba Monteserin, Susana/Fernández Asperilla, Ana/Martínez Vega, Ubaldo (2013): Crisis económica y nuevo panorama migratorio en España. Centro de Documentación de las Migraciones de la Fundación 1° de Mayo, Colección Estudios No. 65, May 14, 2015 (www.1mayo.ccoo.es).

Aneesh, Aneesh (2001): "Rethinking Migration: On-Line Labor Flows from India to the United States." In: Wayne A. Cornelius/Thomas J. Espenshade/Idean Salehyan (eds.), The International Migration of the Highly Skilled,. San Diego: Center for Comparative Immigration Studies, pp. 351-372.

Aparicio Gómez, Rosa (2014): Aproximación a la Situación de los Españoles Emigrados: Realidad, Proyecto, Dificultades y Retos. Organización Internacional para las Migraciones, Representación en España, April 30, 2015 (http://www.spain.iom.int/index.php/component/banners/click/56).

Bach, Robert (2001): "New Dilemmas of Policy-Making in Transnational Labor Markets." In: Wayne A. Cornelius/Thomas J. Espenshade/Idean Salehyan (eds.), The International Migration of the Highly Skilled, San Diego: Center for Comparative Immigration Studies, pp. 113-130.

Bertoli, Simone/Brücker, Herbert/Fernández-Huertas Moraga, Jesús (2013): The European Crisis and Migration to Germany: Expectations and the Diversion of Migration Flows. IZA Discussion Paper, No. 7170, May 30, 2015 (http://ftp.iza.org/dp7170.pdf).

Domínguez-Mujica, Josefina/Díaz-Hernández, Ramón/Parreño-Castellano, Juan (2016): "Migrating Abroad to Get Ahead: The Emigration of Young Spanish Adults During the Financial Crisis (2008-2013)." In: Josefina Domínguez-Mujica (ed.), Global Change and Human Mobility, New York: Springer, pp. 203-224.

Faist, Thomas (2009): "The crucial meso-level." In Marco Martiniello/Jan Rath (eds.), Selected Studies in International Migration and Immigrant Incorporation, Amsterdam: Amsterdam University Press, pp. 59-90.

Faraco Blanco, Cristina/Castillo Castilla, Esther/Krausslach, Marianne/Montero Lange, Miguel (2013): Proyecto Nueva Emigración. Informe final. Coordinadora Federal del Movimiento Asociativo en la RFA/Bundesverband spanischer sozialer und kultureller Vereine e.V., April 30, 2015 (http://www.iree.org/mediapool/132/1325651/data/PNM_Informe_final_30.9_1_.pdf).

Fernandez, Bina (2013): "Traffickers, Brokers, Employment Agents, and Social Networks: The Regulation of Intermediaries in the Migration of Ethiopian Domestic Workers to the Middle East." In: International Migration Review, No. 47, pp. 814-843.

Fuchs, Johann/Kubis, Alexander/Schneider, Lutz (2015): Zuwanderungsbedarf aus Drittstaaten in Deutschland bis 2050. Bertelsmann Stiftung, May 10, 2015 (www.bertelsmann-stiftung.de).

Ganau, Joan/Porsche, Corinna (2014): "De nuevo emigrantes. Las nuevas dinámicas de emigración de la población española y la formación de un mercado laboral europeo (2008-2014)." In: XIV Congreso Nacional de Población, AGE, Sevilla, September 9, 2015 (http://www.agepoblacion.org/images/congresos/sevilla/DOC27.pdf).

González Enríquez, Carmen/Martínez Romera, José Pablo (2014): Country Focus: Migration of Spanish nationals during the crisis. Elcano Royal Institute, Madrid, April 15, 2015 (http://www.realinstitutoelcano.org/wps/portal/web/rielcano_en/contenido?WCM_GLOBAL_CONTEXT=/elcano/elcano_in/zonas_in/gonzalezenriquez-martinezromera-espana-emigracion-espanoles-crisis-spain-migration-crisis).

González-Ferrer, Amparo (2013): "La nueva emigración española. Lo que sabemos y lo que no." In: Laboratorio de la Fundación Alternativas, ZoomPolítico 18, May 14, 2015 (http://www.fundacionalternativas.org/public/storage/publicaciones_archivos/5785a8486ea7ec776fd341c9ee8f4b7b.pdf).

Hernández-León, Raúl (2013): "Conceptualizing the migration industry." In: Thomas Gammeltoft-Hansen/Ninna Nyberg Sorensen (eds.), The Migration Industry and the Commercialization of International Migration, London: Routledge, pp. 24-44.

Herrera, María Jesús (2014): "Migración cualificada de trabajadores de España al extranjero." In: Anuario de la Inmigración en España 2014, Barcelona: CIDOB, September 30, 2015 (http://www.cidob.org/es/articulos/anuario_de_la_inmigracion_en_espana/2014/migracion_cualificada_de_profesionales_de_espana_al_extranjero).

Hess, Barbara (2009): Zuwanderung von Hochqualifizierten aus Drittstaaten nach Deutschland, Working Paper 28 der Forschungsgruppe des Bundesamtes für Migration und Flüchtlinge, September 30, 2015 (http://www.bamf.de /SharedDocs/Anlagen/DE/Publikationen/WorkingPapers/wp28-hochqualfizie rte.html?nn=1663566).

Izquierdo, Mario/Jimeno, Juan Francisco/Lacuesta, Aitor (2014): "La emigración de españoles durante la Gran Recesión (2008-2013)." In: Cuadernos Económicos de ICE, No. 87, May 14, 2015 (http://www.revistasice.com /CachePDF/CICE_87___6BDA4E47903E58D055F14CAC795721E7.pdf).

Kraußlach, Marianne/Stapf, Tobias (2014): "Das Forschungsprojekt Bestandserhebung Neue Arbeitsmigration." In: Christian Pfeffer-Hoffmann (ed.), Arbeitsmigration nach Deutschland. Analysen zur Neuen Arbeitsmigration aus Spanien vor dem Hintergrund der Migrationsprozesse seit 1960, Berlin: Mensch & Buch Verlag, pp. 110-212.

Lester, Stephanie E. (2012): La Generación Ni Ni and the Exodus of Spanish Youth: National Crisis or Functioning European Union Market? Scripps Senior Theses, Paper 83, September 15, 2015, (http://scholarship.claremont. edu/scripps_theses/83).

Li, F.L.N./Findlay, Allan M./Jowett, A.J./Skeldon, Ronald (1996): "Migration to Learn and Learning to Migrate: A Study of the Experiences and Intentions of International Student Migrants." In: International Journal of Population Geography, vol. 2, pp. 51-67.

ManpowerGroup (2014): Studie Fachkräftemangel Deutschland 2014. May 10, 2015 (https://www.manpower.de/neuigkeiten/).

Martinez Calero, Mercedes/Rohloff, Sigurdur (2014): "Spanische Migrantinnen und Migranten der ersten Generation und ihre Nachkommen in Deutschland: Zum Zusammenhang zwischen bürgerschaftlichem Engagement und Bildungserfolg." In: Christian Pfeffer-Hoffmann (ed.), Arbeitsmigration nach Deutschland. Analysen zur Neuen Arbeitsmigration aus Spanien vor dem Hintergrund der Migrationsprozesse seit 1960, Berlin: Mensch & Buch Verlag, pp. 312-354.

Massey, Douglas S./Arango, Joaquín/Hugo, Graeme/Kouaouci, Ali/Pellegrino, Adela/Taylor, J. Edward (1998): Worlds in Motion. Understanding International Migration at the End of the Millennium. International Studies in Demography, Oxford: Clarendon Press.

Montero Lange, Miguel (2014): "Innereuropäische Mobilität am Beispiel der neuen spanischen Arbeitsmigration nach Deutschland." In: Christian Pfeffer-Hoffmann (ed.), Arbeitsmigration nach Deutschland. Analysen zur Neuen

Arbeitsmigration aus Spanien vor dem Hintergrund der Migrationsprozesse seit 1960, Berlin: Mensch & Buch Verlag, pp. 12-105.

Moreno Díaz, José Antonio (2013): "Emigración española: frente a los abusos y la desinformación, asesoramiento e intervención sindical." In: Revista de Estudios y Cultura, No. 56, diciembre, 61, November 20, 2015 (http://www.1mayo.ccoo.es/nova/files/1018/Revista56.pdf).

Muñoz Sánchez, Antonio (2012): "Una introducción a la historia de la emigración española en la República Federal de Alemania (1960-1980)." In: Iberoamericana, XII(46), pp. 23-42.

Navarrete Moreno, Lorenzo et al. (2014): La emigración de los jóvenes españoles en el contexto de la crisis. Análisis y datos de un fenómeno difícil de cuantificar. Serie Estudios del Observatorio de la Juventud en España, Servicio de Documentación y Estudios, Madrid, April 30, 2015 (www.injuve.es).

Nyberg Sorensen, Ninna/Gammeltoft-Hansen, Thomas (2013): "Introduction." In: Thomas Gammeltoft-Hansen and Ninna Nyberg Sorensen (eds.), The Migration Industry and the Commercialization of International Migration, London: Routledge, pp. 1-23.

Petuya Ituarte, Begoña/Muñoz Sánchez, Antonio/Montero Lange, Miguel (2014): Die Forschungsreihe: "Annäherung an die Situation der spanischen Bürger/- innen in Deutschland." In: Christian Pfeffer-Hoffmann (ed.), Arbeitsmigration nach Deutschland. Analysen zur Neuen Arbeitsmigration aus Spanien vor dem Hintergrund der Migrationsprozesse seit 1960, Berlin: Mensch & Buch Verlag, pp. 241-280.

Santos Ortega, Antonio (2013): "Fuga de cerebros y crisis en España: los jóvenes en el punto de mira de los discursos empresariales." In: Areas, No. 32, pp. 125-137.

Sevillano Canicio, Victor (2014): "Der Bildungserfolg der spanischen Migrant/-innen in Deutschland, ein Zufall? Eine Einführung in die Unterstützungsnetzwerke und ihre Akteure (1960-1990)." In: Christian Pfeffer-Hoffmann (ed.), Arbeitsmigration nach Deutschland. Analysen zur Neuen Arbeitsmigration aus Spanien vor dem Hintergrund der Migrationsprozesse seit 1960, Berlin: Mensch & Buch Verlag, pp. 355-395.

Thränhardt, Dietrich (2014): "Der Bildungs- und Integrationserfolg der spanischen Einwander/-innen in Europa." In: Christian Pfeffer-Hoffmann (ed.), Arbeitsmigration nach Deutschland. Analysen zur Neuen Arbeitsmigration aus Spanien vor dem Hintergrund der Migrationsprozesse seit 1960, Berlin: Mensch & Buch Verlag, pp. 281-311.

Xiang, Biao/Lindquist, Johan (2014): "Migration Infrastructure." In: International Migration Review, No. 48, pp. S122-S148.

9. Recruiting from Spain – a qualitative insight into Spanish-German labor migration projects

PHILLIP MEINARDUS

ABSTRACT

This paper focuses on the institutional framing of migration processes, with particular emphasis on the strategy and implementation in the recruitment process. With regard to demographic changes in Germany, a change of mentality can be noted, admitting that not only the achievements of the migrants, but also the accomplishments of German society are of importance.

The main research question was to identify the decisive procedures for a successful recruitment of employees from abroad, as well as the implementation of these procedures. Additionally the origins of the projects as well as the contacts between the participating actors were analyzed. The study is based on expert interviews, which were conducted mostly with individuals at the management level, including civil servants and diplomats. Besides officials also those persons central to the topic – the migrants – got a chance to express their point of view.

It turned out that a 'welcoming culture' is especially important in order to successfully integrate skilled workers from abroad. In case of shortcomings of the welcoming environment, migration projects have to balance this shortcoming. This implies assistance at every stage of the migration process. Of particular importance, but nevertheless often underestimated, is the opportunity to learn German. In general the need for assistance seems to be decreasing with increasing age and level of education. Depending on the branches, the willingness to take the economic risk and invest money and effort into the adaptation process of labor migrants differs considerably. In comparison to past migration, all projects are aimed at the recruitment of qualified persons or of persons who are going to be qualified in Germany.

Keywords: Demographic change, Economic crisis, Skilled migration, Welcoming culture

INTRODUCTION AND RESEARCH FOCUS

The German labor market has experienced a remarkable recovery in the past decade. Unemployment currently seems no longer to be the main challenge. Due to the well known structural processes of demographic change, with Germany's decreasing and ageing population, this situation is not expected to change in the medium or even in the longer term (cf. Friedrich/Schlömer 2013; Laux 2012; Ragnitz 2008; Statistisches Bundesamt 2015). On the contrary, predictions assume a bottleneck in the potential labor supply for the next decades (Fuchs et al. 2011: 1-4; Maier et al. 2012: 4-5).

However, within the labor market, demand and supply differ considerably, depending on the grade of education and the line of occupation (Kalinowski/Quinke 2010: 111-115). In the past supply as well as demand developed towards high levels of qualification (Koppel/Plünnecke 2009: 8). This trend towards flexibility, education and qualification is assumed to be ongoing due to lasting structural and technical changes. Human capital has and will become more important than in past decades (Hardege/Klös 2008: 23-24, Hummel et al. 2010: 98).

The cited studies give an overview on a highly aggregated scale, neglecting regional and sectoral differentiation, which are considerable in the case of Germany. First, each situation differs significantly depending on the geographical location and the region's economic orientation. Second, in a highly differentiated economy, highly specified qualifications become more and more important. This concerns qualified jobs at all levels of education. That means that a supply gap can occur in a small geographical or occupational context, even if a supply surplus is apparent on a higher scale (Maier et al. 2012: 9). Currently, in a nationwide context, there is no supply gap existing (Bundesagentur für Arbeit 2012: 3). Nevertheless, some branches in some regions are under pressure, and regarding the health sector this is the case in nearly all regions and at all educational levels (Bundesagentur für Arbeit 2012: 8-10). Referring to technical occupations, demand is high in the high qualified occupations in the fields of, for example, machine construction, automobile construction, electrical engineering and information technology. But even on the level of skilled workers some bottlenecks still are apparent. These are mainly concentrated in the western part of Germany (Bundesagentur für Arbeit 2012: 4-6).

To react to this development, different approaches are discussed, aiming to raise the labor supply and adapt labor force to changing demands through continuous education and qualification processes. In doing so, the mobilization of the domestic potential seems to be most promising (Bundesagentur für Arbeit 2011a: 16-25), even if a full balancing can hardly be reached (Hülskamp et al. 2008: 130). As one measure, the recruitment of skilled employees from foreign countries has become more and more topical.

In the face of the economic crisis in southern European states, a huge number of well-educated young people have seen themselves confronted with almost no prospect for entering the domestic labor market. Not surprisingly, the migration flows from the countries in crisis to Germany began to increase significantly, from less than 10,000 migrants per year in 2008 up to nearly 35,000 in 2014 (Statistisches Bundesamt 2015; cf. Glorius 2016). The scientific research indicates clear differences to past migration flows from Spain to Germany, which were dominated by unskilled workers ('guest worker'). Nowadays the majority of migrants are well educated and qualified (Domínguez Mujica et al. 2016).

Beside individual migration, some organized forms exist. Companies, employers' associations or even public stakeholders are trying to fill existing or supposed gaps in the labor market by recruiting skilled migrants from abroad. All these projects have in common that they act in a quite new field, often missing any previous practical experience. Even mutual exchange hardly exists. Up to now, scientific research examining and evaluating such initiatives is scarce.

This study aims at giving an initial insight into such migration initiatives brought into being in the context of the economic crisis in southern European countries. Data was collected in the context of a diploma thesis in 2013 at the University of Würzburg. The research focus was on identifying the aspects and measures that are indispensable for a successful recruitment of foreign employees. In the following section the methodological approach, the scope of the study, the observed projects and the results from expert interviews are presented.

RESEARCH STRATEGY AND METHODOLOGICAL APPROACH

Facing the lack of scientific research and studies available about current Spanish-German recruitment projects, the study pursues a qualitative approach, focusing on experts with special insights into the field. Due to their professional involvement, their knowledge regarding technical and procedural steps as well as their interpretation are of special relevance (Bogner 2009: 71-73).

The empirical data was collected by means of problem-focused expert interviews. Giving a framework, semi-structured interview guides were developed. They had to be adapted to each actor's respective role. In the run-up to the interviews, information about the initiatives – if available – was picked, structured and added to the prevailing interview guide (Lamnek 2010: 364). This approach provides a framework for structuring and analyzing the collected material while staying open to new perspectives.

Following a sequential selection, further interview partners can be detected, and the interview guidelines are to be modified on a continuous basis (Meier Kruker 2005: 76). The main concern has been to identify the decisive procedures for successfully recruiting skilled workers from abroad, and the way these procedures were implemented. Accordingly the prevailing study focused on best practice-projects. Experts' insights and contacts were crucial for extracting promising projects from a whole range of existing initiatives. In this context, especially the role of the Spanish Embassy in Berlin has to be mentioned, which apparently has the best overview about existing projects and mediated contact persons for further investigation.

The expert interviews were held in the usual working environment of the interviewed persons. The interviews were recorded on the scene and transcribed. The analysis was done by means of a structuring content analysis (Mayring 2002: 114-121). Important information was marked in a first step. In several following steps a paramount system of categories had to be formed, giving a structure to the collected information. As this is a dynamic working process, these categories had to be modified continually. Finally a comparison of the evaluated projects with regard to the most important aspects was carried out.

Altogether 14 interviews with 18 persons were held between April and August 2013 (table 9.1). They focused on projects that recruited Spanish migrants for the German labor market. The nine cases that were selected for this study contain mainly projects that supported, facilitated and organized recruitment and thus acted as intermediators between migrants and companies (table 9.2). Within those projects, a large number of actors appeared, among them representatives of state authorities (embassy, ministries), non-governmental organizations (chambers, labor agencies), and private entrepreneurs. The interview partners came from the leadership positions in these projects. It goes without saying that the goals, procedures and capabilities of these actors differ considerably depending on their own roles and the way they give meaning to their professional role. Also it is to be noted that all projects were in different stages of the recruitment process. Even if not highlighted during the interviews, nearly all observed projects were controversial within their own institution or company, as accompanying research evinced.

Three of the examined nine projects were implemented by stakeholders from the public sector, and again these projects are distinct from one another. One project was carried out by a small municipality in the northern part of Bavaria (Wunsiedel, about 10,000 inhabitants), the second by the social ministry of Hessen, and the third by the job agency of a city in the southern part of Bavaria (Regensburg, more than 135,000 inhabitants). All of these projects operated as mediators between employers and migrants.

The other six projects were carried out by private actors. Especially employers' associations played an important role. Two different projects were launched by chambers of crafts, another by a bio-cluster and the fourth by the educational institute of the Bavarian chamber of economy. Whereas these associations represent different companies and also appeared as mediators, two employers initiated projects directly at their own companies; both were larger clinics from the southern part of Germany (table 9.2).

To get a more comprehensive picture, some other experts from closely linked fields were called in. First to mention is the Spanish Embassy in Berlin (Department of Work and Social Affairs), which seems to have the best overview of current migration initiatives. Also interviews with specialists from the Federal Employment Agency (*Bundesagentur für Arbeit – BA*), the Federal Office for Migration and Refugees (*Bundesamt für Migration und Flüchtlinge – BAMF*) and the German Federation of Trade Unions (*Deutscher Gewerkschaftsbund – DGB*) were conducted. Another interview was performed with an employer (automotive, about 300 employees) who participated at the mentioned project of the job agency Regensburg. All in all, the experiences of three employers could be evaluated. To complete the picture, also the migrant's view was captured by an interview with a young Spanish migrant, who participated in one of the observed projects.

Table 9.1: Interview partners

	Institution/ Organisation	Interview partner (position, sex, age)	Int.-nr.
Public sector			
	City of Wunsiedel Social Ministry of Hessen	Mayor of Wunsiedel; male; 55 to 60 years	Int_02
	Social Ministry of Hessen	Expert in the social ministry of Hessen, male, 50 to 60 years	Int_10
	Ministry of Economy, Traffic and State Development	Head of the division for vocational training in the Ministry of Economy in Hessen; male, 50 to 60 years	
	Ministry of Economy, Traffic and State Development	Expert of the division for vocational training in the Ministry of Economy in Hessen, female; 30 to 40 years	
	Job Agency Regensburg	Corporative director; male; 30 to 40 years	Int_03
	Embassy of Spain, Berlin	Expert of the division for labor and social affairs; male; 40 to 50 years	Int_05
	Federal Office for Migration and Refugees (BAMF)	Head of the division in the Federal Office for Migration and Refugees; responsible for the occupational language classes (ESF-BAMF); male; 35 to 40 years	Int_06

Private sector			
	Chamber of Trade and Crafts München	Employee of the chamber of Trade and Crafts; female; 20 to 30 years	Int_08
	Educational Institute of Bavarian Economy (BBW)	Expert from the BBW; male; 40 to 50 years	Int_07
	Bio Cluster (Anonymous)	Head of a Biotech-Cluster; male; 55 to 60 years	Int_01
	Clinic 1 (anonymous)	Care manager; male; 30 to 40 years	Int_04
	Clinic 2 (anonymous)	Regional personal manager; male; 40 to 50 years	Int_11
	AVL Software and Functions Regensburg	Chief executive; male; 50 to 60 years	Int_12
	AVL Software and Functions Regensburg	Employee and Spanish migrant; engineer; female; 25 to 30 years	Int_13
	German Federation of Trade Unions, Bavaria	Expert for policy and international affairs; male, 50 to 60 years	Int_14

Source: own survey

MOTIVATION AND CONSIDERATIONS REGARDING RECRUITMENT FROM SPAIN

In the following section, the main stakeholders, their motivation and target groups dependent on their role within these projects are examined.

Main stakeholders and their motivation

A view on the required educational levels and occupations in the examined projects confirms the main needs of the German labor market, as discussed above.

First we can differentiate regarding education level and work experience (table 9.2). Five of the nine observed projects dealt with the recruitment of people with vocational degree and some work experience. Two projects concentrated on highly qualified persons, while working experience was not required. Two other projects focused on the recruitment of apprentices ready to receive vocational training in Germany.

Regarding the branches, the abovementioned occupations were dominating (table 9.2). The two projects with focus on highly qualified persons aimed at recruiting engineers and IT-specialists. Nursing staff (in clinics and homes for the elderly), partly with very special qualifications, was the target group of three other projects. With main emphasis to avoid shortages in special fields of qualified craftspeople, two projects focused especially on system mechanics, roof slaters, electricians and metalworkers. Only one project had no specific target group. All observed projects dealt with the recruitment of qualified persons or persons that were meant to start vocational training.

Table 9.2: Branch and required experience/educational level

Nr.	Project initiated by	Branch	Required experience/ educational level
1	City of Wunsiedel	Craftsmen: no special focus	Experienced/vocational degree
2	Social Ministry of Hessen	Nursing staff/geriatric care	Experienced/vocational degree
3	Job Agency Regensburg	IT-specialists/engineers	Experience subordinated/high qualified
4	Chamber of Skilled Crafts Franfurt/Main	Craftsmen: esp. roof slater, electricians, system mechanics	Experience subordinated/apprentices
5	Chamber of Trade and Crafts München	Craftsmen: esp. electricians	Experienced/vocational degree

6	Educational Institute of Bavarian Economy (BBW)	Craftsmen: esp. metalworker, electricians	Experience subordinated/apprentices
7	Bio-Cluster (Anonymous)	IT-specialists/engineers	Experience subordinated/high qualified
8	Clinic 1 (Anonymous)	Nursing staff	Experienced/vocational degree
9	Clinic 2 (Anonymous)	Nursing staff	Experienced with special qualification

Source: own survey

There were also significant variations in the time frame within the action was to yield results, reaching from immediate over medium-term to long-term strategies. All projects within the health sector had a clear concentration in the recruitment aspect, as there are severe labor force shortages in this field, thus calling for immediate action. A head of a unit in the Social Ministry of Hessen describes the situation:

"[...] we don't have a bottleneck, but a lack of skilled employees. [...] In the area of [our federal estate we have] more than 3,500 vacant jobs. That's why we started to think outside the box."[1]

This statement also holds true for the other observed projects in the health sector. The engagement in international recruiting was clearly motivated by the companies' needs, as the following statement clarifies:

"[...] the decisive factor are needs in the companies. [...] It is not about doing a charitable act for Spanish adolescents. The approach is clearly economic, business[-oriented] [...]. We have a demand for skilled employees."[2]

---

1 "Da ist es so, dass wir keinen Fachkräfteengpass haben, sondern wir haben einen Fachkräftemangel. [...] Im Bereich [...][unseres Bundeslandes haben wir] über 3.500 unbesetzte Stellen. [...] deshalb die Initiative, über den Tellerrand hinauszuschauen." (Int_10, 25.07.2013, pp. 4-5)

Indeed, all projects only recruited employees with definite job offers. But, in contrast to the projects in the health sector, the strategic approach was more important in the other projects, anticipating that the effort would pay off maybe not immediately, but in the long run. The main goals include gathering experience in international recruitment while anticipating a challenging future. The number of recruited persons was not the crucial factor. Consequently all projects defined themselves as pioneer projects. A competitive situation in Europe was highlighted by several interviewed persons. In their opinion, especially Germany, with its missing migration tradition, had to make a greater effort than other countries.

What does this mean? Collecting experience in this context has a double-faced character: first, experience was necessary concerning the essential steps in recruiting skilled people from abroad. Whom to ask? Who are my partners? Where to look for applicants? What costs are connected to a recruiting process from Spain?

Second, experience relates to the creation of a 'welcoming culture' in Germany. Especially the projects initiated from the public branch accentuated the positive impacts for Germany as a destination country for migrants. Raising the attraction of the whole country or a special region by implementing a welcoming culture is one important side effect. Currently additional requirements in comparison to other countries are seen as indispensable by the majority of the interviewed persons. But signal effects are not only outward-orientated. Hesitancy towards international recruitment in the society as a whole is seen as objection. Beside obstacles by authorities, even companies and employers' associations had insufficient visions for how to act in this field. In respect to these, the projects also are meant to stress the positive impact and the feasibility of international recruitment.

Finally, the research tried to find out why the geographical focus of those recruitment initiatives was concentrating on Spain. Due to the economic situation in the context of the crisis, all initiators became attentive to the topic in general and to Spain in particular. The high education level of the younger Spanish generation was an important aspect. Also the similar cultural background in comparison to migrants from other countries was assessed as an advantage. But also the acceptance by the German population was an argument, as some respondents pointed out; there are fewer prejudices against Spanish migrants as compared to

---

2   "[…] der entscheidende Faktor [sind] Bedarfe in den Unternehmen. […] Weil es eben nicht den Hintergrund hat, wir machen hier jetzt eine große Sozialtat für spanische Jugendliche. Der Ansatz ist ganz klar volkswirtschaftlich, betriebswirtschaftlich […]: wir haben einen Fachkräftebedarf." (Int_07, 19.07.2013, p. 15)

others, in particular from Eastern Europe. Furthermore, in two cases, strong personal ties of the interviewees drew the attention to Spain.

Aims and target definition

In accordance with the underlying motivations and the different roles of the actors, the aims and target definitions within these projects are distinct. Apart from the general objective of gaining experiences in international recruitment and how to develop a 'welcoming culture', the actors pursued tangible, measurable goals, defining benchmarks for evaluation of the projects' success.

Depending on the actor's role, the target definitions differ considerably. Some interviewees act as an agent or mediator between employers and employees. From this point of view, the aspect of matching is the most important indicator of success. Given a specific job offer, adequate candidates had to be selected and afterwards brought together with the potential employers. Data indicates that this aspect worked out quite well. In most cases the vacant positions could be filled, even if some adjustments had to be taken into account.

Whereas mediators concentrate on the matching between employers' needs and the candidates' profiles, the employers focus on the sustainability of the recruitment process, meaning that the candidate would stay in the company for a considerable time and thus pay off the initial investment of money and efforts. A certain decrease is seen as inevitable by the interviewed employers, but within a time span of about five years, a retention rate of about 80 per cent is assessed as indicator of successful recruitment. In light of the necessary investment, employers see this as an economic imperative. Only if the investment is rewarding will such a project be judged as successful. A method of measurement would be to calculate costs in relation to the hired individuals and compare it to other recruiting processes.

Those projects that dealt with the recruitment for apprenticeships had a differing perspective, mainly defining the successful completion of vocational training as benchmark. However, considering the young age of the trainees and anticipating problems of social integration, the interviewees were cautious regarding long-term expectations, anticipating adaptation difficulties especially in case of the migrants of young age.

Recruitment procedure

The following passage deals with the contacts and partners in Germany as well as in Spain, and reveals concrete recruitment measures within the examined projects before clarifying a number of enlistments and – as far as possible – the financial costs.

Network partners in Germany

It seems to be a simple fact, yet it must be stated that one basic condition for recruiting foreign skilled employees is the existence of a person in charge who is willing to take on the risk within their own institution, company or association. From this starting point, the majority of initiatives acted in networks. All initiators had a good overview of and deep insights into the labor market.

The two employers from the health sector worked mainly on their own, only calling in experts for special tasks (for example language acquisition). The other projects acted within wider networks, cooperating with employers, public sector, civil society and employers' associations in Germany. Thus risks and costs could be divided.

As the health sector is under far more pressure than other branches, the numbers of recruited individuals and the willingness to take recruitment risks seem to be higher. Another difference occurred considering the varying capabilities of the actors. Small and medium-sized companies seemed to be more dependent on cooperation recruiting international labor force. Huge companies in contrast could afford to take on costs and risk on their own.

In all of our nine examined projects (table 9.2), stakeholders had good contacts to potential companies and therefore an insight in potential bottlenecks on the local labor market. However, in contrast to the often articulated needs, the first challenge was finding companies that were willing to participate in the project. Moreover, the willingness to participate decreased continuously in the course of the projects. Respondents explained this behavior through the still-existing supply within the market and insufficient awareness regarding the consequences of demographic change. As the data shows, the most important reason for the decline were the costs of international recruiting. In the examined projects, the mediating institutions only accepted employers who were fully aware of the efforts to be done during the integration process. That was considered as an absolutely essential precondition, as the following statement of a person in charge from the southern German job agency shows:

"The employers are prepared by us, in the run-up to a project, in a way that [...] [it is better if] he jumps off and he knows why he jumped off, [...] before we disappoint some individual candidates. That is not necessary."[3]

Developing the concept and defining concrete steps and requirements, specialists were called in. Preferential partners were clearly the employers' associations, but in one case even the local job agency was involved. Exchange with vocational schools also turned out to be useful. The Federal Office of Migrants and Refugees (BAMF), which provides for language and integration classes, played an outstanding role regarding language acquisition. In the political sphere, contacts to the ministries concerned were useful. In two cases, ministries (social and economic) from the Federal State of Hesse were directly involved. Also the collaboration with the Federal Ministry of Work and Social Affairs and its subordinated authority, the International Placement Service (Zentrale Auslands- und Fachvermittlung – ZAV), was of great importance. This authority is in charge of the MobiPro-EU program, which supports the recruitment of foreign apprentices to Germany.[4] Two examined projects (BBW and Chamber of Skilled Crafts, Frankfurt am Main) participated within the MobiPro-EU program. Contacts to the local ethnic community of Spaniards were also useful, especially when it came to integration measures.

Also of outstanding importance was the role of the Spanish embassy in Berlin: all examined projects were in direct contact with the Spanish embassy. The contact was either established by initiators or actively by the Spanish embassy itself. Having deep insights into different projects, the embassy played an important role as advisor. On the other hand, there were no networking activities or even any direct contacts between various migration projects. This might be due to the early stage and the geographic distance of the projects. However, as one respondent conceded, even rivalry plays a partial role in that context.

Networks and partners in Spain

Before analyzing the partner and recruiting channels in Spain in detail, a view on the regions and especially their selection mode is of importance. Similarity in

---

3 "Wir seifen die Arbeitgeber im Vorfeld so tief mit der Materie ein, dass [...] [es besser ist, wenn] [...] er [...][ab] springt und weiß aber dann auch, warum er abgesprungen ist [...] bevor wir irgendwelche Menschen da enttäuschen. Und das muss nicht sein." (Int_03, 19.06.2013, p. 16)

4 Information about the program: https://www.thejobofmylife.de/en/home.html.

economic structure and size of source and destination region was an explicit selection criterion, as two respondents accentuated. Other initiatives developed their projects along already existing ties between actors of different fields (especially the political and economic sphere). Even though not highlighted equally, a certain coincidence in scale and economic structure was also given.

Other projects had no preliminary selection apart from concentration on bigger agglomerations. Only two out of nine projects had no regional focus and recruited nationwide.

As an example, the BBW initiative (table 9.2) intentionally tried several options in three different regions. The Basque region was selected due to their metalworking industry corresponding to the structure and needs of the represented Bavarian companies. By choosing the capital Madrid, connections and contacts to the central government should be implemented. Last but not least, the existing ties between the industries in Catalonia and Bavaria caused the third core area.

In order to avoid "blind recruitment"[5], competent partners on-site had to be found. Throughout the cases, there was a wide range of partners and considerable difference of strategies, as the following statement indicates:

"We have different partners. In Santander our contact on-site is a FLM, a Fundación Laboral de Metal[6] [...]. In Madrid we collaborate with the Communidad de Madrid very close. There are even different training centers like in Santander. In Barcelona we collaborate with the Goethe Institute. We collaborate with [...] the Catalonian labor administration and in principle with the education authority of the Generalidad de Catalonia."[7]

Without any practical experience in the international recruiting process, different approaches were used. It is to be assumed that, on the one hand, selection of partners to a certain degree depended on the availability of given structures or

---

5 "[...] blindes Anwerben [...]." (Int_06, 12.07.2103, p. 11)
6 Author's note: among other functions they operate training centers. More information: http://fundacionlaboraldelmetal.com/.
7 "Wir haben von den Partnern her ganz unterschiedliche. In Santander ist unsere Ansprechorganisation vor Ort eine FLM, eine *Fundación Laboral de Metal*. [...] In Madrid arbeiten wir mit der *Communidad de Madrid* sehr eng zusammen. Dort gibt es auch entsprechend viele Bildungszentren, ähnlich wie in Santander. In Barcelona arbeiten wir mit dem Goethe-Institut intensiv zusammen. Wir arbeiten mit [...] der katalanischen Arbeitsverwaltung [...] zusammen und grundsätzlich noch mit der Bildungsbehörde der *Generalidad* in Katalonien." (Int_07, 19.07.2013, pp. 2-3)

organizations on-site. On the other hand a multichannel approach seems to reduce risk and enables different learning experiences.

Also the other initiatives collaborated with several contacts, but usually there was one of special importance. Also, the cooperation with the international placement service (ZAV) and their contacts to the Spanish job centers were of importance. The same applies for associations and actors from the political sphere. Even the Goethe Institute's role as first contact especially to young people in Spain has to be mentioned. The initiators tended to make contacts with institutions or organizations corresponding to their own, in regard to the line of business or branch as well as to the actor's level within this area.

Recruiting process and its outcomes

With respect to recruiting processes some general patterns, but also some differences, were identified.

Six out of nine projects organized recruiting events in Spain. In most cases job advertisements were published by the Spanish partner before the events took place. The whole range of information channels was used (nevertheless mainly internet and newspapers). After a pre-selection of candidates, invitations to information events were pronounced and carried out on-site. Usually the employers were directly involved. Afterwards the job interviews were carried out, sometimes face to face, sometimes via Skype. It is to be stated that being present on site is a quite expensive issue, as the following statement illustrates:

"We were in Madrid with 30 employers and 110 job advertisements and there came about 400 applicants [...]. The Spanish partner of the Federal employment agency [...] organized the venue. On the other hand they selected the candidates. The employers [...] presented their companies [...] and the applicants were able to inform themselves about the employers. There were ten interpreters on-site for facilitating the job interviews [...].The amount of organizational work was relatively high. But I think it was necessary doing it that way. Really a first step. I don't think we will do it the same way again in the future. [...] But in the starting period of this model project, this effort surely was necessary."[8]

---

8 "Wir waren mit 30 Arbeitgebern in Madrid, 110 offenen Stellenangeboten und es kamen dann ungefähr 400 Bewerber. [...] das ist gelaufen über [...] die spanischen Partner von [...] der Bundesagentur für Arbeit, die uns den Raum gestellt haben. Die auf der anderen Seite die Auswahl der Bewerber sichergestellt haben. [...] die Arbeitgeber [...] haben ihre Unternehmen vorgestellt. Und die Bewerber hatten dann die Möglichkeit, sich die verschiedenen Arbeitgeber anzuschauen. Es waren zehn Dolmetscher

Those projects that dealt with the recruitment of apprentices chose an alternative way. The companies were not directly present on-site. After an information event, the initiators selected a range of adequate candidates (up to three) and the companies chose their favorites. In case of interest on both sides, the next step was a short probationary period in Germany (from some days up to one month), followed by a joint decision whether or not to start an apprenticeship. With respect to the outcomes and financial cost the data is incomplete, as most of the projects treated this information as confidential. Nevertheless some basic information can be given. Within eight projects (one respondent made no statement) 195 persons were hired. One employer estimates the additional expenses for one foreign skilled employee at about 5,000€ in the first months (project from the medical branch: clinic 2; table 9.2). An employers' association that recruited 51 foreign apprentices parallely created seven full-time positions to assist the integration process. In another case, 44 apprentices were engaged, the total costs were calculated at about 200,000€. Further indirect costs arise out of the fact that the employees or apprentices take language classes during the work time. Even though these calculations seem rather provisional and incomplete, it becomes clear that recruiting from foreign countries is connected with additional costs.

RECEPTION AND INTEGRATION OF FOREIGN EMPLOYEES AND APPRENTICES

German migration policy was traditionally focused on low-educated workers. After the recruitment stop of 1973, Germany pursued a very restrictive labor market policy with regards to labor migration and migration in general (OECD 2013: 67-70). Only since the end of the 1990s the attitude towards immigration gradually changed. The implementation of the German Migration Law in 2004 (*Aufenthaltsgesetz*) can be interpreted as a statement of being an immigration country, detailing immigration and labor market entry for third country nationals for the first time. This was followed by a public debate on the integration conditions of German society. The key term concerning the reception and integration conditions was the notion of a 'welcoming culture' (Kober 2012: 13-15). The

---

vor Ort, um tatsächlich auch Bewerbungsgespräche zu führen […]. Das war vom Organisationsaufwand auf relativ hohem Level. Das war aber, glaube ich, auch notwendig, das so zu machen. Tatsächlich ein erster Schritt. Ob man das in Zukunft so machen muss, glaube ich nicht. […] der Aufwand [war] im Rahmen des Modellprojektes sicher notwendig." (Int_10, 25.07.2013, p. 8-9)

connection between those new stances towards immigration and the consequences of demographic change with respect to the labor supply are obvious. The debate intensified in 2010, when the German economy took an upswing and thus labor force demands increased (Schammann et al. 2012: 30-31).

A 'welcoming culture' in a broader sense can be understood as an "attraction of a society [...] that refers to the general contact with diversity within society" (Bertelsmann Stiftung 2012: 2).[9] A 'welcoming culture' must be based on a legislation that supports diversity, but it also covers efficient structures or institutions – public and private – giving support to newly arriving immigrants. Even if the term – and its underlying political claim – is criticized for being a simple "buzzword" (Kober 2012: 14), the concept is helpful as an analytic instrument.

Following the recommendations of the advisory council of the representative of the federal government for migration, refugees and integration (figure 9.1), the development of a 'welcoming culture' can be seen as a temporal sequence divided into different stages (Beirat der Beauftragten der Bundesregierung 2012):

The first two steps – pre-integration and first-integration – refer to all attitudes and measures in the country of origin and during the arrival in the receiving country. The third step aims at appreciation of diversity and is to be understood in a mid- and long-term context (Schammann et al. 2012: 33; cf.: Beirat der Beauftragten der Bundesregierung 2012; Bertelsmann Stiftung 2012). In the next passage, indicators and aspects that can be perceived as part of a 'welcoming culture' will be analyzed.

Information policy

Migration projects and employers have to advertise their proposal. A transparent information policy is of fundamental importance, as respondents clearly stressed. This holds true even in the pre-integration stage, and contains open information about an employer's motivation in recruiting foreign employees, as well as detailed job-related information. An adequate job description including working conditions and salary is seen as essential, especially during recruitment. An applicant's appreciation in this context means payment according to someone's education level. "We want you and we need you"[10] has to be the basis of recruit-

---

9 "Die Attraktivität einer Gesellschaft kann als 'Willkommenskultur' verstanden werden.[...] Zur Willkommenskultur gehört auch der generelle Umgang mit Vielfalt in einer Gesellschaft." (Bertelsmann Stiftung 2012, p. 2)

10 "[...] wir wollen Dich und wir brauchen Dich." (Int_07, 19.07.2013, p. 6)

ment, as a person in charge strongly underlined. Wrong expectations or non-transparent behavior should be avoided. Not only "hard facts" are of significance. Even information about daily life has to be communicated, as an example illustrates:

Figure 9.1: Development of a 'welcoming culture'

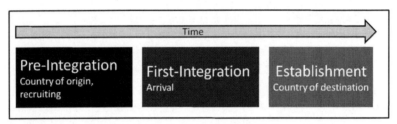

Source: Beirat der Beauftragten der Bundesregierung 2012: 7; own design

"[we informed them about] life in Bavaria. [...] First, Bavaria is not only Munich and Olympia stadium and Oktoberfest. Bavaria consists mostly of totally diverse regions. The companies offering apprenticeships were more in peripheral regions. [...] We had to show how it is to live in Cham, or Furth im Wald, or Marktredwitz. That this is different than Oktoberfest and Munich. We told [them about] social and community structures. [...] like associations, et cetera [...]. Of course we intensively gave information about language acquisition. That is a special issue. [We talked about] costs of living. We tried to describe life in all details. [...]." (Int_07 19.07.2013, S. 4-5).[11]

Avoiding wrong expectations through transparent handling seems to be a precondition of successful recruitment. As far as possible, all upcoming questions should be answered during the job interview or during the first temporary stay of

---

11 "[...] Leben in Bayern [informiert]: erstens, Bayern ist nicht nur München und Olympiastadion und Oktoberfest. Bayern besteht mehrheitlich mal aus ganz anderen Regionen. Die Unternehmen, die Ausbildungsplätze zu vergeben haben, haben sich bei uns interessanterweise fast wie eine Perlenschnur rund um Bayern aufgereiht. [...] wir mussten auch darstellen, wie sieht denn Leben in Cham oder in Furth im Wald oder in Marktredwitz aus. Dass das was anderes ist, als wenn man das Oktoberfest und München im Kopf hat. Wir haben [über] Gesellschaftsstrukturen [geredet]. [...] Vereinsleben et cetera [...]. Wir sind natürlich umfangreich auf dieses ganze Sprachthema eingegangen. Das ist dann ein Extrakomplex. Wir sind [auf] Lebenshaltungskosten [eingegangen]." (Int_07, 19.07.2013, pp. 4-5)

the candidate, as respondents declare. Applicants should be "taken seriously"[12] in their concerns. As the statements illustrate, transparent handling even means talking about difficulties connected to living in a foreign country. Candidates had to be fully aware of what they had to expect about their job and life in Germany, in order to avoid that a candidate accepts an offer based on wrong expectations or insufficient preparation, as a respondent pointed out.

Language acquisition

Not surprisingly, language acquisition is seen as a basic condition and most challenging factor for successful recruitment. Generally, the German language is considered as disadvantageous in comparison to other European countries, as an expert of the BAMF stated clearly:

"For us the big problem – that is in quotation marks the 'disadvantage' of Germany – that we have this [challenge in language acquisition]. The [...] biggest obstacle shaping migration to Germany is simply the language."[13]

The interviewee – a declared expert in this field and contributor of the ESF-BAMF integration classes – identified most problems within migration initiatives in the context of communication. He emphasizes the need for intensive language training in the first months or even half a year. In his opinion, learning by doing is not sufficient at all, and even the expectations in this context are to be held down. This is true for employers as well as employees.

Data confirmed his opinion. Nearly all projects underestimated the time and efforts regarding language acquisition and had to reconsider their expectations. In daily practice, the outstanding importance of this topic became clear:

"[...] the biggest problems [...] [are connected] simply to language. [...] if competence in German is a given, orientation time is the same as for our own employees. [...] But lan-

---

12 "ernst genommen." (Int_10, 25.07.2013, p. 23)
13 "Bei uns ist die große Hürde – [...] das ist in Anführungszeichen der Nachteil von Deutschland – dass wir hier eben diese [Herausforderungen beim Spracherwerb] haben [...]. Das [...] größte Hindernis, um die Zuwanderung nach Deutschland zu gestalten, ist einfach die Sprache." (Int_06, 12.07.2103, p. 13)

guage. Language, language, language. The better they speak German, the faster they integrate in the whole team."[14]

Expenditure in time for language acquisition differed between the examined projects. Some started with classes still in Spain and continued while already working in Germany. Others only started classes in Germany. Differences in details do not seem to be decisive; the important aspect is language acquisition as essential basic for successfull integration. As a consequence, time and assistance have to be provided. Employers

"[...] really have to spend money [...] and to increase their interest in integrating their employees during months [...]." [15]

This appears as an essential precondition, as an initiator's statement underlined:

"[...]decisive [was][...] what the company invested. They have to agree to support employees regarding language acquisition. [...] It was important that the companies made employees available for language classes during work time. Even that's part of a welcoming culture."[16]

Applicability during this time is limited. Of course differences exist depending on target groups and environment, as the different projects reveal. Working in a

---

14 "[...] größten Probleme [...] einfach [in der] [...] Sprache. [...] Der Einarbeitungsaufwand an sich, wenn die Sprachkompetenz da ist, ist nicht größer wie bei unseren eigenen Mitarbeitern [...]. Aber die Sprache. Sprache, Sprache, Sprache [...]. Je besser die Sprache ist, desto schneller läuft diese Integration im Team [...]." (Int_04, 27.06.2013, p. 12)

15 "[...] tatsächlich Geld in die Hand nehmen [...] und damit sein Interesse an der Integration dieser Mitarbeiter tatsächlich auch Monate einbringen [...]." (Int_10, 25.07.2013, p. 7)

16 "[...] entscheidend [...], was investiert der Betrieb. [...] Sie müssen sich bereit erklären, den Mitarbeiter hier auf der einen Seite zu unterstützen, was den Sprachunterricht betrifft an sich. [...] Und da war auch wichtig, dass die Betriebe auch gesagt haben, O.K., wir gewähren den Mitarbeitern gewisse Zeiten zu, wo sie während der Arbeitszeit Deutsch lernen. Auch das gehört zu einer Willkommenskultur mit dazu." (Int_03, 19.06.2013, p. 8)

small craft enterprise in a rural area of Bavaria, communication with customers is inevitable. So importance of speaking German from the beginning is quite higher than in an international company in a bigger town, where highly qualified employers, colleagues and costumers are able to switch to English. Also it is to be assumed that learning a new language for people with an academic background is easier.

Some employers had a special strategy supporting their staff in learning German. The Spanish employees were inserted in a decentralized manner, so they could not fall back on their separated Spanish group within the company.

Assistance on site

Support measures within the projects were executed in a wide range. In the following section, the most important ones identified by the interviewed persons will be explained. The decisive and most important aspect in the sense of a successful first-integration is, that there is someone who cares about all needs and question of the new employees, as the following statement indicates:

"[...] this question is decisive for project's success or failure. If you have someone who cares, then the project will be successful. Someone who is attentive, open-minded. If you have no one, the project will fail."[17]

All examined projects had such persons in charge. The provided assistance and information on exploring the new environment, bank connections, mobile phones, health insurance or contact to authorities. Assistance should be flexible, depending on the employee's needs and requirement, as an employer stated:

"The most important issue is avoiding the problems in the beginning. That starts with easy issues. Someone who makes the first contact and previously cares [...] That we keep in touch and assist with [...], preconditions, apartments... all this authority stuff, we accompany them. Every new employee gets a mentor."[18]

---

17 "[...] an dieser Frage entscheidet sich der Erfolg oder Misserfolg eines Projektes. Und wenn Sie jemand haben, der sich kümmert, dann wird das ein erfolgreiches Projekt sein, der zugewandt ist, der offen ist. Und wenn Sie [...] niemand haben, wird das Projekt daran scheitern." (Int_10, 25.07.2013, p. 17)

18 "Naja, das Wichtigste ist eigentlich so die Anfangsprobleme auf die Seite zu räumen. Das geht mit ganz einfachen Themen an. Jemanden, der den Erstkontakt dann macht und sich schon im Vorfeld ein bisschen kümmert. [...] Ab und an fragt, was denn so

All dimensions of daily life are seen as important:

"Where are the best bars [...]? Or one Spaniard rowed at a high level. Regensburg Rowing Club, and so on. That's part of a project. These are some small issues. Where we have to put in a lot of energy is looking for an apartment [...]. The first impression counts twice. Two weeks with nobody caring about me ... very bad. If someone cares four weeks before I come, before I go abroad, you can start very differently. Because you are always very positive."[19]

As all projects and even the interviewed migrant underlined, finding an accommodation is the most important issue. Some projects provided apartments to their employees, other guaranteed the rent to the owner or even established the contract. In this context, many employees had to face prejudices and as a consequence difficulties in finding decent housing.

SUMMARY AND OUTLOOK

This study aimed to explore new recruitment processes of German labor market institutions that came up during the Spanish financial and economic crisis. The topic is framed by important societal and policy changes in Germany: On the one hand, Germany claimed to be a non-immigrant country until the 2000s and still is rather reluctant to establish immigration policies. On the other hand consequences of demographic change and the long term goals of economic development call for new strategies, which are developed and tested on different policy levels in cooperation with non-governmental institutions. Before this background, the study tried to give first insight into those newly developing recruit-

---

für Voraussetzungen, Wohnung... [...] das ganze Behördenzeugs, da begleiten wir. Jeder der neuen Mitarbeiter kriegt einen Mentor." (Int_12, 09.08.2013, pp. 2-3)

19 "Wo sind die besten Kneipen in Regensburg? Das ist bei denen, jetzt zum Beispiel bei unseren Spaniern natürlich ein Thema gewesen. Oder einer der Spanier [...] hat relativ auf hohem Niveau gerudert. Ruderverein Regensburg und so weiter. [...] Aber das gehört dazu einfach. Das sind so ein paar kleine Themen. Wo wir viele Energie reinstecken ist Wohnung.[...] Und wie überall, der erste Eindruck zählt doppelt. Das heißt zwei Wochen kümmert sich keiner um mich... ganz schlecht. [...] Vier Wochen bevor ich überhaupt ankomme und aus dem Ausland komme und die kümmern sich schon, fliegen Sie ganz anderes rein oder fahren Sie ganz anders rein zum neuen Arbeitgeber. Weil Sie immer positiv besetzt sind." (Int_12, 09.08.2013)

ment structures and depict motives and strategies of stakeholders involved. Even though the sample of nine projects was rather small, some general conclusions can be drawn.

Regarding the initial motivation of companies and mediating institutions to engage in international recruitment from Spain, we can clearly determine the economic need as decisive factor, however to a varying degree. While in some branches – like in the health sector – labor force shortages were already critical and called for immediate action, other branches pursued a strategic approach and sought to gain initial experiences with international recruitment procedures, anticipating the need for such measures in the near future. Thus, we can interpret those strategies as active adaptation to processes of demographic change. Given the fact that the perception of demographic change is still underdeveloped in many regions and branches, the engagement of non-governmental institutions and even small companies in this field is rather surprising. In comparison to the period of guest-worker recruitment, the political and institutional frame has changed considerably. The European integration process, processes of globalization and transnationalization as well as manifold personal contacts between Spain and Germany clearly facilitates the engagement of the actors in our case study. Personal contacts and regionalized knowledge not only facilitated the initiation of recruitment projects, but also determined their regional catchment area, thus matching regions with high similarity regarding economic and settlement structure.

Second, all projects focused on the recruitment of qualified persons, or persons who are going to be qualified in Germany. That is an important difference to former migration flows and coincides to the structural changes and resulting needs on the labor market. Such an orientation implicates another, stronger positioning of migrants. In view of the participating companies, the migrants are needed. Whereas in former decades, the supply of unskilled workers from foreign countries went on without considering individual profiles, recruitment of qualified labor force requires far more appreciation.

Third, also the recruitment procedures and the positioning of employers and job seekers differed considerably. While recruitment of guest-workers mainly responded to needs of the employer side without giving any choice to the candidate concerning field of work or regional distribution, the recent recruitment processes are multi-step processes based on building up trust through face-to-face-contacts. This underlines the fact that the labor market needs switched towards skilled labor, with high gains however preceded by considerable costs of recruitment and integration. Thus, in the eyes of employers, only in cases of long-term residency in the receiving country will international recruitment pay off and can be considered an option in the future.

This argument directly leads to our fourth finding, considering the assessment of integration processes and the role of society in the country of destination, notably the existence of a 'welcoming culture'. Throughout our research, integration was not solely assigned to the migrants, but as a collective, long-term process involving (at least) the migrants, recruitment initiatives and recruiting companies. Within the projects the awareness of the complexity of migration processes was evident, leading to the assumption that an effective recruitment process is based on constant efforts from all sides. Crucial elements are transparency in all steps of the recruitment process, language acquisition as well as personal mentoring before, during and after the migration. The necessity for personal mentorship may derive from the fact that a 'welcoming culture' is still missing within German society and especially among authorities, although differences exist. Depending on a company's field, the amount of time and expenditures with respect to these measures differ considerably. Integration into an international English-speaking work environment is quite easier than into a rural crafts enterprise. Generally, the younger and less educated a migrant is, the higher is the need for assistance. Due to structural changes, a migrant's position in the market surely is far better than in the past, especially in comparison to guest worker recruitment.

Nevertheless, all these circumstances imply costs for companies and initiators. But without the willingness to take on these costs a migration project will fail. In the mid- and long-term perspective, international recruitment will be an option only if companies evaluate their investment as a rewarding one. Depending on learning effects in our society and abroad, as well as supply and demand in an international context, this will never be a static situation.

REFERENCES

Beirat der Beauftragten der Bundesregierung für Migration, Flüchtlinge und Integration (2012): "Willkommen. Working and Living in Germany – Your Future!" Empfehlungen für einen gesamtgesellschaftlichen Paradigmenwechsel in der Einwanderungspolitik im Sinne einer Willkommenskultur, Berlin, September 03, 2016 (http://www.bundesregierung.de/Content/DE/_Anlagen/IB/2012-04-28-working-and-living-lang.pdf?__blob=publicationFile).

Bogner, Alexander (ed.) (2009): Experteninterviews. Theorie, Methoden, Anwendungsfelder, Wiesbaden: Verlag für Sozialwissenschaft.

Bott, Peter/Helmrich, Robert/Schade, Hans-Joachim/Weller, Sabrina-Inez (2010a): "Datengrundlagen und Systematiken für die BIBB-IAB-Qualifikations- und Berufsfeldprojektionen." In: Robert Helmrich (ed.), Beruf und Qualifikation in der Zukunft. BIBB-IAB-Modellrechnungen zu den Entwicklungen in Berufsfeldern und Qualifikationen bis 2025, Bielefeld: Bertelsmann, pp. 63-80.

Brücker, Herbert/Brunow, Stephan/Fuchs, Johann/Kubis, Alexander/ Mendolicchio, Concetta/Weber, Enzo (2013): Fachkräftebedarf in Deutschland (IAB-Stellungnahme 1), Nürnberg: IAB.

Bundesministerium des Innern (2011): Demografiebericht. Bericht der Bundesregierung zur demografischen Lage und künftigen Entwicklung des Landes, Berlin, June 6, 2013 (https://www.bmi.bund.de/SharedDocs/Downloads/DE/ Broschueren/2012/demografiebericht.pdf?__blob=publicationFile). Bundesagentur für Arbeit (BA) (2012): Fachkräfteengpässe in Deutschland. Analyse Dezember 2012, Nürnberg: BA.

Domínguez-Mujica, Josefina/Diaz-Hernandez, Ramón/Parreño-Castellano, Juan: "Migrating Abroad to Get Ahead: The Emigration of Young Spanish Adults During the Financial Crisis (2008-2013)." In: Josefina Domínguez-Mujica (ed.), Global change and human mobility, Berlin: Springer, pp. 203-223.

Drosdowski, Thomas/Wolter, Mark Ingo (2010): "Entwicklung der Erwerbspersonen nach Berufen und Qualifikation bis 2025, Modellrechnung mit dem BIBB-DEMOS-Modell." In: Robert Helmrich (ed.), Beruf und Qualifikation in der Zukunft. BIBB-IAB-Modellrechnungen zu den Entwicklungen in Berufsfeldern und Qualifikationen bis 2025, Bielefeld: Bertelsmann, pp. 125-152.

Friedrich, Klaus/Schlömer, Claus (2013): "Demographischer Wandel. Zur erstaunlich späten Konjunktur eines lang bekannten Phänomens." In: Geographische Rundschau 65/1, pp. 50-55.

Fuchs, Johann/Zika, Gerd (2010): Arbeitsmarktbilanz bis 2025: Demografie gibt die Richtung vor (IAB Kurzbericht 12), Nürnberg: IAB.

Glorius, Birgit (2016): "New 'Guest Workers' from Spain? Exploring Migration to Germany in the Context of Economic and Societal Change." In: Josefina Domínguez Mujica (ed.), Global change and human mobility, Berlin: Springer, pp. 225-248.

Hardege, Klaus/Klös, Hans-Peter (2008): "Der deutsche Arbeitsmarkt im Spiegel der wirtschaftlichen Megatrends." In: Institut der deutschen Wirtschaft (ed.), Die Zukunft der Arbeit in Deutschland. Megatrends, Reformbedarf und Handlungsoptionen, Köln: Dt. Inst.-Verlag , pp. 9-30.

Helmrich, Robert (ed.) (2010): Beruf und Qualifikation in der Zukunft. BIBB-IAB-Modellrechnungen zu den Entwicklungen in Berufsfeldern und Qualifikationen bis 2025, Bielefeld: Bertelsmann.

Helmrich, Robert/Zika, Gerd/Kalinowski, Michael/Wolter, Mark Ingo (2012): Engpässe auf dem Arbeitsmarkt: Geändertes Bildungs- und Erwerbsverhalten mildert Fachkräftemangel (BIBB Report 18), Bonn: BIBB.

Hummel, Markus/Thein, Angelika/Zika, Gerd (2010): "Der Arbeitskräftebedarf nach Wirtschaftszweigen, Berufen und Qualifikationen bis 2025." In: Robert Helmrich (ed.), Beruf und Qualifikation in der Zukunft. BIBB-IAB-Modellrechnungen zu den Entwicklungen in Berufsfeldern und Qualifikationen bis 2025, Bielefeld: Bertelsmann, pp. 81-102.

Kober, Ulrich/Süssmuth, Rita (2012): "Nachholbedarf: Vom Einwanderungsland wider Willen zu einem Land mit Willkommenskultur." In: Bertelsmann Stiftung (ed.), Deutschland, öffne dich! Willkommenskultur und Vielfalt in der Mitte der Gesellschaft verankern, Gütersloh: Bertelsmann Verlag, pp. 13-24.

Koppel, Oliver (2007): Wertschöpfungsverluste durch nicht besetzbare Stellen beruflich Hochqualifizierter in der Bundesrepublik Deutschland. Studie im Auftrag des Bundesministeriums für Wirtschaft und Technologie, Berlin, Köln: IAB.

Koppel, Oliver/Plünnecke, Axel (2009): Fachkräftemangel in Deutschland. Bildungsökonomische Analyse, politische Handlungsempfehlungen, Wachstums- und Fiskaleffekte, Köln: IW Medien.

Lamnek, Siegfried (2010): Qualitative Sozialforschung. Lehrbuch. 5. Auflage. Weinheim, Basel: Beltz.

Laux, Hans Dieter (2012): "Deutschland im demographischen Wandel." In: Geographische Rundschau 64/7-8, pp. 38-44.

Mayring, Philipp (2002): Einführung in die qualitative Sozialforschung. Eine Anleitung zu qualitativem Denken. 5. Auflage, Weinheim [u.a.]: Beltz (Beltz-Studium).

Maier, Tobias/Helmrich, Robert/Zika, Gerd/Hummel, Markus/Wolter, Mark Ingo/Drosdowski, Thomas/Kalinowski, Michael/Hänisch, Carsten (2012): Alternative Szenarien der Entwicklung von Qualifikation und Arbeit bis 2030. Bonn: Bundesinstitut für Berufsbildung.

Meier Kruker, Verena (2005): Arbeitsmethoden der Humangeographie. Darmstadt: Wissenschaftliche Buchgesellschaft (Geowissen kompakt).

OECD (2013): Zuwanderung ausländischer Arbeitskräfte: Deutschland (German version), OECD Publishing, September 02, 2016 (http://dx.doi.org/ 10.1787/9789264191747-de).

Ragnitz, Joachim (2008): "Wirtschaftliche Implikationen des demographischen Wandels." In: Dresdner Geographische Beiträge 13, pp. 57-79.

Sachverständigenrat zur Begutachtung der gesamtwirtschaftlichen Entwicklung (2011): Herausforderungen des demografischen Wandels. Expertise im Auftrag der Bundesregierung, Paderborn: Bonifatius GmbH Buch-Druck-Verlag, September 02, 2016 (http://www.sachverstaendigenrat-wirtschaft.de/filead min/dateiablage/Expertisen/2011/expertise_2011-demografischer-wandel.pdf).

Statistisches Bundesamt (2015): Bevölkerung Deutschlands bis 2060. 13. Koordinierte Bevölkerungsvorausberechnung, Wiesbaden: Statistisches Bundesamt.

Statistisches Bundesamt (2015): Bevölkerung und Erwerbstätigkeit. Vorläufige Wanderungsergebnisse 2014, Wiesbaden: Statistisches Bundesamt, September 02, 2016 (https://www.destatis.de/DE/Publikationen/Thematisch /Bevoelkerung/Wanderungen/vorlaeufigeWanderungen5127101147004.pdf? __blob=publicationFile).

Part III: Perceptions and discourses

10. The recent international emigration of young Spaniards
The emigrants' narrative versus the official and media perception

RAMÓN DÍAZ-HERNÁNDEZ AND JUAN M. PARREÑO-CASTELLANO

ABSTRACT

Since the beginning of the financial crisis in 2008, and especially with the implementation of tight fiscal control measures in the public sector, the employment prospects of young Spaniards have worsened substantially. The adverse economic situation has made an increasing number of young people decide to emigrate to countries across the globe, especially Europe and Latin America. Despite being highly qualified, these young Spaniards have been denied the opportunity to enter the job market, been made redundant, or forced to cope with job insecurity.

The emigration experience has sparked a wide range of emotional responses among Spanish youth and their families. Disappointment, indignation and a sense of failure mingle with the hope of a better life abroad. In contrast, official and media discourses range from outright denial of the phenomenon to incomprehension, criticism and even irony.

The aim of this study is twofold: firstly, to analyze the opinions of young Spaniards who have gone abroad in order to determine how they perceive their migration experience, the reasons why they left, and their current frame of mind and future expectations; and secondly, to analyze how this phenomenon is perceived by Spanish society, based on the image projected by the government and the mass media.

The methodology of this study is based on a survey of young emigrants using non-probability sampling and the qualitative analysis of a significant number of publications drawn from various mass media sources (newspapers, blogs, podcasts, comics, etc.).

Keywords: Economic crisis, Media, Migration, Spain, Qualified young

INTRODUCTION

Data on outbound migration shows that the number of Spaniards between the ages of 20 and 39 who emigrate has been steadily rising since 2010 (table 10.1). Year after year, the ranks of emigrants continue to swell, with the sharpest spike registered in 2014. The provisional data for 2015 released by the Spanish National Statistics Institute (*Instituto Nacional de Estadística Español* (INE)) reflects an even higher figure, bringing the total to approximately 50,000 emigrants.

Table 10.1: Emigration of Spain-born citizens in selected age groups

	Age 20 to 24	Age 25 to 29	Age 30 to 34	Age 35 to 39	Total
2008	1,909	4,817	5,196	3,333	15,255
2009	1,821	4,455	5,579	3,586	15,441
2010	2,183	4,898	6,130	4,272	17,483
2011	2,930	6,828	8,740	6,622	25,120
2012	3,252	6,967	8,574	6,668	25,461
2013	4,197	8,564	10,723	8,696	32,180
2014	4,886	10,217	12,147	9,688	36,938

Source: Migration Statistics. INE

This trend has been accompanied by a similar rise in the Census of Spanish Citizens Abroad (*Padrón de Españoles Residentes en el Extranjero* (PERE)). The number of Spain-born citizens residing abroad has increased by 100,000 since 2009, reaching 733,387 in 2015.

Some researchers (González Enríquez 2012; González Ferrer 2013) and young emigrants' associations (Marea Granate 2015) claim that the INE is understating its figures for both technical and political reasons. They point out that the INE prepares its statistics (PERE) with data supplied to it by Spanish consulates and ignores a second type of consular register known as ERTA (Spaniards Temporarily Residing Abroad-*Electores Residentes en España Temporalmente Ausentes en el Extranjero*). Furthermore, the INE does not take into account that some emigrants fail to report their departure to municipal population census offices and do not register with consular offices abroad.

In fact, a survey conducted by the *Real Instituto Elcano* in 2013 showed that only one-third of young Spaniards who had left the country since 2008 were officially registered (González Enríquez 2014). Another study carried out by *Marea Granate* (Maroon Wave, a transnational network for Spanish emigrants)[1], based on local social security and population census data in the UK, USA, Uruguay, Germany, Austria, Norway, Iceland, Denmark and Ireland, identified 58,000 more emigrants than the official INE statistics (Marea Granate 2015). This was confirmed by the *Instituto de Juventud* (Youth Institute), an agency of the Spanish Ministry of Health, Social Services and Equality, after analyzing the official data on record in each foreign country (Navarrete Moreno 2014).

Setting aside the issue of official emigration statistics, it is also important to consider that this phenomenon includes other forms of migration, such as individuals who leave Spain with a contract to work abroad, or those who simply set out to try their luck but return after a few months if things don't work out. Additional categories include interns who go abroad to study or do research, employees of Spanish companies on international assignment, international aid workers, government employees and military personnel, beneficiaries of family reunification programs, etc. (Domínguez-Mujica/Díaz-Hernández/Parreño-Castellano 2016).

The general trend is a slightly male-dominated migration flow of highly qualified young people. According to the 2013 survey conducted by the *Real Instituto Elcano* (2015), 91 per cent of emigrants had a university degree, primarily in engineering (31 per cent) and economics and business administration (17 per cent).

Certain countries in South America and northern and western Europe are the main destinations of most Spanish emigrants, although the sample did represent a diverse array of host countries, in consonance with current globalized migration flows. They usually reside in major cities within their host countries and work in the service sector, though their occupations vary widely (Parreño-Castellano/Domínguez-Mujica/Díaz-Hernández 2016).

---

1 Cp. López-Sala in this volume.

Spanish academic literature has taken a keen interest in this emigration of young qualified professionals, as it represents a dramatic shift from Spain's migration patterns of the previous fifteen years, characterised by the massive influx of migrants from every nation and walk of life.

Many studies on this subject have been published recently, especially after the second recession began in 2011. Most reports and studies rely on official statistical data (Díaz-Hernández/Domínguez-Mujica/Parreño-Castellano 2015), and some researchers have even obtained data from the host countries themselves, such as records of Spaniards who have been issued work permits or registered with local Social Security offices in each foreign country. Some research projects also include ad hoc surveys, most of which are closed-ended questionnaires of the semi-structured or structured variety. Only a few studies have used open-ended questionnaires or in-depth interviews (Aparicio Gómez 2014; Navarrete Moreno 2014). Our study falls into the latter category, as it attempts to characterise the migration phenomenon by using the narrative discourses of the emigrants themselves. To this end, we focused our analysis on the open-ended questionnaires used in several preliminary studies and an online survey we conducted in 2013. The results of this survey have already been partially presented in other papers, but the narratives themselves, given their particular complexity, have not been studied in sufficient detail. This is precisely one of the goals of this study, to determine the motivations and feelings of Spanish emigrants by examining their own words, the substance of what they freely chose to share with us.

The public and private mass media, social networks and cultural circuits have also reflected this reality, adopting very different approaches governed by equally disparate criteria. In this study we attempt to reveal the relevance and disparity of reactions to this mass exodus of qualified young professionals as portrayed by the media. By analyzing the perspectives of the emigrants themselves and of the cultural and mass media, we will be able to determine the variance between how emigrants narrate their personal experiences in first person, how this phenomenon is portrayed through the lens of prevailing ideologies in the media, and how these facts are presented to Spanish society, depending on the degree of affinity or discrepancy with the official government position.

DATA SOURCES

The two primary sources used in this study are a survey of young adult emigrants conducted in 2013 and the systematic compilation of information appearing in different media.

The survey included 170 questionnaires completed by Spanish citizens born in Spain between the ages of 25 and 40 who had emigrated to another country. The online questionnaire was implemented over a ten-month period, between March and December 2013. The method used was snowball sampling, with an initial random set of informants that eventually made it possible to survey young people living in 37 different countries. The questionnaire, distributed by email, contained both open and closed-ended questions.

We chose this sampling method for several reasons: it is well-suited to situations where population size is not precisely established – we have already mentioned the difficulty of estimating the real number of Spaniards abroad – and locating potential respondents poses a challenge, given the lack of adequate records and their geographical dispersion; and it is an efficient means of encouraging potential respondents to participate.

However, we must bear in mind that this method can partially bias the results, as it is based on previous contact with initial informants, and emigrants whose experience in their host countries has not been satisfactory might be more reluctant to participate.

This survey was particularly interesting as it contained a combination of open and closed-ended questions, allowing us to perform quantitative and qualitative analyses of the results. The survey is divided into five parts. In the first part, personal data of respondents are collected, such as age, sex, place of birth, year of leaving Spain, city and country of residence at the time of the survey, profession and education level. In the second block fifteen questions about the decision to leave Spain are included. The questions asked about the labor and economic situation of respondents before emigrating, the job performed in the host country, the way in which the emigrants got this job and, finally, if the emigration abroad was a free decision.

The third block includes fifteen questions about the reception and integration in the country of destination. These questions were devoted to the working conditions, the job mobility, the difficulties in finding housing, the support they have had from institutions, family and networks of friends and expats as well as the main obstacles to integration.

The fourth section focuses on the relationship that the respondents have with Spain. This block is interesting since it includes some questions about the contact with homeland, remittances and the decision to return. Furthermore, the section addresses other questions that allow us to detect whether the respondents are immigration intermediaries looking for work for friends and family members, or starting up a process of family reunification.

The last block of the survey consists of two open questions. In one of them the emigrants can send a message to the whole of Spanish society, including institutions and entrepreneurs, with regard to the economic crisis and emigration. In the other, they are encouraged to tell their feelings, their thoughts, their personal situation and any additional information they want to provide.

These open-ended questions were especially valuable for our purposes, as they gave respondents the opportunity to express their opinions freely and create a personal narrative of their experiences and feelings. The presentation of the results included the explanation of the argumentative lines of the respondents and their exemplification by means of quotations. Previously, a partial statistical lexicological analysis was performed. This analysis consisted of, on the one hand, the selection of keywords and the coding and quantification of frequencies and, on the other hand, the categorization of ideas and feelings as well as the segmentation of the discourses in terms of these categories. Therefore, the challenge was to transfer the individual ideas and feelings to collective categories and to identify the mentioned argumentative lines.

With regard to the profile of survey participants, men accounted for 55 per cent of the sample, with those between the ages of 30 and 34 being the predominant age group. The average age of the women surveyed is slightly lower, as maternity reduces their inclination to go abroad.

The other principal data source of this study was obtained by systematically collecting and analysing mentions of this topic in the private and public mass media and other specialised media run directly by emigrants' associations and groups in foreign countries. In the category of national printed press, we consulted the dailies *El País, El Mundo, ABC* and *La Razón*, while our digital press sources were *El Confidencial, Público, Libertad Digital, El Diario, Voz Populi, Huffington Post, Periodista Digital* and *Nueva Tribuna*. Local press sources were limited to the Canary Islands, specifically the dailies *La Provincia-Diario de Las Palmas* and *La Opinión de Tenerife*. In the area of national radio, we obtained data from *Radio Nacional de España, Cadena Ser, Onda Cero, ABC Punto Radio* and *Cadena COPE*. In television, we reviewed part of the material broadcast by the national TV stations *Televisión Española, Antena 3, Telecinco, La Sexta, Canal Plus* and *Cuatro TV*, and by the regional stations *Telemadrid, Canal Sur* (Andalusia) and *Televisión Autonómica Canaria*.

This ample selection of media ensured an ideologically diverse sample, as we included media sympathetic to Spain's current conservative administration as well as those that tend to be more critical of the government discourse.

With regard to specialized media for the Spanish emigrant population, often run by emigrants themselves, we consulted *El Ibérico* (London), *Círculo Crea-*

tivo London, El Northern (Manchester), *The Spanish Herald* (Sydney), *Polska Viva* (Poland), *Berlunes* (Berlin) and *El Correo del Golfo* (United Arab Emirates). We also reviewed other media based in Spain that target the expat community (*Pasaporte, Carta de España, La Región Internacional* and *Crónicas de la Emigración*).

The priority was obtaining a broad base of newspaper articles and radio recordings and carrying out their transcripts. Other audiovisual sources such as movies, comics, and television entertainment programs were also included in order to provide an overview on the cultural and media impact that the new Spanish emigration is generating.

The analysis has been made as a presentation of preliminary results of the qualitative processing of the contents. Since the selection of newspaper articles, we have made a study of the terms used describing the migration process. This data processing has also led to generate a file for each of the analyzed transcripts in which we summarize the way the media shows the migration phenomenon, e.g., quoting a few contradictory examples: migration as a linear course – migration as complex process; migration as a successful experience – migration as a negative life lesson, etc. All this allows us to present some ideas about how the emigration of young Spaniards is depicted depending on the type of media and its ideological tendency.

NARRATED REASONS AND FEELINGS

Reasons for emigrating

All studies focused on the migration of Spaniards since 2008 cite the existence of serious dysfunctions in the Spanish job market as the primary reason for emigrating. In the survey funded by the *Real Instituto Elcano* on "The emigration of Spain-born citizens after the crisis", conducted in 2013, 30 per cent of respondents declared that they were unemployed, 19 per cent that they had no possibility of improving their employment situation, 14 per cent that they received very low pay, and 48 per cent that they saw no hope of change, leading them to believe that there was no future for them in Spain. Our survey also points in this direction: 46.1 per cent of respondents stated that either unemployment or job insecurity motivated them to leave Spain.

Therefore, the situation of the labor market was the cause of emigration for at least half of those surveyed. A similar percentage of emigrants cited other reasons. Many of them left with the goal of improving their education. In the *Real*

Instituto Elcano survey, 32 per cent claimed that this was their motivation. In our study, 36.7 per cent of survey participants indicated that they emigrated to further their education or training or to acquire professional experience. In fact, many of them combine study and work in their host countries.

Of the people surveyed by the *Real Instituto Elcano*, 27 per cent declared that they had emigrated for the sake of a new experience, to have an adventure; 7 per cent cited the relocation of a partner as their reason for going abroad; and 6 per cent had been transferred out of Spain by their employers.

These surveys, with structured or semi-structured formats, confirm that emigration is in fact a multifaceted phenomenon involving many different profiles and factors. Although the economic situation is also identified as the primary cause of emigration in open-ended questions, the narratives tend to focus more on the responsibility of individuals than on general economic phenomena.

Firstly, a large proportion of migrants blame their current situation on the inability of politicians and leaders to prevent and mitigate the negative effects of the financial crisis. The importance they attach to this factor is evidenced by the fact that their narratives mention the word "government" (referring to the Spanish administration) more often than "work" or "economy", to name but a few of the most relevant key words in the discourses of the 102 respondents (figure 10.1).

Figure 10.1: Most frequently used words in respondent narratives

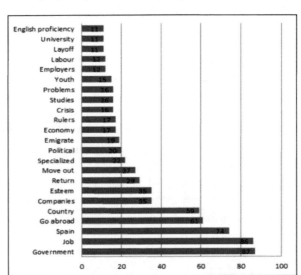

Source: Survey, 2013 (102 respondents)

They criticize both the uncontrolled public expenditure of the early years of the recession and the lack of economic countermeasures to support workers and small business owners. In particular, they mention the inefficacy of labor reforms and political class's indifferent attitude towards these and other measures to combat youth unemployment and underemployment. In this respect, a number of emigrants attribute their situation to poor political management of the crisis, which has only benefited big business:

"[I wish] employers were not so unscrupulous and would stop taking advantage of the situation in which the rest of society finds itself, offering abusive contracts, when many of their companies are making even bigger profits than before the crisis." (Elba, Vienna, Austria)

Moreover, they believe that the negligence of political leaders has led them to maintain policies with long-term consequences. This is illustrated by their opinions of the Spanish educational system, incapable of producing individuals with initiative. "We studied to work for other companies, whereas in foreign countries young people study to found their own companies" (Jonay S., Cheltenham, UK). In general, in their heated narrative discourses, emigrants see themselves as "victims" of a productivity model that benefits the privileged few and of employers and politicians.

Furthermore, in their narratives public administrators are often associated with corruption. "I would ask the political class to stop stealing, all we want is for our taxes to be used to promote employment." (Fernando M., West New York, USA)

"[I wish] the system of cronyism and corruption that most politicians promote would disappear, and that they would follow the example of more developed [Scandinavian] countries. Of course, this is just a pipe dream, and we'll never be able to change the system unless we change our culture. So, regretfully, I do not expect the situation to change in the near future." (Juan A., México FD)

"[...] most of the problems stem from the fact that access to political power is not regulated. It's inconceivable that decisions of paramount importance are made by people whose sole merit is a long history of affiliation with a political party. I would insist on intellectual qualifications." (David, Edinburgh, UK)

Reasons for not returning

When deciding whether or not to return, young emigrants weigh expulsion factors against attraction factors. In other words, they compare what they will find if they return to Spain with their current situation in the host country.

In our survey, three out of four emigrants described their experience outside of Spain as positive, particularly as their working conditions are better abroad. Most believed that they were better paid, although some of them stated that they had to take jobs for which they were overqualified or poorly paid. A similar percentage (78.2 per cent) felt that they were well integrated in the host society. The principal obstacles to integration are language differences (Germany being the most representative case), the job market limitations that foreigners face in some countries, difficulty finding accommodation other than temporary shared housing, legal and bureaucratic complications derived from their foreign status, and access to adequate healthcare. However, many respondents seem to lead very active social lives, especially with fellow Spaniards, colleagues and neighbors. They frequently join emigrants' associations and turn to them for advice on different matters in the host country. A smaller percentage also stated that they had made friends among the host country's native population. The results of these surveys are conditioned by the fact that many respondents left Spain quite recently, and attraction factors such as family ties do not yet carry much weight; however, in general the narratives give the impression that they are not unhappy with their situation abroad.

With regard to the future, the majority of those surveyed have little hope that the situation in Spain will change and feel that they are experiencing a prolonged or permanent process of exclusion. Many do not believe that employment prospects in Spain will allow them to return in the medium term: "The problem is when I think back on Spain, I believe I'll probably never have the same opportunities as I do abroad, even though I speak four languages." (Martín D., Mexico FD) Others feel that social rights have been lost and there is little hope of recovering them:

"It pains me to think that my children won't grow up in Spain, but I won't condemn them to live in a country where healthcare and education are increasingly treated as privileges rather than rights, where opportunities are reserved for a privileged few, and where employers ask for personal photos with every CV, I don't know why." (Olmo, Edinburgh, UK)

More than a few opine that the political changes they feel are necessary in order to even consider a future in Spain will not occur in the short term.

"With each passing day, I feel less inclined to return. I believe there is a real obstacle to a group of people who criticise, debate, make proposals, etc. Our leaders are OK, but the opposition [parties] should be proposing a recovery plan, working in cooperation with social organisations like Marea Granate." (Sara, Pau, France)

It is therefore not surprising that, in 2013, 52 per cent of emigrants expected to spend five years or more in their current host countries or relocate to another foreign country, and only 12 per cent planned to return to Spain within the year (Real Instituto Elcano 2015). Moreover, 80 per cent of emigrants are not actively seeking employment in Spain, according to our survey.

Thus, Spanish emigrants feel that their current situation in their host countries, though not ideal in many cases, is better than what they would hypothetically experience if they returned to Spain. Not only that: in the medium term, they feel that their prospects are better in their host countries than at home. For these reasons, the majority of respondents do not feel that returning to Spain is an option. Additionally, they believe that the authorities currently in power have not made an effort to recover the human resources which Spain lost during the recession.

Narrated feelings

The open-ended questions allowed emigrants to explain how they feel about their current situation. These feelings are shaped not only by their experiences in the host countries and what they left behind, but also by their perception of the consideration and concern for their situation shown by Spanish society and the political class.

As stated earlier, in general their narratives convey feelings of exclusion. Their self-perception as excluded individuals frequently leads them to emphasise that the decision to emigrate was not made freely. The slogans chanted at these groups' political demonstrations, such as "We're not leaving, we're being forced out", clearly illustrate this idea.

"Emigration is a very enriching experience, but leaving without knowing if you'll ever be able to return is less so, because it's more of an obligation. It's very frustrating to live in a place where you don't want to stay, not knowing if you'll ever be able to go home, and knowing that it's all the fault of those people who squandered and stole and don't care about fixing the problem now because they're living very well. [...] I truly believe that they want us to stay away. Firstly, because it's a way of solving the unemployment problem, and secondly, because they don't want the bother of dealing with critical thinkers." (Mónica, Dublin, Ireland)

The lack of support from Spanish government agencies abroad, the red tape involved in exercising their right to vote, and problems with maintaining healthcare coverage in Spain only exacerbate this sense of rejection or expulsion. In general, they feel that Spanish society does not understand the gravity of the problem, and there is no lack of commentaries about the population's complacent attitude in this respect. They see no signs of change or measures to reorganise and support the emigration process.

The combination of these factors inspires strong feelings of frustration and confusion in this stage of their lives.

"After five weeks on probation, I was offered a permanent position, in the very same capacity I had in Spain, with one slight difference: my salary was double. Plus, I was pregnant when I started working, and corporate management was aware of this fact when they made me the offer. I worked right up until giving birth, and I was promoted immediately after resuming my duties. Can anybody explain to me what's going on in Spain? I don't need consolation, just an explanation, but it can't possibly have anything to do with common sense." (María, Erl-Kufstein, Austria)

Although most keep close tabs on current events in Spain, a large number of emigrants – surprisingly large, considering how recent the migration process is for many of them – expressed strong feelings of disaffection and even sadness with regard to Spanish society and politics in their narratives.

"I would like to express the sadness I feel about the image of our country abroad, about how we got into this depressing situation, with wages that are embarrassing in comparison with other countries, and about how a handful of people shattered the stability of an entire nation, triggering a mass exodus." (David B., Edinburgh, UK)

However, there are plenty of emigrants who have adopted a more defiant, outspoken attitude and claim that they are committed to political activism, often by supporting grassroots initiatives like *Marea Granate* or the *15-May movement.* In these cases, emigration was the spark that ignited their political consciousness and inspired them to develop a spirit of collaborative camaraderie, even though this was not generally part of their previous lives in Spain. Some respondents decided to express this mentality by joining support networks like *Oficinas Precarias* (Precarious Workplaces). "Spain should stop bragging so much about its 'brand image' and get its act together, because if things continue in this vein, draining the nation of qualified people, it's going to end up at the tail-end of the queue." (Jonathan R., Lüneburg, Germany)

"Thanks to opportunism and threats, widespread dishonesty, clientelism as a standard operating procedure in government institutions, and populism as the 'new' political philosophy, political and business leaders have managed to paralyze citizens who don't know how to react to outrageous conduct. But citizens are looking for new channels and means of expression, new ways of organizing themselves in order to repair or transform an abusive, obsolete government and financial/corporate system." (Noemí, Pichincha, Ecuador)

We also feel it is important to point out the strong sense of self-affirmation conveyed in their narratives. Their experience abroad is making them grow as individuals and as citizens, in their own words. Yet the keen awareness of having lost the freedom to decide their own future pushes these positive emotions into the background.

THE PERSPECTIVE OF THE SPANISH GOVERNMENT AND MASS MEDIA

Migration is not a real issue for the Spanish government

In a session on 13 May 2015, the president of Spain stood before the Congress of Representatives and flatly refused to acknowledge that 500,000 young people had left Spain as a result of the financial crisis when the question was put to him by the opposition. In his rebuttal, Mariano Rajoy recalled that, according to the latest working population survey, the youth employment rate was up 4.7 per cent and social security records showed that employment had risen by 9.2 per cent. Prior to this session, the Secretary-General of Immigration and Emigration, Marina del Corral, had already stated that the exodus of young Spaniards could not be attributed solely to the financial crisis, citing other factors such as the "adventurous spirit of youth". In statements made to *El País* (November 30, 2012) during the presentation of a report on the emigration of qualified professionals, she insisted, "It's true that the domestic situation influences that capacity to set their sights further afield, but I believe there are no grounds for the claim that the departure of qualified Spanish workers is solely and exclusively attributable to the situation of recession." The fact that qualified Spanish workers "have finally ceased to be local", she added, should be viewed as an "essentially positive" thing, placing them "on an equal footing with the qualified workers of our European partners in terms of their international reputation".

Meanwhile, the Minister of Employment and Social Security, Fátima Báñez, had also informed the Spanish Congress on 17 April 2013[2] that "it's true there are a lot of young people who have left Spain in search of opportunities due to the crisis, and that's what we call international mobility, because some people go out and look for educational and work opportunities." In her opinion, "It's a reality that didn't just appear overnight." This mobility, Báñez explained in response to the question of a representative in the opposition, "leads to an idea of exchange", as in 2012 there were already 17,300 Spaniards living in other European countries due to the crisis, but thousands of young people from Italy, France, Germany and the UK had also come to work in Spain.

In short, in their public statements and through the pro-government media, the successive Spanish administrations have consistently downplayed the importance of this "new mobility", voicing opinions that range from assessments of these international movements as something normal and typical of a particular age group to openly contemptuous remarks. Euphemisms like "adventurous spirit", the "search for new experiences", "exchange in the logical pursuit of an international reputation" or "internationalized job mobility" have tried – unsuccessfully – to deny the impact of this mass exodus of Spain's youth in order to pacify public opinion, understating the magnitude of the phenomenon. While the official denial of such an obvious reality is surprising, the speed at which the media and social networks have spread these counter-messages is no less astonishing, managing to shake up public opinion and spark a heated social and political debate.

The Spanish mass media: between realism and sensationalism

The majority of national, local and online newspapers have, with an impeccable sense of timing, given extensive coverage to the recent emigration of young Spaniards in the form of news articles, special reports, editorials, interviews, photographs, etc. Their treatment of this phenomenon has varied widely, from serious, professional journalism to the most exaggerated tabloid sensationalism. The headlines have made liberal use of evocative, eye-catching words and

---

[2] http://www.libremercado.com/2013-04-17/banez-sobre-la-inmigracion-masiva-de-jovenes-eso-se-llama-movilidad-exterior-1276487768/.

phrases: "expat exodus", "neo-nomads", "brain drain", "forced exile", "loss of talent", "crisis driving out talent", "economic exile", "loss of human capital", "losing the best", "Euro exiles", etc. With these arresting one-liners, the media have attempted to get different messages across: expressing the citizens' disapproval of how the crisis is being managed, dramatizing the consequences of the recession in terms of decapitalization and difficulties, and even announcing the impossibility of reversing the situation, although a few merely indulged in thoughtless trivialization, treating this new version of the migration phenomenon as if it were some kind of reality TV show.

Coverage from a professional journalistic perspective was provided by the leading national newspapers and radio stations, as well as the majority of regional and provincial media. By way of example, the most widely circulated daily in Spain, *El País*, published a total of 246 news items – features, editorials, op eds, analyses, investigative articles, interviews, photo reports, etc. – on this topic between January 1, 2009 and January 31, 2015.

In the same way, the rest of the national, regional and provincial newspapers offered their readers detailed and reiterative information on this phenomenon, occasionally going the extra mile with rare initiatives like the transnational investigation conducted by the online daily *El Confidencial* and the web page created by a local paper, *La Opinión de Tenerife*, to map the diaspora of Canary Islanders across the globe. As of February 1, 2015, this map had registered a total of 452 individuals scattered across 74 foreign countries, which corroborated some of the trends we have observed in this new migratory reality, such as the fact that emigrants today can end up practically anywhere in the world.

Radio stations (both national and local) have also followed this mass departure closely, featuring the experiences of the young emigrants in numerous shows. For example, *Cadena Ser* (Spain's top radio in audience share) has devoted a large number of interviews, commentaries, debates, panel discussions and reports to this issue in its daily programming, all of which are stored in podcasts. Other examples of radio coverage of this reality are the special shows broadcast by *ABC Punto Radio, Radio Nacional de España, Onda Cero, Cadena COPE* and other regional and provincial stations.

However, the media sector that has probably dedicated more time to the emigration of young Spanish adults than any other is television. National and local channels alike have enthusiastically tackled the topic in reportage shows with identical format and similar titles: *Españoles por el mundo* (Spaniards round the World) and its regional variations, *Madrileños por el mundo, Andaluces por el mundo, Canarios por el mundo, Valencianos por el mundo*, etc. This medium is undoubtedly responsible for spreading the most distorted view of the phenomenon, focusing on success stories that bear little or no resemblance to the experience of the majority. The central message conveyed by such programs is that "Spain causes a furor abroad". These special reports usually feature Spaniards who live in different foreign countries showing off their comfortable homes and pleasant family and work environments, where certain situations and phrases tend to pop up repeatedly: "We Spaniards export our food, culture and customs", "Wherever we go, we make our mark", "Here we're going to look for that mark, the imprint of Spain", "The Japanese/Chinese/Australians/Polish/Canadians/Argentinians love everything to do with Spain: the language, flamenco, ham", and so on.

The film industry has also rallied to this cause. Motivated by the current situation in Spain and the knowledge that large numbers of young people are leaving in search of better job opportunities, Spanish film directors like Icíar Bollain (*En tierra extraña*) and the journalists Alba Casilda and Ana Callejo (*Destino emigrante*) decided to shoot documentaries in 2014 and 2015, respectively, in which these new emigrants were given the chance to be heard. Nacho García Velilla (*Perdiendo el Norte*) and Jaime Rosales (*Hermosa juventud*) also produced two timely films that reflect the lives of young Spaniards who go abroad to find work, their everyday experiences and the difficulties and problems they encounter in their host countries. More recently, in February 2015, Antena 3 Televisión began broadcasting a series called "Buscando el norte" in which a group of young people decide to move to Berlin in light of their dismal job prospects in Spain.

In summary, the majority of Spanish media – whether or not they are mouthpieces for the government's official position – have worked to shape the public perception of these "mass departures", fuelled by the more or less subjective testimonies of emigrants and their family members, who narrate their experiences live and in person (motivations, feelings, difficulties or facilities encountered, pros and cons, future plans, etc.). Looking beyond their absolute or relative numbers and the objectivity or subjectivity of their coverage, what we find is that the media and pundits have exploited the images, phrases and symbols of this phenomenon in such a simplistic way that, with a few rare exceptions (editorials, op eds and certain reports), they never made a serious effort to investigate the heart of the matter and inform their audiences of the underlying causes of this new mobility and its attendant complexities.

Based on our analysis, we can conclude that most news items and reports published or broadcast on this new migration process paint a picture of a mass, unidirectional emigration (returnees are usually ignored); yet the statistics, despite understating the true magnitude of the phenomenon, do not support this notion of emigration on a massive scale, especially when compared with migration flows in the past (the 1960s, for instance). The nature of mobility in this era of globalization also demands consideration of multi-directional, multi-causal and return flows, yet these receive little or no attention in the media. Moreover, the standard profile presented to the public is that of an emigrant with no previous ties to the larger world, overlooking the relevance of other cases such as Spaniards who move from one foreign country to another, Spanish children of foreign citizens who emigrate to their parents' country of origin or to others where job opportunities are available, and Spanish expatriates whose mobility can be explained by the business activities of many Spanish firms in foreign countries and of the transnational companies that employ them. Finally, the reports with the widest reach – especially on television – depict the migration experience as a story of adventure and success, glossing over the difficulties and conflicts that emigration frequently entails and presenting a distorted if not completely unrealistic image.

In this respect, it is important to recall that the immigration of foreigners during the years of economic prosperity (1996-2007) received similar treatment in the media, who subjected readers, listeners and viewers to such a constant barrage of news and images of aliens entering Spain – especially those who did so without proper authorization – that the native population was whipped into an anxious state of mounting alarm. In fact, during the years of the property market bubble, anything related to immigration was a hot topic in the media, which employed alarmist terms such as "immigrant invasion", "immigration wave", "migration tsunami", etc., and the phenomenon was highlighted and even stigmatized in certain cases as an overwhelming, unsettling threat to national security.

The realistic discourse of emigrant-created media

The expatriation-emigration phenomenon has also spawned a new school of journalism, created by the protagonists of those migration processes as well as by private companies, civic platforms and government agencies. Earlier we listed the principal media of this type operating in Spain and abroad. This new journalism is aimed at emigrants and attempts to satisfy their need for a special blend of news from Spain and their respective host countries. Some of these media were founded by Spaniards who departed in previous emigration waves, but now they are being modernized, reinvented and multiplied. Many connect with their readers via websites, text messages or social networks. They are often critical of the Spanish government and corporate world, on which they place the ultimate blame for their situation.

To these we must add the *Portal for Spanish Citizens Abroad* (CEXT), operated by the Directorate-General of Migrations and the Office of the Secretary-General of Immigration and Emigration, a department of the Spanish Ministry of Employment and Social Security, whose purpose is to make Spain's government institutions more accessible to Spaniards living abroad. Naturally, in this case the discourse is more aseptic.

Special reference must be made of the blogs, websites and other creative forms of communication that have proliferated among communities of young Spaniards abroad, with highly critical content and information about the new migration processes as well as personal accounts of the migrants' own experiences. A case in point is *La Blogoteca, Pepas y Pepes 3.0*, where these experiences are presented in a succinct manner that contrasts sharply with the overly-descriptive, self-satisfied perspective usually presented by the conventional media.[3]

Spanish emigration has also inspired a number of new comics and web series, yet another example of the many creative, unconventional communication initiatives found on social media and the internet in general. The majority of these web series have a substantial following on YouTube and social networks (Facebook, Twitter, Instagram, LinkedIn, etc.). Their success is owed in part to the treatment of emigration as a central factor, along with current events, humor, music and a shared, critical, endearing spirit of camaraderie.

As we stated earlier, the prevailing discourse in most of the media created by emigrants/expatriates is one of dissatisfaction and unhappiness with the financial crisis and how the Spanish government has handled it. In most cases, these outlets for expression also provide information, advice and assistance to any Spanish emigrants/expatriates in need of their expertise. From the reports, articles and information they publish, we can deduce that the young people who decided to emigrate are entrepreneurial individuals with initiative and drive who are prepared to take on the challenge of adjusting to life in other societies and different places, but who also maintain close contact with their families and roots thanks to social networks and certain transnational communication tools (e.g., Skype), although they bear little resemblance to the emigrants of previous eras who sent regular remittances to their home countries. In our estimation, this is probably a fairly accurate characterization of the typical Spanish emigrant of the recession years.

---

3 See the following websites for further information: http://lablogoteca.20minutos.es/pepas-y-pepes-30-33052/l/;http://leavingspaincomic.blogspot.com.es/2013/05/1-2_4.html; http://spaniardsinlondon.com/.

Conclusions

The emigration rate of young qualified Spanish professionals born in Spain has risen rapidly in recent years, especially since the financial crisis began in the late 2000s. In this paper, we have analyzed how the phenomenon is perceived by the emigrants themselves and compared that perception with the image projected by government channels, the mass media and specialist media for the emigrant community.

The emigrants' perspective was gleaned from the narrative discourses provided by 170 survey respondents. Our analysis of these narratives focused on three main aspects: their motivations for leaving Spain, their expectations of returning, and how they perceive their situation.

To get a general picture of the image projected by the media, we consulted official press releases, a large number of printed articles and editorials, and the content of various radio and television programs. Finally, we rounded out our analysis by reviewing both conventional (films) and alternative (blog libraries, comics, web series, etc.) cultural productions.

In general, we can conclude that emigrants develop a personal discourse which leads them to specify, and in some cases personify, the reasons why they left. Meanwhile, the media tend to target the financial crisis and, in rare cases, the way it has been handled. The affected individuals place the blame directly on politicians, managers and business owners, and believe that the emigration phenomenon is related not only to the crisis but also to the direction being taken in the process of economic recovery. What is more, they feel that their departure is attributable to a secret agenda of personal gain for a select minority of Spanish society while imposing measures of economic austerity on the majority.

Respondents also point to a direct link between emigration and political corruption, especially when discussing their prospects for the future, although this connection is not clearly defined in most of the messages conveyed by the media. It is quite interesting to note how emigrants associate economic prosperity with democratic quality and political transparency. Again, this association is less clear in the media, where corruption is frequently related to the misappropriation of public resources.

Another noteworthy aspect is how the media present the emigration of these young qualified professionals and how the migrants perceive their own experience. The differences between the various images conveyed to society are striking. Government channels of communication tend to downplay the importance of the phenomenon or dismiss it as a natural consequence of the globalization of the job market; in the political discourse, and especially in the context of European integration, this is presented as a positive thing, generating new job opportunities, providing an outlet for personal freedom, and creating wealth. The depiction of migration projects as success stories, especially in programs broadcast on public television networks, is one of the most subtle ways of camouflaging the new wave of Spanish emigration, associating it with entertainment.

Another segment of the mass media has opted for a sensationalist approach, at times with intensely dramatic content, which, though presented from a different angle, offers an equally distorted view of this reality. Only some media – primarily those catering for the emigrant community – tend to offer a more realistic perspective, presenting the everyday difficulties that emigrants face and allowing them to speak for themselves.

We were not surprised to find that a significant number of respondents complain of a lack of sensitivity to their plight in Spanish society. Emigrants bemoan the public sector's deafness to their needs – hence the existence of movements like *Oficina Precaria* – as well as society's general failure to acknowledge their problems, which is closely related to the way in which the media narrate this reality and the importance they attach to it.

This is particularly relevant in light of the growing sense of rejection or exclusion among young emigrants. In general, they feel that they are not wanted, and they therefore exhibit attitudes of growing mistrust and disaffection with Spanish government institutions and society. It is important to bear in mind that this new wave differs substantially from the migration movements of previous decades in Spain. Emigration is now a personal decision rather than a family centered strategy. Emigrants do not send remittances and are not sure when or, in many cases, *if* they will ever return. In light of these circumstances, it is understandable that their narratives express feelings of emotional detachment from Spain and frequently allude to a sense of rootlessness, a feeling that they do not belong here, there or anywhere.

The image conveyed by specialist media aimed at emigrants is undoubtedly the one closest to their discourses, especially because they reflect the idea of self-affirmation mentioned in many of the young migrants' narratives. Overcoming challenges and making personal progress are the elements that best define their day-to-day existence in the host countries, and this is apparent in the discourse of those alternative media, which frequently employ terms such as "initiative", "self-improvement" or "overcoming the odds".

In conclusion, the contrast between the emigrants' own narratives and the discourses employed by the media reveals the needs of those affected by this phenomenon – to be visible in Spanish society, to be heard and understood – and underscores the fact that, in many cases, the media is failing to adequately meet these needs.

REFERENCES

Aparicio Gómez, Rosa (2014): Aproximación a la Situación de los Españoles Emigrados: Realidad, Proyecto, Dificultades y Retos, Madrid: OIM España.

Díaz-Hernández, Ramón/Domínguez-Mujica, Josefina/Parreño-Castellano, Juan M. (2015): "Una aproximación a la emigración española durante la crisis económica: herramientas de estudio." In: Ar@cne. Revista electrónica de recursos en Internet sobre Geografía y Ciencias Sociales, 198, pp. 1-26, December 10, 2015 (http://www.ub.edu/geocrit/aracne/aracne-198.pdf).

Dominguez-Mujica, Josefina/Díaz-Hernández, Ramón/Parreño-Castellano, Juan M. (2016): "Migrating Abroad to Get Ahead: The Emigration of Young Spanish Adults During the Financial Crisis (2008-2013)." In Josefina Domínguez-Mujica (ed.), Global Change and Human Mobility, Singapore: Springer.

González Enríquez, Carmen (2012): La emigración desde España, una migración de retorno, Madrid: Real Instituto Elcano, November 02, 2015 (http://www.realinstitutoelcano.org/wps/portal/rielcano/contenido?WCM_GLOBAL_CONTEXT=/elcano/elcano_es/zonas_es/ari4-2012).

González Enríquez, Carmen (2014): Fuga de cerebros, Madrid: Real Instituto Elcano, November 02, 2015 (http://www.realinstitutoelcano.org/wps/portal/web/rielcano_es/contenido?WCM_GLOBAL_CONTEXT=/elcano/elcano_es/zonas_es/demografia+y+poblacion/comentario-gonzalezenriquez-fuga-de-cerebros-espana-braindrain-spain#.VOZuXPnz0Ro).

González-Ferrer, Amparo (2013): La nueva emigración española. Lo que sabemos y lo que no, Madrid: Fundación Alternativas.

Granate, Marea (2015): "El Gobierno minimiza deliberadamente los datos de la emigración española". June 25, 2015 (http://mareagranate.org/2015/06/el-gobierno-minimiza-deliberadamente-los-datos-de-la-emigracion-espanola).

Navarrete Moreno, Lorenzo (2014): La emigración de los jóvenes españoles en el contexto de la crisis. Análisis y datos de un fenómeno difícil de cuantificar, Madrid: Observatorio de la Juventud en España.

Parreño-Castellano, Juan/Domínguez-Mujica, Josefina/Díaz-Hernández, Ramón (2016): "Migrations and mobility abroad of Spaniards at a time of crisis. The state of the question." In: Rosa Cañada Torrecillas (ed.), Aportación Española al 33rd International Geographical Congress, Madrid: AGE.

Real Instituto Elcano (2015): "La emigración de los españoles autóctonos tras la crisis.", November 02, 2015 (http://www.realinstitutoelcano.org/wps/portal/ rielcano/PrensaVista?WCM_GLOBAL_CONTEXT=/elcano/elcano_es/ prensa/notas/encuesta-emigracion-espanoles-crisis).

11. The new emigration issue in the public and political debate in Spain
Official discourses and new forms of mobilization

ANA LÓPEZ-SALA

ABSTRACT

Spanish emigration has become the subject of intense debate in the national press, leading to a large number of academic studies and reports that have sought to characterize this new emigration in terms of labor and migration expectations. Despite the heated social and media debate, the current government has not considered containing this outflow a priority or an issue to be included in the Spanish political agenda. On the contrary, the attitude of the current government has oscillated between indifference and denial. Faced with the government's inaction, which can be referred to as a policy of 'disengagement', different profiles of emigrants, all of whom can be identified as economic exiles, have united to fight for what they refer to as their 'right to return' by developing new forms of mobilization and protest against austerity measures and the erosion of their economic, social and political rights. This has created a new kind of external citizenry that is highly critical of the current government. Known collectively as the *Maroon Wave*, this movement is just one facet of a broader reconfiguration of Spanish society and political life brought about by the economic crisis. The *Maroon Wave* is in part a reaction to the inaction and indifference of the Spanish government to the plight of economic exiles, but also an aspect of the general detachment from and lack of trust in Spanish institutions and traditional political parties observed in many sectors of Spanish society. However, for many economic exiles their mistrust has not increased their feeling of detachment from Spanish society, but rather had the opposite effect: it has activated a desire to influence the political and social dynamics in the society of origin, with the objective of bringing about structural changes that will allow them to return. Their protest actions and message have struck a resonant chord with the complaints of other sectors of Spanish society and with the emerging political parties, becoming key issues in the recent general election held in December 2015.

Keywords: Economic crisis and mobilization, External Spanish Citizenry, *Maroon Wave*, Social Movements, Spain, Spanish emigration

INTRODUCTION

Starting in 2012 the growing number of Spanish nationals moving abroad as a consequence of the economic and employment crisis has been given a great deal of attention by the media, public opinion, and academics in Spain. After more than a decade of intense immigration, the emigration of Spanish nationals, especially significant among the young, has come to symbolize a particularly painful dimension of the profound economic, social and institutional crisis that Spain has suffered over the past five years, as it is reminiscent of the Spain's still recent past of scarce prosperity and general poverty. Although Spain's economic crisis began in 2008, the emigration of nationals did not emerge in public debate until the start of 2012, coinciding with the publication of the first statistics revealing not only that Spanish emigration had been increasing since 2010, but also that the return of Spanish nationals living abroad was slowing down. Statistics reveal the inversion of the migration cycle, with Great Britain, France, the United States and Germany being the main destinations of these new and previously unexpected flows from Spain (Domingo/Sabater 2013; Domingo/Blanes 2015; Domínguez-Mujica et al. 2016; López-Sala/Oso 2015).

Spanish emigration has become the subject of intense debate in the national press and has led to a large number of academic studies and reports whose objective has been to characterize this new emigration in terms of labor and migration expectations[1] (Alba/Fernández-Asperilla 2015; IOM 2014; Navarrete 2014; Pumares 2015). The national media's interest in this issue has spread to the European press and international experts, who have reported on the large numbers of young people leaving Spain and other European countries due to the crisis (Papademetriou 2015; Glorius 2016; Glynn et al. 2015; Glynn 2015; Cavounidis 2015; Triandafyllidou/Gropas 2014).

---

1 For a complete review of the studies carried out on Spanish emigration over the past several years, cp. Díaz-Hernández et al. 2015.

To a certain extent, the new Spanish emigration has eclipsed immigration as the major concern of public opinion. In 2013 various important analysts of the phenomenon highlighted that the "media have made the emigration of young Spanish nationals a media star whose brilliance blots out all other aspects of the migration issue" (Aja et al. 2013: 13). This was coupled with the results of the Sociological Research Centre (CIS) barometer published in February 2012[2] indicating that in 2011, 17 per cent of the people surveyed had thought about living abroad and that 48 per cent were very willing or somewhat willing to live outside of Spain, with Germany, Great Britain, France and the United States viewed as the most desirable destinations.[3]

Recent studies have provided more detail regarding the volume of this outflow and have characterized it with greater precision, revealing a much more heterogeneous profile among the emigrants than the stereotypical image provided by the media suggests[4] (Domingo/Ortega-Rivera 2015). However, there is no doubt that the impact of this phenomenon on the media is due to the fact that it is perceived as a symptom of the failure of the Spanish economic and social model, the lack of opportunities affecting broad social sectors and the general lack of trust in public institutions that has devastated the country since 2011.

However, this broad social and media debate on the new Spanish emigration has not had a significant impact on the position of the current conservative Spanish government, which has not included this emerging phenomenon in its agenda during the current legislature (2012-2015). On the contrary, the Spanish government has maintained positions on this issue ranging from indifference to denial, a position that has been broadly condemned not only by public opinion and part of the political class, but also by the increasingly organized Spanish community living abroad. The government's attitude toward the emigration issue has starkly contrasted with the importance it has acquired in political and public debate over the past few years, which led to it becoming a key issue during the general election campaign at the end of 2015.

---

2   These Barometers are carried out on a monthly basis – except in August – and their main objective is to measure Spanish public opinion at that time. They involve interviews with around 2,500 randomly-chosen people from all over the country (cp. www.cis.es).

3   Cp. Glorius in this volume.

4   This outbound flow includes other profiles, such as former immigrants who had acquired Spanish nationality, as well as descendants of immigrants born in Spain. For more on these distinctions, cp. Domingo et al. 2014.

The objective of this chapter is to examine the social and political debate that has been generated by the emigration issue over the past several years in Spain. The analysis reveals the discrepancies between the response of the current Spanish government and the concerns of Spanish society, and more specifically, with the new community of Spanish nationals residing abroad. Faced with the inaction of government institutions, the new Spanish diaspora has created an effective political movement, known as the *Maroon Wave*, that has reshaped and infused the emigrant community with new significance and resilience, despite the erosion of their social and political rights.

The analysis presented in this chapter draws on various official and public statements made by representatives of the Spanish government, official documents and reports, the database of speeches given in parliamentary debates, the press, websites and secondary literature. Press material displayed on their websites and Facebook and Twitter accounts was used to characterize the *Maroon Wave* social movement.

STATE-DIASPORA RELATIONS IN THE CASE OF SPAIN

Spain has a long tradition of protecting Spanish communities residing abroad that dates back to the start of the 20th century (Sánchez-Alonso 2011). Although the Spanish Civil War and the two decades of international isolation imposed on the Francoist regime limited the implementation of measures directed at the Spanish community abroad for more than 30 years, the end of the 1950s marked the start of what could be considered a Spanish emigration policy. At that time the regime's new political elites began to consider emigration as "an important advantage for the triumph of Spain's economic development and modernization" (Fernández-Vicente 2009: 279). This vision underlies the optimism around the link between migration and development, something that has been repeatedly indicated by migration theory (Delano/Gamlen 2014). At the institutional and legislative level, this policy was articulated through the creation of the Spanish Emigration Institute and various Emigration laws (in 1960 and 1971) that over the following decades consolidated the State's very active intervention in regulating Spanish migration flows and the social protection of emigrants and their families (Calvo-Salgado et al. 2009; Fernández-Vicente 2005).

With the return of democracy, the objectives of this policy were broadened, focusing on guaranteeing the social, economic and political rights of nationals residing abroad, all of which were acknowledged in the 1978 Spanish Constitution.[5] However, although these rights were formally guaranteed, their practical implementation left much to be desired, due to the limited resources available and also because they were partial or limited in their orientation. By the 1990s the focus was on providing assistance for emigrants who had returned to Spain, improving the external election census and promoting cultural and linguistic initiatives. It is important to point out that over the past few decades the orientation of this policy was shaped by three aspects: the advanced age of the Spanish diaspora; its demographic importance in the electoral census in some regions, such as Galicia, where it represented close to 15 per cent of the voting population; and finally, by the desire of successive Spanish governments to use the community residing abroad to disseminate the Spanish language and improve its cultural influence in Europe and Latin America.

However, it was not until 2006, during the first Socialist government of Jose Luis Rodríguez Zapatero, that the Spanish Citizenry Abroad Statute was enacted.[6] This is the first integral regulation of Spanish nationals residing abroad, guaranteeing them the same rights as those living in Spain. It focused on strengthening the ties between Spain and its diaspora, increasing the concession and practical implementation of their social and healthcare rights, improving their participation in all initiatives that could affect them through the creation of the General Council of Spanish Citizenry Abroad, and promoting cultural and educational policies (Goig 2010).

The promises offered by this new statute have been partially undermined by changes in the economic and social policies provoked by the onset of the economic crisis in 2009. In addition to this, as a consequence of the recent Spanish emigration, the profile of the Spanish community living abroad has undergone a profound change in terms of demographic characteristics, class structure, political culture, welfare prospects and migration projects. We should remember that the social and generational reconfiguration of this community could be particularly significant in determining the links that are created between it and the Spanish State over the next few years.

---

5   Art. 42 of the Spanish Constitution of 1978 states that "the State will especially protect the economic and social rights of Spanish workers abroad". The right to vote is acknowledged by art. 68.
6   Law 40/2006 on Spanish External Citizenry.

BETWEEN INDIFFERENCE AND DENIAL: THE POSITION OF THE SPANISH GOVERNMENT ON THE EMERGING PHENOMENON OF EMIGRATION (2012-2015)

Despite the intense social and media debate surrounding the new Spanish emigration, the position of the current Spanish government has oscillated between indifference and denial. The austerity measures and structural reforms implemented by the Spanish government since the end of 2011, which included a dramatic reduction in social spending and a labor reform that has provoked even more severe forms of precarious and short-term employment, provoked this new outflow. The economic situation in Spain has reduced the possibilities and expectations of entering the labor market and finding stable employment for large segments of Spanish society, especially for the youngest generations[7] (Dolado et al. 2013; Villar 2014), which have the highest level of education and training in Spanish history. In this scenario, emigration has quickly and unexpectedly become one of the few alternatives to find not only employment, but stable, quality employment, and to improve the social and employment expectations of a population that had undergone an extraordinary improvement in its education level over the past three decades.[8] This has led to a new culture of emigration, especially among sectors of Spanish society that have the highest levels of educational and social capital, in a country that has produced little emigration since the end of the 1970s.

This new generation of youths and young adults, many of whom are from the urban middle class and raised in the years of Spain's greatest economic abundance, have witnessed and in many cases actively participated in the social mobilization provoked by the austerity measures of the conservative Spanish government and whose most well-known expression was perhaps the anti-austerity

---

[7] Accordingly to Eurostat in April 2015, the youth unemployment rate was 20.7% in the EU28 and 22.3% in the Euro area. The lowest rates were observed in Germany (7.2%), Austria and Denmark (both 10.1%), and the highest in Greece (50.1%), Spain (49.6%), Croatia (45.5%) and Italy (40.9%). The mismatch of young workers' skills with jobs and over-qualification are a widespread phenomenon in Spain.

[8] In Spain in 2014, according to the data provided by the Spanish Statistical Office (INE), 36.8% of men and 47.8% of women between 30 and 34 had higher education studies. The European Union 28 percentages were lower than Spain's, both for women (42.3%) and men (33.6%).

movement known as the *Indignants* or *15-M Movement*[9] (Perugorría/Tejerina 2013; Cameron 2014; Sampedro/Lobera 2014; Flesher-Fominaya 2015; Campos Lima/Artiles 2013; Moreno-Caballud 2015).

During 2011 the Spanish government remained silent on this issue. However at the end of 2012 the first public statements were made, generating a very strong reaction, even an uproar, in public opinion. First of all, because the position of the Spanish government has been to deny a link between emigration and its austerity policies, as well as to minimize its magnitude and importance. More specifically, the official discourse has maintained that emigration is fundamentally the result of economic globalization, the demand for highly-skilled workers and the freedom of movement of European Union workers.[10] This discourse highlights external variables as the explanation, while denying that internal variables (such as the high rate of youth unemployment, overqualification and the high rates of job instability) stimulate migration.[11]

For example, along these lines we find statements made in 2012 by the former Spanish Minister of Education, Jose Ignacio Wert, indicating that the emigration of Spanish youth was not a negative phenomenon or a brain drain (*El País*, February 23, 2012), but rather the result of the globalization of high skilled jobs in Europe; or those of Esperanza Aguirre, former president of the Community of Madrid (and one of the most noteworthy figures of the governing conservative Popular Party), who stated that youth emigration was "a reason to be proud and optimistic, because it demonstrated the excellent training of Spanish youth" (*El País*, April 27, 2013). One of the most important leaders of the Popular Party (PP) and currently a MEP, Esteban González Pons (*El Diario*, June 2,

---

9 The *Indignants* movement is an autonomous social movement that demands a radical change in Spanish politics. They protest against economic and political disempowerment and arose in the form of concerted and sustained manifestations of mass indignation. They view their struggles as a means to a better future, not solely for themselves but also for their peers. It is also a movement of ordinary citizens rather than activists.

10 Cp. for example, the official position on this issue in Boletín Oficial Congreso (BOCG), October 18, 2012.

11 As Santos points out, the position of the Spanish government reflects "the hegemonic and neoliberal discourse on the international mobility of talent insistently recommended by the business world" (Santos 2013: 126) who avoids mentioning the negative consequences of that mobility on workers (cp., for instance, Sennet 1998).

2013), stated in 2013 that working in the European Union was like working at home.[12]

At the end of 2012 yet another controversial declaration was heavily criticized by Spanish society, becoming the object of ridicule by the press and on different internet platforms. The Secretary of Immigration, Marina del Corral, claimed in an interview that Spanish youth also emigrated because of their "adventurous spirit" (*El País*, November 30, 2012). After the indignant response of the general public, the Spanish government (among them the Minister of Labor and Immigration Fátima Bañez [*El Mundo*, 17 April 2013], or Rubén Urosa [*Europapress*, August 5, 2014], the director of the Spanish Youth Institute, INJUVE) has sought to avoid making declarations on this subject at all costs, despite the insistence of the press, and has avoided using the term emigration in its official discourse, substituting it with the euphemism external mobility.

The position of the Spanish government can be interpreted by various motives. First of all, it has to be highlighted that the fundamental goal of the policies developed by the government during this legislature (2011-2015) has been to reduce public spending. This very short-term vision does not take into consideration the loss of human resources caused by job instability and the lack of employment and promotion opportunities. Second, because the new Spanish migrants residing abroad (including young researchers and highly skilled professionals) have been one of the sectors most critical of government austerity in regards to its labor, economic and R&D policy.

In a recent study two important historians of Spanish emigration interpreted that the position of the current Spanish government was a "return to the positive vision of emigration inherited from the Francoist technocracy" (Gil/Fernández-Vicente 2015: 16); reviving the idea that emigration was a way to return to equilibrium, like an escape valve for social discontent.

The Spanish government's "disengagement" position (Gamlen 2006) has activated responses and forms of resistance among the new emigrants that have coalesced into a politically conscious movement. This transnational "voice"

---

12 This position starkly contrasts with the attitude of politicians in Italy. In 2013 then Prime Minister Enrico Letta publically apologized to all young Italians who had been forced to leave the country, declaring that the emigration of educated youth was an unforgivable failure of Italian policy (La Stampa, June 2, 2013) (cp. Montanari/Staniscia in this volume). In 2014, Italy's new Prime Minister Matteo Renzi, promised to make unemployed youth one of his main priorities by offering incentives to companies that hire young people and helping university graduates find jobs and internships through the Youth Guarantee Program.

(Hirschman 1970) shows how strongly these new emigrants are politically engaged in domestic issues, producing new aspects of external Spanish citizenship and revitalizing old ones.

ADDRESSING THE EMIGRATION PROBLEM? MUCH ADO ABOUT NOTHING

Since the end of 2013 representatives from the rest of the political parties, echoing the social unrest, have denounced the government's lack of action to contain emigration and promote the return of young Spaniards. They have proposed urgent action plans, including a new R&D policy that could reduce the emigration of highly skilled workers and researchers from Spain.[13] Additionally, Spanish unions have incorporated protecting the labor rights of Spanish workers living abroad into their agenda. To achieve this they have recently started to develop initiatives to coordinate with union organizations in the countries of destination.[14]

The changes in the Spanish political panorama since 2014, with the emergence of new parties, such as *Podemos* and *Ciudadanos*, and the renewal of the leadership of other parties, like the *Socialist Party* (PSOE) and *United Left* (IU), have revitalized proposals in this area.[15] The development of specific plans, not so much to contain emigration but to promote returns, have been mentioned in official statements by almost all parties on the political spectrum. For example, the main opposition party, *PSOE*, has defended since the end of 2014, the establishment of a Plan to Return Scientific and Professional Talent, in collaboration with universities and businesses, designed to promote the return of young Span-

---

13 Since 2009 Spain has lost around 11,000 researchers. The main Spanish research agency, the CSIC, lost around 15% of its research staff between 2011 and 2014 due to the lack of contract renewals for young researchers.
14 For example, one of the major Spanish Trade Unions (Comisiones Obreras, CCOO) has carried out various coordination actions with the DGB *(Deutscher Gewerkschaftsbund,* Confederation of German Trade Unions) aimed at providing information, guidance and support for Spanish workers (cp. Meinardus in this volume).
15 In August, 2014, The Spanish Youth Council initiated a campaign for government policies to contain the outflow of young people abroad and to promote their return. The Spanish Youth Council is a forum for coordination, communication, training and cooperation of organizations that comprise the youth association movement.

ish citizens living abroad.[16] Various political representatives have affirmed that the government has used its parliamentary majority to block any non-law proposition or specific action in this area.[17] However, these initiatives have not resulted in actual measures being taken, even on the regional level, in autonomous communities governed by opposition parties, such as Andalusia or Catalonia.

The results of the municipal elections of May, 2015, which revealed growing support for the new political parties, signaled a change in course and consolidation of the emigration issue in party platforms. The inclusion of emigration in the political agenda, which over the past few months has centered on reforming the law regulating absentee ballots from abroad, was activated, however, by the mobilization and protests of the Spanish emigrant community, especially through the *Maroon Wave* social movement, which has very effectively channeled the powerful voice of the new Spanish emigrant community.

FROM MOBILITY TO MOBILIZATION: THE CASE OF THE *MAROON WAVE*

The *Maroon Wave* is a transnational social movement made up of Spanish emigrants. It arose in 2013 with the goal of providing visibility to Spanish citizens who have been forced to leave Spain as a consequence of the economic crisis. This movement, that is not affiliated with any political party, is largely a response to the position of the current Spanish government, which has tried to downplay the volume of Spanish emigration and given little importance to its causes. In this sense its goal is to fight, from outside the country, against the causes that have led to the economic and social crisis that has forced thousands to emigrate.

The *Maroon Wave* was born in the heat of other social movements that have appeared in Spain in recent years.[18] Its origins are found in large part in the *Indignants* movement, more specifically in one of its subsidiary social movements, called *Youth Without Future* (Santos/Martín 2012). The *Youth Without Future* movement demands reforms that would allow young people to join the labor

---

16 At the end of 2013, the government even publically declared that it was working on a young entrepreneurs plan that could contain emigration and promote self-employment. However, nothing concrete has come of it in the following years.

17 Cp. for example, the non-law proposal presented by the Socialist parliamentary group in the 10th legislature (BOCG, 261; May 7, 2013).

18 Cp. http://mareagranate.org/.

market and lead a dignified life in Spain.[19] In April 2013 *Youth Without Future* organized the "You are not going to get rid of us"-campaign, which was the starting point for the *Maroon Wave*.[20]

The *Maroon Wave* has adopted the form and denomination of what are known within this protest movement as *Citizen Waves*. *Citizen Waves* are ongoing protests that have arisen in response to the cuts to social spending and austerity policies implemented by the Spanish government since 2011.[21] Among the most significant examples are the *White Wave* (made up of healthcare professionals against cuts to public healthcare) or the *Green Wave* (of teachers against cuts to education) (Ferrer 2014). The color of this wave is maroon like the color of the Spanish national passport. This is the first wave that is acting outside of Spanish borders, and it has become a symbol of what they understand as forced migration.

Members of the *Maroon Wave* are quite diverse and fall into three kinds of migrant profiles: a) highly skilled young workers who as a result of the economic crisis have seen their prospects of joining the Spanish labor market dwindle to such a degree that they have been forced to emigrate to further their professional careers (either because they are unemployed or because they had precarious working conditions that were not in line with their qualifications); b) young adult workers who left Spain, either individually or with their families, simply to find any kind of job that allowed them to live independently and c) a third profile of young people who emigrated temporarily before the crisis (either to receive education or training, or to work), with the idea of spending time outside of Spain

---

19 *Youth Without Future* highlights the awareness of young Spaniards that they are part of a social class trapped in the lowest socio-labor rungs through its motto "No home, no job, no pension, no fear". The members of *Youth Without Future* denounce the disconnect between education, employment and housing that make it difficult for young people to emancipate themselves and the absence of public intervention which could be a bulwark against these difficulties" (Santos/Martín 2012: 108). (Cp. www.juventudsinfuturo.net and http://www.nonosvamosnosechan.net/)

20 To commemorate its third anniversary, in June 2016 the *Maroon Wave* posted a video on the social networks describing the movement's ongoing struggle and demands. This Spanish language video was widely covered by the digital press. It was directed at both Spanish expats and Spanish society. The motto of the campaign is "Feliz Lucha [...], desde todas partes" (Happy Struggle, from Everywhere). (Cp. https://www.youtube.com/watch?v=IVF0PXClyBU)

21 Since 2011 spending per capita on education and healthcare in Spain has been reduced by 21%. (Pérez-García et al. 2015)

and later returning home, who have found that the current employment situation in Spain made a homecoming impossible.

The element that unites members of the *Maroon Wave* is that they all see themselves as economic exiles who were forced into emigration and they all demand what they call their right to return. That is, they feel that although they might want to live temporarily abroad to improve their work experience or skills, the economic crisis has frustrated their desire to live in Spain permanently. In addition, they feel that the migration experience is very difficult, even for those who have good jobs, because it involves leaving behind family and friends and this difficulty is even more acute when the economic conditions in Spain limit or impede their return.

Another aspect that unites members of the *Maroon Wave* is a deep mistrust of Spain's institutions and political class, who they feel are responsible for their country's political system becoming what they refer to as a low intensity democracy, suffering from increasing inequality and discrimination and plagued by high levels of corruption, which has been incapable of responding to the country's main social and economic issues (Torcal 2014; Campos-Lima/Artiles 2013).[22] Because members of the wave feel that the State and its institutions have turned their backs on them they have assumed the responsibility of organizing themselves to denounce and expose the situation and to initiate actions that improve the conditions and rights of Spanish citizens living abroad.

The *Maroon Wave* has established itself as a horizontal movement, with regular face to face and virtual meetings at the local and global level. This approach is fostering new forms of participation, self-organization and demands for rights beyond borders. In this sense members of this social movement are voting with their feet and fighting with their voice. With this goal it has established a network of international assemblies (called nodes) capable of coordinating joint, simultaneous actions around the world directed at denouncing the policies and actions of the current Spanish government that have led to the economic and social problems that have forced them to emigrate. Currently and since its creation in 2013, the *Maroon Wave* is made up of different nodes in America, Europe, Asia and Oceania.

---

22 This lack of trust is widespread in Spanish society. According to data provided by the latest Sociological Research Centre (CIS) barometer, from December 2015, the Spanish felt that the main problem in the country was unemployment, followed by corruption. European studies carried out in other Southern European countries coincide with this lack of faith in institutions as a determining factor in emigration. (cp. Triandafyllidou/Gropas 2014)

In addition to providing visibility to the emigrant community through information campaigns and by maintaining close contact with various media outlets, the *Maroon Wave* has also directed its actions at strengthening the external citizenry, which they feel has been increasingly weakened over the past few years.

First of all, the wave seeks to support and assist other new Spanish emigrants by creating offices in different countries (called *Oficinas Precarias*) that offer mainly labor assistance and practical information for new arrivals about their labor rights, how to find work, rent a flat or where to take language courses. Currently these offices exist in London, Berlin, Paris, Prague, Edinburgh and Vienna. Along these lines they have created somewhat formal support networks for new arrivals, in response to the Spanish government's lack of action to protect new migrants residing abroad. Emigrants with greater experience offer support and information in increasingly formalized ways to newer arrivals through weekly meetings and internet-based support services. This is a direct response to one of the most common complaints made by its members, not only is there a lack of attention provided by Spanish authorities, but there is also lack of information provided by the poorly run Spanish consulates.[23]

The second important element on the *Maroon Wave*'s agenda has been to fight for the healthcare rights of Spanish emigrants in Spain through the creation of a specific work and action group known as *Maroon Wave Healthcare*. At the end of 2013 a legal reform was passed that made significant changes to healthcare services, including denying Spanish citizens who reside abroad for more than three months a year access to healthcare services in Spain. Although it is true that this right can be recovered once the individual returns to Spain, it involves an administrative procedure that can take some time to resolve. A second element introduced by this reform indicates that the European Health Card will only be issued to Spanish workers with permanent contracts in Spain. All others will receive a provisional certificate valid for 90 days. For this reason, many Spanish citizens living abroad for more than three months do not have access to the healthcare coverage provided by the European Health Card, despite having jobs (the European card requires the Spanish healthcare system to cover the healthcare costs of Spanish citizens abroad). In April, 2015 the wave launched a campaign called *"They won't take away our healthcare"* with the goal of not only condemning this situation, but also creating a registry of complaints regarding healthcare exclusion (denominated REDES) for Spanish citizens residing abroad

---

23 This aspect has even been included in reports by the Defensor del Pueblo (Spanish Ombudsman), due to the increased number of complaints by the Spanish community living abroad.

by compiling individual cases. Currently the organization is creating a series of guides to provide information on how to recover healthcare rights after returning to Spain, as well as national guides to help its members navigate the healthcare systems in the different countries in which they reside.

Thirdly, the members of the wave believe it is necessary that migrants maintain a voice in Spanish political and social life. Therefore, a large part of the initiatives over the past two years have focused on providing information about the external vote and denouncing the growing difficulties involved in participating in elections from abroad. This has been one of the questions that has had the greatest impact on public opinion, creating a bitter controversy that forced political parties to confront this issue during their election campaigns in December, 2015.

It should be noted that in 2011 the General Electoral Regime Law was modified to introduce two major changes (García-Mahamut 2012). First of all the right of Spanish citizens residing abroad to vote in local elections was eliminated. Second, it introduced a formal request to vote that is referred to as the *voto rogado*. This is a procedure through which Spanish citizens living abroad must request to vote through a formal application in the electoral census offices in Spain or in a Spanish consulate, during a period that is usually very short. Once the request is made the electoral census offices send the citizens their ballots so they can vote either in the consulates or by mail. This is a major change, because until 2011 ballots were sent to all Spanish citizens registered in a consulate by default, with no application necessary. As mentioned, the time periods during which these formal applications must be made are very limited and often even after submitting an application within the ordained period the ballots do not arrive in time to vote, due to enormous bureaucratic problems.

In fact, one of the most respected experts in this area has analyzed this situation and come to the conclusion that these procedural obstacles have made the external vote ineffective and undermined the system of guarantees of the right to vote (García-Mahamut 2012). Although this legal reform was heavily criticized and even led to protests among emigrant communities, it did not become a political issue in 2014, not due to an election period, but rather due to the complaints of the *Maroon Wave*.

The data on the effects of this reform on the external vote are compelling. According to the Spanish Statistics Office (INE), only 5 per cent of the Spanish citizens registered in the Electoral Census of Absent-Residents (CERA in Spanish) voted in the 2011 general elections, while in the 2008 general elections more than 32 per cent of the voters registered in this census had voted. In the European Elections of 2014 this percentage dropped again to below 2 per cent, while in the general election in December, 2015, the percentage increased to 4.7 per cent. For this reason, it seems clear that this reform is producing an increase in induced abstention.[24]

To combat this, in the second half of 2014 and during 2015 the *Maroon Wave*'s *Right to Vote* work group carried out an extensive information campaign leading up to the regional and national elections in 2015, providing information on how to formally request the right to vote, on how to register in the consulates and also started a campaign to repeal the *voto rogado*.[25] Their mobilization was so effective that this reform became an issue in the party platforms during the election campaign in December 2015, with the exception of the governing party *(PP)*, which proposed maintaining the procedure, but making it more efficient. *PSOE* included the elimination of the *voto rogado* and a reform of the legislation regulating the healthcare rights of Spanish emigrants in its platform; *Ciudadanos* claimed it would repeal the law and implement an on-line voting system for those living abroad; *United Left (IU)* wanted to repeal the 2011 reform, eliminating the *voto rogado* and allowing emigrants to once again vote in local elections; and the *Podemos* party platform included repealing the *voto rogado*, reforming the CERA registration system and increasing the periods to exercise the right to vote from abroad.

One of the most paradigmatic campaigns of this mobilization was the "Rescue my Vote"-campaign[26] launched at the end of November, 2015 whose objective was to put people living in Spain who were abstention volunteers willing to vote in someone else's name in contact with emigrants who could not vote. According to data published by the *Maroon Wave*, this initiative, using their termi-

---

24 The complaints by the emigrant community have centered not only the difficulties to apply for a *voto rogado*, but also on the delays in receiving the ballots needed to vote by mail, which have made it extremely difficult to exercise the vote, even among those who had applied for the vote. According to the publication *España Exterior*, only 60% of citizens who applied for the *voto rogado* could vote in the general election of December, 2015. Regarding the election results, the party most voted by those living abroad was *Podemos* (27%), which also became the third most voted party on the whole, after the two traditional parties, *PP* and *PSOE* (España Exterior 868). (Cp. http://www.espanaexterior.com/upload/eimpresa/4541-portada_868.pdf)

25 In the second half of 2015 the *DosMillionesdeVotos* platform was also created, a platform of lawyers that arose with the objective of providing legal and technical aid to Spanish citizens residing abroad so that they could exercise their right to vote. (Cp. http://www.dosmillonesdevotos.org)

26 http://mareagranate.org/rescatamivoto/rescatamivoto.php.

nology, "rescued" more than 3,000 votes in the national elections of December 2015. Again, this campaign was a response to the lack of assistance provided by Spanish consulates in the voting process, because they lack both the means and the political will to do more. The campaign sought to promote the reformation of the election law with the collaboration and involvement of Spanish citizens, an objective that has become central to its demands. The campaign was launched through the *Maroon Wave*'s website (*Vote work group*) and efficiently distributed through the social networks, receiving a great deal of coverage by the media, especially the digital press. The campaign increased public awareness about this civic demand, understood as an exercise in real democracy,[27] and further sparked the public debate in Spain regarding the difficulty of exercising the right to vote from abroad. The nature of this social movement, which is a citizen platform created around the common objective of improving the political and social rights of the new Spanish diaspora, explains the logic behind its actions and strategies, which include seeking alliances with other citizen-based social movements and using social networks as the primary means of disseminating its message and making a political impact. In this sense the wave has moved away from more classic forms of political action in which alliances are formed between the social fabric, political parties and trade unions.

The wave's mobilization has consolidated voting from abroad as a priority of the Spanish political agenda. In February 2016, the movement sent an open letter to all the political parties demanding that they undertake a series of legislative, operational and instrumental initiatives that will eliminate all the current obstacles to exercising the right to vote from abroad and the establishment of a single overseas electoral district. That same month the main opposition party, the *Socialist Party*, proposed a reform of the electoral law in the Spanish Parliament, which led to the approval of a research commission in April 2016 to study the difficulties that Spanish citizens living abroad have in exercising their political rights. In practice this reform has encountered many difficulties due to the inability of the political parties to reach an agreement to form a government during the first months of 2016, leading to a call for new general elections in June 2016.

---

27 *Democracia Real YA* (Real Democracy NOW) was another motto of the *15-M movement*.

Conclusions

The new Spanish emigration resulting from the deep economic, social and institutional crisis that Spain has been suffering during the past five years has had a significant impact on the country's social and political environment and generated serious controversies in the media and parliament. Throughout the last legislature (2011-2015) the current conservative government turned its back on this bitter issue, at first maintaining a posture of indifference regarding the outflow of young, and not so young, Spanish citizens, which later turned into denial. This approach, however, failed to cover up an issue that has deeply affected national pride. On the contrary, the government's attitude, which highlights its disconnection from Spain's social reality, has had the undesired effect of provoking new forms of mobilization, resistance and visibility at the heart of an emerging and increasingly organized Spanish community abroad. Moreover, the rest of Spanish society and the emergent political parties have also thrown their support behind the issues fought for by this community. In response to what we can refer to as the government's disengagement diaspora policy, the last few years have revealed the Spanish emigrant community's growing political engagement in domestic issues, which has very effectively increased its external, transnational voice; solidifying and reshaping the external citizenry in reaction to the erosion of its political, social and economic rights.

References

Aja, Eliseo/Arango, Joaquín/Oliver, Josep (2013): "Crisis, mercado de trabajo y cambiantes tendencias migratorias." In: Eliseo Aja/Joaquín Arango/Josep Oliver (eds.), Inmigración y crisis: entre la continuidad y el cambio. Anuario de la Inmigración en España 2012, Barcelona: CIDOB, pp. 12-24.

Alba, Susana/Fernández-Asperilla, Ana (2015): Nueva emigración exterior y cuestión laboral. Informe 2014, Madrid: Fundación 1º de Mayo.

Calvo-Salgado, Luis/Fernández-Vicente, María José/Kreienbrink, Axel/Sanz-Díaz, Carlos/Sanz-Lafuente, Gloria (2009): Historia del Instituto Español de Emigración. La política migratoria exterior de España y el IEE del Franquismo a la Transición, Madrid: Ministerio de Trabajo e Inmigración.

Cameron, Bryan (2014): "Spain in crisis: 15-M and the culture of the indignation." In: Journal of Spanish Cultural Studies 15/1, pp. 1-11.

Campos Lima, Maria/Artiles, Antonio (2013): "Youth voice(s) in EU coutries and social movements in Southern Europe." In: Transfer. European Review of Labour and Research 19, pp. 345-364.

Cavounidis, Jennifer (2015): The Changing face of Emigration. Harnessing the potential of the new Greek Diaspora, Washington: Migration Policy Institute.

Delano, Alexandra/Gamlen, Alan (2014): "Comparing and theorizing state-diaspora relations." In: Political Geography 41, pp. 43-53.

Díaz-Hernández, Ramón/Domínguez-Mujica, Josefina/Parreño-Castellano, Juan (2015): "Una aproximación a la emigración española durante la crisis económica: herramientas de studio." In: Aracne 198, pp. 1-26.

Dolado, Juan/Jansen, Marcel/Felgueroso, Florentino/Fuentes, Andrés/Wölfl, Anita (2013): "Youth Labour Market Performance in Spain and its determinants. A micro-level perspective." In: OCDE Economics Departament Working Papers 1039, pp. 1-71.

Domingo, Andreu/Sabater, Albert (2013): "Crisis económica y emigración: la perspectiva demográfica." In: Eliseo Aja/Joaquín Arango/Josep Oliver (eds.), Inmigración y crisis: entre la continuidad y el cambio. Anuario de la Inmigración en España 2012, Barcelona: CIDOB, pp. 61-87.

Domingo, Andreu/Sabater, Albert/Ortega-Rivera, Enrique (2014): "¿Migración neohispánica? El impacto de la crisis económica en la emigración española." In: Empiria 29, pp. 39-66.

Domingo, Andreu/Blanes, Amand (2015): "Inmigración y emigración en España: estado de la cuestión y perspectivas de future." In: Joaquín Arango/David Moya/Josep Oliver/Elena Sánchez-Montijano (eds.), Flujos cambiantes, atonía institucional. Anuario de la Inmigración en España 2014, Barcelona: CIDOB, pp. 94-122.

Domingo, Andreu/Ortega-Rivera, Enrique (2015): "La emigración española. Esa vieja desconocida." In: Cristobal Torres (ed.), España 2015. Situación Social, Madrid: Centro de Investigaciones Sociológicas, pp. 207-215.

Domínguez-Mujica, Josefina/Díaz-Hernández, Ramón/Parreño-Castellano, Juan Manuel (2016): "Migrating Abroad to Get Ahead: The Emigration of Young Spanish Adults During the Financial Crisis (2008-2013)." In: Josefina Domínguez-Mujica (ed.), Global Change and Human Mobility, Berlin: Springer, pp. 203-223.

Fernandez-Vicente, Maria José (2005): "De calamidad nacional a baza del desarrollo. Las políticas migratorias del Régimen Franquista." In: Migraciones & Exilios 6, pp. 81-100.

Fernández-Vicente, María José (2009): "El Estado español y la emigración, 1880-1985." In: Ángeles Escrivá/Anastasia Bermúdez/Natalia Moraes (eds.),

Migración y participación política, Madrid: Consejo Superior de Investigaciones Científicas, pp. 265-295.

Ferrer, Nadia (2014): "Rethinking social theory in contemporary social movements." In: Contention 1/2, pp. 27-45.

Flesher-Fominaya, Cristina (2015): "Debunking Spontaneity: Spain's 15M/Indignados as Autonomous Movement." In: Social Movement Studies: Journal of Social, Cultural and Political Protest 14/2, pp. 142-163.

Gamlen, Alan (2006): Diaspora Engagement Policies: What are they, and what kinds of states use them? Working Paper 32, Oxford: Centre on Migration, Policy and Society.

García-Mahamut, Rosario (2012): "La reforma electoral (LO 2/2011) y el voto de los españoles en el exterior. La inefectividad del derecho de sufragio de los españoles en el exterior. Una necesaria revisión." In: Teoría y Realidad Constitucional 30, pp. 259-289.

Gil-Lázaro, Alicia/Fernández-Vicente, María José (2015): Los discursos sobre la emigración española en perspectiva comparada. Principios del siglo XX-principios del siglo XXI. Madrid, Universidad de Alcalá.

Glorius, Birgit (2016): "New 'Guest Workers' from Spain? Exploring Migration to Germany in the Context of Economic and Societal Change." In: Josefina Domínguez-Mujica (ed.), Global Change and Human Mobility, Berlin: Springer, pp. 225-247.

Glynn, Irial/Kelly, Thomas/Pairas Mac Éinrí (2013): Irish Emigration in an age of austerity, Cork: University College of Cork.

Glynn, Irial (2015): "Just one of the PIIGS or a European outlier. Studying Irish emigration from a comparative perspective." In: Irish Journal of Sociology 23/2, pp. 93-113.

Goig-Martínez, Juan Manuel (2010): "Derechos de la ciudadanía española en el exterior." In: Revista de Derecho UNED, 7, pp. 325-372.

Hirschman, Albert (1970): Exit, Voice and Loyalty: responses to the decline in Firms, Organizations, and States, Harvard University Press, Cambridge.

IOM (2014): Aproximación a la situación de los españoles emigrados. Realidad, proyectos, dificultades y retos, Madrid: IOM.

López-Sala, Ana/Oso, Laura (2015): "Inmigración en tiempos de crisis. Dinámicas de movilidad emergentes y nuevos impactos sociales." In: Migraciones 37, pp. 9-27.

Moreno-Caballud, Luis (2015): Cultures of Anyone. Studies on Cultural Democratization in the Spanish Neoliberal Crisis, Liverpool: Liverpool University Press.

Navarrete, Lorenzo (coord.) (2014): La emigración de los jóvenes españoles en el contexto de la crisis, Madrid: Observatorio de la Juventud en España.

Papademetriou, Demetrius (2015): Rethinking Emigration. Turning Challenges into Opportunities, Washington: Migration Policy Institute.

Pérez-García, Francisco/Cucarella, Vicent/Hernández, Laura (2015): Servicios Públicos, diferencias territoriales e igualdad de oportunidades, Valencia: Valencia Institute of Economic Research and BBVA Foundation.

Perugorría, Ignacia/Tejerina, Benjamín (2013): "Politics of the encounter: Cognition, emotions, and the networks in the Spanish 15M." In: Current Sociology 61/4, pp. 424-442.

Pumares, Pablo (2015): Cosas que hacer en Brighton mientras escampa la crisis. El atractivo de Brighton para los jóvenes españoles en tiempos de crisis, Granada: Congreso Nacional de Migraciones, September 2015.

Sampedro, Víctor/Lobera, Josep (2014): "The Spanish 15-M Movement: a consensual dissent?" In: Journal of Spanish Cultural Studies 15/1, pp. 61-80.

Sánchez-Alonso, Blanca (2011): "La política migratoria en España. Un análisis de largo plazo." In: Revista Internacional de Sociología 1, pp. 243-268.

Santos, Antonio/Martín, Paz (2012): "La juventud española en tiempos de crisis. Paro, vidas precarias y acción colectiva." In: Sociología del Trabajo 75, pp. 93-110.

Santos, Antonio (2013): "Fuga de cerebros y crisis en España: los jóvenes en el punto de mira de los discursos empresariales." In: AREAS, Revista Internacional de Ciencias Sociales 32, pp. 125-137.

Sennett, Richard (1998): The Corrosion of the Character, New York: W.W.Norton.

Torcal, Mariano (2014): "The Decline of Political Trust in Spain and Portugal. Economic Performance or Political Responsiveness?" In: American Behavioral Scientist 58/12, pp. 1542-1567.

Triandafyllidou, Anna/Gropas, Ruby (2014): "Voting with their feet: Highly skilled emigrants from Southern Europe." In: American Behavioral Scientist 58/12, pp. 1614-1633.

Villar, Antonio (2014): "No es país para jóvenes." In: Panorama Social 20, pp. 53-69.

List of figures

Fig. 2.1: Crude rate of natural population change — 23

Fig. 2.2: Age Pyramids of selected countries of Northern and Western Europe — 25

Fig. 2.3: Age Pyramids of selected countries of Southern Europe — 26

Fig. 2.4: Net migration rate (base 100) of countries of Northern and Western Europe (2010-2013) — 28

Fig. 2.5: Net migration rate (base 100) of the countries of Southern Europe (2010-2013) — 29

Fig. 2.6: Component Plot in Rotated Space of the countries in Northern, Western and Southern Europe — 32

Fig. 2.7: Dendrogram resulting from Cluster Analysis — 33

Fig. 2.8: Conglomerates resulting from Cluster Analysis — 34

Fig. 2.9: Spaniards residing abroad (people born in Spain) in 2013 — 36

Fig. 2.10: Portuguese residing abroad (people born in Portugal) in 2013 — 39

Fig. 2.11: Italians residing abroad (people with Italian citizenship) in 2013 — 40

Fig. 4.1: Migration Flows (2008-2014) — 80

LIST OF FIGURES

Fig. 5.1: Movements of non-German nationals between Spain and Germany, 1996-2014 — 106

Fig. 5.2: Type of language certificate pursued, own survey — 115

Fig. 5.3: Foreign language proficiency, self-estimation, in per cent of cases — 117

Fig. 5.4: Experiences staying abroad (more than three months), in per cent of cases — 118

Fig. 5.5: "Could you imagine living abroad? Which possible reasons could you imagine?", in per cent of cases — 120

Fig. 5.6: Probability of job search abroad within the following two years, in per cent of cases — 121

Fig. 5.7: Level of preparation for a job related migratory stay in a German-speaking country, in per cent of respondents — 122

Fig. 5.8: Level of preparation for a study related migratory stay in a German-speaking country, in per cent of respondents — 122

Fig. 5.9: Perceptions of Germany, in per cent of respondents — 124

Fig. 5.10: Perceptions of Germany in relation to personal experiences, in per cent of respondents — 125

Fig. 5.11: Perceptions of Spain, in per cent of respondents — 126

Fig. 7.1: Age of study participants — 166

Fig. 7.2: Year of migration — 167

Fig. 7.3: Main reason for migration — 168

Fig. 7.4: Number of close German friends in Germany — 173

Fig. 7.5: Employment status — 174

Fig. 7.6: Intended duration of residence in Germany   176

Fig. 9.1: Development of a 'welcoming culture'   232

Fig. 10.1: Most frequently used words in respondent narratives   252

List of tables

Tab. 2.1: Population change in the countries analyzed during the stages of economic expansion and recession	21
Tab. 2.2: Population change in 2001-2007 and its demographic drivers	22
Tab. 2.3: Population change in 2008-20014 and its demographic drivers	22
Tab. 2.4: Net migration rate of the countries of Southern Europe (2001-2008)	28
Tab. 2.5: Annual growth rates in the number of residents born in Greece, Italy, Portugal and Spain (2004-2008 and 2009-2014)	35
Tab. 2.6: Outflows from Italy, Spain, Portugal and Greece in 2013, in per cent of total outflow	37
Tab. 3.1: Some relevant figures concerning youth migration in Italy	63
Tab. 4.1: Overview of media articles reviewed	84
Tab. 5.1: Main characteristics of survey participants	113
Tab. 5.2: Reasons for studying German	116
Tab. 5.3: Level of internationalization of respondents	118

Tab. 5.4: Which means of information are you using for collecting
information on study and job opportunities in a German
speaking country? 123

Tab. 6.1: Interviewees' profiles 158

Tab. 7.1: Correlations between study variables 178

Tab. 9.1: Interview partners 222

Tab. 9.2: Branch and required experience/educational level 224

List of contributors

Díaz-Hernández, Ramon, PhD, is a Professor of Human Geography since 1992. Nowadays, he teaches in this discipline at the University of Las Palmas de Gran Canaria (Spain). His research is focusing on population geography, where he has carried out a high number of publications.

Domínguez-Mujica, Josefina, PhD, is a Professor of Human Geography at the University of Las Palmas de Gran Canaria. She has devoted most of her research to the study of migrations from the perspective of Human Geography. She has collaborated with and conducted different research projects funded by Spanish public institutions and has participated in two Expert Committees on the subject of immigration to the Canary Islands. Since 2012 she is the Chairperson of the International Geographical Union Commission on Global Change and Human Mobility, specialized in a new reading of traditional population movements and forms of mobility. She also conducts the Research Group on Atlantic Societies and Spaces at the University of Las Palmas de Gran Canaria.

Glorius, Birgit, Dr. rer. nat., works as Professor for Human Geography of East Central Europe at Chemnitz University of Technology. She was trained in Geography, Geology and Political Sciences at the Universities of Erlangen-Nürnberg, Würzburg and the University of Texas at Austin (Tx.). She earned a diploma in Human Geography from the University of Würzburg and a Doctoral degree from the University of Halle-Wittenberg. Her research interests and majority of publications are in the fields of international migration, demographic change and geographies of education. She carried out plenty of research projects within these fields of interest, especially in Eastern Germany, Poland, Bulgaria and the Western Balkans.

Godenau, Dirk, Dr., Department of Applied Economics and Quantitative Methods, University of La Laguna, Tenerife, Spain. Dirk Godenau is Senior Lecturer of Applied Economics at the University of La Laguna (Spain). His research in the field of Population Economics includes irregular migration, mobility in local labor markets and demo-economic interactions in island contexts. At present he is the Director of Research Activities at the Tenerife Immigration Observatory (www.obiten.net).

Grammatikas, Dimitris, studied Anthropology and History at the Utrecht University. For the last 15 years he worked as advisor on EU-migration and integration for the Dutch government. He has various publications about EU-migrants and the implementation of EU-legislation in the Netherlands. Nowadays he studies the influence of digital communities and social media on EU network migration.

Hatziprokopiou, Panos, DPhil, is Assistant Professor at the School of Spatial Planning and Development, Aristotle University of Thessaloniki, Greece. He has studied Economics (BA, Macedonia), Sociology (MA, Essex) and Human Geography (DPhil, Sussex). His research and publications touch upon aspects of migration and migrants' incorporation, with a focus on labor market integration and on diversity and urban change.

Labrianidis, Lois, PhD, is Secretary General for Strategic and Private Investments of the Greek Ministry of Economy, Development & Tourism, and Professor in the Department of Economics, University of Macedonia, Greece. He is an economic geographer (BA–Aristotle University of Thessaloniki, MA–Sussex, PhD–LSE) and has done research and published on topics such as industrial location, the spatial aspects of subcontracting, development of rural areas, rural entrepreneurship, delocalization of economic activities and international migration.

López-Sala, Ana, PhD, holds a PhD in Sociology and is a Tenured Research Fellow at the Institute of Economics, Geography and Demography (IEGD) at the Spanish National Research Council (CSIC) in Madrid. She is the author of Immigration and the Nation-State (Anthropos, Barcelona, 2005), Migration and Borders (Icaria, Barcelona, 2010) and Human Trafficking in Spain (Immigration Spanish Ministry, 2011). She was a Rockefeller Fellow (at Bellagio Program) and member of LINET (Independent Network of Labour Migration and Integration Experts, IOM and EC). Currently, she is researcher in charge of the MIND

Project ("Non-state actors in migration control policies") supported by the Spanish Research Program.

Meinardus, Phillip, Dipl. Geogr., holds a degree in political science and in geography from Julius-Maximilians-University Würzburg. He works in the field of urban and rural development in Nürnberg.

Montanari, Armando, Prof. Dr., is President of the Degree in Tourism Sciences, Sapienza University of Rome and teaches Geography of Tourism and Human Mobility. Coordinator of numerous international research projects in the past, he is now P.I. of the HORIZON 2020 YMOBILITY Project (2015-18). He has published 240 articles and volumes in Italian, English, French, Spanish and Japanese.

Parreño Castellano, Juan M., PhD, is senior lecturer in Human Geography and chairman of Department of Geography at the University of Las Palmas de Gran Canaria (Spain). His research focuses on Social and Urban Geography, in particular, migratory and tourist mobility and urban and tourist planning.

Pérez-García, Tanausú, is a Graduate in Geography at the University of Las Palmas de Gran Canaria and a geographical information systems technician. He has participated as a predoctoral researcher in different projects on the issue of demography and migrations. He has been the author of most of the maps in the articles and books published by the members of the Atlantic Societies and Spaces Research Group at the University of Las Palmas de Gran Canaria.

Pratsinakis, Manolis, PhD, is a Marie Curie IF postdoctoral fellow at the University of Macedonia, Greece, studying the new crisis-driven Greek emigration, and a research fellow at the University of Amsterdam where he previously worked as a lecturer in Sociology. He has studied Human Geography (BA), Sociology (MA) and Anthropology (PhD) and has done research and published on migration, ethnicity and everyday nationhood.

Pumares, Pablo, PhD, is a Professor of Human Geography at the University of Almería, Dept of Geography, History and Humanities. PhD by the Complutense University of Madrid (1994) and research award by the Fundació La Caixa (1995). He is the current director of the Centre for Migration and Intercultural Relations (CEMyRI) and he is leading the Spanish team participating in the

H2020 project YMobility: Youth Mobility: maximizing opportunities for individuals, labor markets and regions in Europe.

Staniscia, Barbara, PhD, is the Scientific Secretary of the IGU Commission on "Global change and human mobility-Globility" and Research Scientist at Sapienza University of Rome. She is currently member of the research teams of the international projects on "Youth mobility: maximizing opportunities for individuals, labour markets and regions in Europe (YMobility)" and on "Brain drain or brain gain? Skilled migration from Southern Europe to the new emerging Mexican cities".

Wassermann, Maria, holds a degree in psychology from Humboldt University, Berlin. Her doctoral research in the field of Positive Occupational Health Psychology focuses on occupational success, well-being and personal resources among immigrants from southern European countries.

Social Sciences

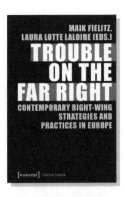

Maik Fielitz, Laura Lotte Laloire (eds.)
Trouble on the Far Right
Contemporary Right-Wing Strategies
and Practices in Europe

2016, 208 p., 19,99 € (DE),
ISBN 978-3-8376-3720-5
E-Book: 17,99 € (DE), ISBN 978-3-8394-3720-9
EPUB: 17,99 € (DE), ISBN 978-3-7328-3720-5

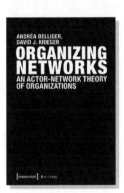

Andréa Belliger, David J. Krieger
Organizing Networks
An Actor-Network Theory of Organizations

2016, 272 p., 34,99 € (DE),
ISBN 978-3-8376-3616-1
E-Book: 34,99 € (DE), ISBN 978-3-8394-3616-5

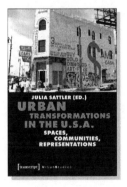

Julia Sattler (ed.)
Urban Transformations in the U.S.A.
Spaces, Communities, Representations

2016, 426 p., 39,99 € (DE),
ISBN 978-3-8376-3111-1
E-Book: 39,99 € (DE), ISBN 978-3-8394-3111-5

All print, e-book and open access versions of the titels in our entire list
are available in our online shop www.transcript-verlag.de/en!

Social Sciences

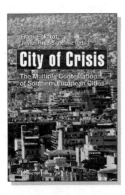

Frank Eckardt, Javier Ruiz Sánchez (eds.)
City of Crisis
The Multiple Contestation
of Southern European Cities

2015, 264 p., 29,99 € (DE),
ISBN 978-3-8376-2842-5
available as free open access publication
E-Book: ISBN 978-3-8394-2842-9

Derya Özkan (ed.)
Cool Istanbul
Urban Enclosures and Resistances

2014, 172 p., 29,99 € (DE),
ISBN 978-3-8376-2763-3
E-Book: 26,99 € (DE), ISBN 978-3-8394-2763-7

Michael Friedman, Samo Tomsic (eds.)
Psychoanalysis: Topological Perspectives
New Conceptions of Geometry and Space
in Freud and Lacan

2016, 256 p., 34,99 € (DE),
ISBN 978-3-8376-3440-2
E-Book: 34,99 € (DE), ISBN 978-3-8394-3440-6

All print, e-book and open access versions of the titels in our entire list
are available in our online shop www.transcript-verlag.de/en!